BEHIND THE BACK PAGE

THE ADVENTURES OF A
SPORTS WRITER

KNOW THE SCORE BOOKS SPORTS PUBLICATIONS

CULT HEROES	Author	ISBN
CARLISLE UNITED	Mark Harrison	978-1-905449-09-7
CELTIC	David Potter	978-1-905449-08-8
CHELSEA	Leo Moynihan	1-905449-00-3
MANCHESTER CITY	David Clayton	978-1-905449-05-7
NEWCASTLE	Dylan Younger	1-905449-03-8
NOTTINGHAM FOREST	David McVay	978-1-905449-06-4
RANGERS	Paul Smith	978-1-905449-07-1
SOUTHAMPTON	Jeremy Wilson	1-905449-01-1
WEST BROM	Simon Wright	1-905449-02-X

MATCH OF MY LIFE	Editor	ISBN
DERBY COUNTY	Johnson & Matthews	978-1-905449-68-2
ENGLAND WORLD CUP	Massarella & Moynihan	1-905449-52-6
EUROPEAN CUP FINALS	Ben Lyttleton	1-905449-57-7
FA CUP FINALS 1953-1969	David Saffer	978-1-905449-53-8
FULHAM	Michael Heatley	1-905449-51-8
LEEDS	David Saffer	1-905449-54-2
LIVERPOOL	Leo Moynihan	1-905449-50-X
MANCHESTER UNITED	Ivan Ponting	978-1-905449-59-0
SHEFFIELD UNITED	Nick Johnson	1-905449-62-3
STOKE CITY	Simon Lowe	978-1-905449-55-2
SUNDERLAND	Rob Mason	1-905449-60-7
SPURS	Allen & Massarella	978-1-905449-58-3
WOLVES	Simon Lowe	1-905449-56-9

GENERAL FOOTBALL	Author	ISBN
2007/08 CHAMPIONS LEAGUE YEARBOOK		978-1-905449-93-4
BURKSEY	Peter Morfoot	1-905449-49-6
MY PREMIERSHIP DIARY	Marcus Hahnemann	978-1-905449-33-0
OUTCASTS	Steve Menary	978-1-905449-31-6
PARISH TO PLANET	Eric Midwinter	978-1-905449-30-9
A History of Football		
TACKLES LIKE A FERRET	Paul Parker	1-905449-47-X
(England Cover)		
TACKLES LIKE A FERRET	Paul Parker	1-905449-46-1
(Manchester United Cover)		
UNITED THROUGH TRIUMPH AND TRAGEDY	Bill Foulkes	978-1-905449-78-1

CRICKET	Author	ISBN
MOML: THE ASHES	Pilger & Wightman	1-905449-63-1
GROVEL!	David Tossell	978-1-905449-43-9
The 1976 West Indies Tour of England		
MY AUTOBIOGRAPHY	Shaun Udal	978-1-905449-42-2
WASTED?	Paul Smith	978-1-905449-45-3
LEAGUE CRICKET YEARBOOK	Andy Searle	978-1-905449-70-5
North West edition		
LEAGUE CRICKET YEARBOOK	Andy Searle	978-1-905449-72-9
Midlands edition		

RUGBY LEAGUE	Editor	ISBN
MOML: WIGAN WARRIORS	David Kuzio	978-1-905449-66-8

FORTHCOMING PUBLICATIONS

GENERAL FOOTBALL	Author	ISBN
THE BOOK OF FOOTBALL OBITUARIES	Ivan Ponting	978-1-905449-82-2
THE DOOG	Steve Gordos & David Harrison	978-1-905449-02-9
THE RIVALS GAME	Douglas Beattie	978-1-905449-79-8

BEHIND THE BACK PAGE
THE ADVENTURES OF A SPORTS WRITER

by CHRISTOPHER DAVIES

www.knowthescorebooks.com

First published in the United Kingdom by Know The Score Books
Limited, 2008 Copyright Christopher Davies, 2008

Know The Score Books Limited
118 Alcester Road, Studley, Warwickshire, B80 7NT
Tel: 01527 454482
Fax: 01527 452183
info@knowthescorebooks.com www.knowthescorebooks.com

Mixed Sources
Product group from well-managed
forests and other controlled sources
www.fsc.org Cert no. TT-COC-2082
© 1996 Forest Stewardship Council
FSC

A CIP catalogue record is available for this book from the British Library
ISBN: 9781848185067

Printed and bound in Great Britain
By Cromwell Press, Trowbridge, Wiltshire

PRAISE FOR CHRISTOPHER DAVIES AND BEHIND THE BACK PAGE

"Christopher Davies has a wealth of experience as a national newspaper journalist – and a wealth of stories to go with it. He tells them with great wit too... A funny guy. Funny haha, that is."

Ian Ridley, Mail on Sunday

"Journalists like to imagine that theirs is a serious, stressful profession. The truth, at least as far as football reporters is concerned, is that it is a great life. Christopher Davies happily acknowledges that truth and his book takes the reader behind the scenes for a peek at the privileged, joyful business of being in the football media and a close-up view of some of the biggest names and biggest events of the game."

Mick Dennis, Daily Express

"When people ask about sports writing, it's difficult to convey to them the excitement, the frustration, the adrenaline, the anecdotes and the characters. Now there's no need. Just tell them to read Behind The Back Page. It's all in there."

Nick Szczepanik, The Times

"Prepare to be entertained."

Alan McKinlay, Daily Mirror

"A personal, often hilarious and honest insight into life on the road as a sports writer."

Matt Lawton, *Daily Mail*

"Roguish, wickedly acerbic and containing elements of Bill Bryson at his best in observing the humdrum and the everyday through a lens of hilarity."

Vince Hogan, *Irish Independent*

"Laugh out loud stuff. Christopher Davies adds a new perspective to sports writing. With his years of Fleet Street experience he brings to the reader a catalogue of hilarious stories and incidents from the unpredictable and sometimes incongruous world of soccer reporting."

John Ley, *Daily Telegraph*

"Christopher Davies is one of those sports hacks who has never forgotten how lucky he is. If playing sport is the absolute dream profession, then watching it is a privileged second-best. With an almost childlike 'kid-in-a-sweetshop' enthusiasm, he articulates the routine relish.

"Some of the reminiscences will have fellow journalists purring nostalgically and empathising with the frustrations of life on the road – dodgy hotel rooms, faulty laptops, deaf copy-takers. But, at the same time, all sports fans will love to read how it really is. I've heard some of the Jack Charlton stories on the circuit, but – even sitting alone in my lounge – I was still helpless with laughter as Christopher retold the tales of those vintage days with Ireland.

"If you were making a documentary about life on the frontline as a national sports journalist, then this would be your script: humour, reality and – above all – a genuine sense that the author remembers (when other hacks sometimes forget) just what a wonderful professional life he's been fortunate to live."

Peter Drury, ITV *Sport*

"An absorbing, entertaining and amusing journey through the world of sport's journalism. From the inside story of Roy Keane's explosive departure from the 2002 World Cup to paying a prostitute for a lift in rain-lashed Glasgow, Christopher Davies captures the highs and lows of life on the road."

Jon Brodkin, *Guardian*

"Christopher Davies has the ability to make the reader feel as if he is there with him, enjoying every adventure during a thrilling roller-coaster ride of emotions."

Neil Silver, *The People*

"Christopher Davies knows how to write a story, including his own. One of the more approachable national scribes, his humour and enthusiasm always prevail no matter how big the bags under the eyes. If you think writing about sport for a national daily is champagne and caviar all the way, read this. The author has had a front row seat for some of the most gripping sport of recent decades and has never fallen out of love with the game. This isn't the story of a cynical old hack, just one who sometimes felt like throwing his laptop out of the window of the nearest tall building."

Simon Brotherton, *BBC Radio 5Live and Match of the Day commentator*

ACKNOWLEDGEMENTS

I think I have probably bought everyone here a drink or three at some stage. Hangovers are temporary but friendships can last forever.

I have been lucky, very lucky to enjoy such a wonderful career even if I didn't always realise it at the time. So the largest of glasses must be raised both to what Pelé called the beautiful game and to some slightly less beautiful football writers who have made the job such fun.

The person who taught me most about football news reporting was Colin Gibson. We worked together for seven years on the *Daily Telegraph* when he was the football correspondent before becoming sports editor of the *Sunday Telegraph*. Colin's news sense and inspirational personality are unsurpassed.

During my 20 years with the *Telegraph* I could ask for no more loyal colleague than John Ley. Paul Hayward and Mick Dennis, both *ex-Telegraph* before landing at the *Daily Mail* and *Daily Express* respectively, remain good friends and superb columnists. Brian Oliver and Ben Findon were supportive sports news editors with Keith Perry an excellent sports editor and friend, while football correspondent Henry Winter maintains a standard of writing few anywhere can equal. On the *Sunday Telegraph*, Patrick Barclay is a class act as a writer and person. Thanks also to Lee Horton of the *People*.

Covering the Republic of Ireland was unforgettable, the Dublin-based journalists adding a new dimension to Anglo-Irish relationships. Apologies for any omissions but … Peter Byrne, John Brennan, Roy Curtis, Garry Doyle, Cathal Dervan, Dion Fanning, Billy George, Vince Hogan, Tom Humphries, Paul Hyland, Paul Lennon, Liam Mackey, Emmett Malone, Gerry McDermott, John O'Brien, Neil O'Riordan, Philip Quinn, Charlie Stuart plus the late Michael Carwood.

The Brit pack who have travelled with Ireland over the years were the best of tourists. John Bean, Jon Brodkin, Simon Brotherton, Neil Custis,

Peter Fitton, Des Kelly, Ian Ridley, Russell Kempson, the late Rob King, Joe Lovejoy, Neil Silver, Tony Stenson, Richard Tanner, Danny Taylor, David Walker, Clive White, Colin Young et al.

American football has blown hot and cold in England but the friendships built up covering the sport remain constant. Special thanks to the following for ensuring I had many nice days in the United States covering the Super Bowl: Pete Abitante, Ken Adam, Ken Elliott, Barry Flatman, Jack Gallagher, Nick Halling, Thomas Hensey, Oliver Holt, Des Kelly, Alan McKinlay, Nick Szczepanik, David Tossell, Simon Veness and Keith Webster.

Others in the football industry have helped me, particularly Graham Poll, Graham Barber, Steve Dunn, Paul Durkin, Rob Styles and John Moules who opened my eyes to the world of refereeing. UEFA's Graham Turner and Rex Gowar of Reuters have been friends and colleagues since the early 1970s.

ITV's Peter Drury and Clive Tyldesley not only talk a good game but are engaging company off mike. Ditto Jonathan Legard and Jonathan Pearce of BBC's Radio 5Live plus talkSPORT's finest Paul Hawksbee and Andy Jacobs.

Special thanks also to Karen Smith, Kelly Scott, Nicky McGovern and Lesley MacDonald (who all did a brilliant job of organising my life at the *Telegraph*) plus Alison, Jackie Monk, Roy Collins, John Kinlough, Patsy Neal, Sue Lawrence, Sonia, Georgia, Terry, Barbara, Joanna, Vicky and Marina.

Last but by no means least, Simon Lowe of Know the Score Books Ltd for having faith in me.

Christopher Davies, March 2008

***The front cover photograph was taken before Shakhtar Donetsk v Arsenal in November 2000. It was minus 10 degrees. We lose the right to complain about sitting out in that sort of temperature for two hours because, unlike the fans who also endure the conditions, we are paid to do so.

CONTENTS

Introduction 17

1. The Early Days (part1) 19

2. The Early Days (part2) 31

3. The Republic of Ireland 39

4. George Best Tells Me I'm The Expert 49

5. 2002 World Cup, Japan/South Korea 57

6. Euro 2004, Portugal 109

7. Super Bowl XXXIX, 2005 133

8. Israel v Ireland, March 2005 141

9. Amsterdam Tournament, July 2005 147

10. Ireland v Italy, August 2005 153

11. France v Faroe Islands, September 2005 157

12. The Republic of Ireland, Autumn 2005 159

13. Super Bowl XL, 2006 171

14. 2006 World Cup, Germany 183

15. Germany v Ireland, September 2006 224

16. France v Italy, September 2006 231

17. Hamburg v Arsenal, September 2006 235

18. Levski Sofia v Chelsea, September 2006 237

19. Super Bowl XLI, 2007 243

20. Barcelona, September 2007 257

21. Milan, January 2008 263

22. The Final Word 267

23. Been There Got The T-shirt 269

24. About The Author 272

To my parents Eileen and Tim,
who are simply the best,
and my son Kerry for putting up
with me.

INTRODUCTION

IN THE FINAL reckoning I counted 64 countries, nine World Cups, nine European Championships, 17 European club finals, almost 200 Republic of Ireland internationals, 18 Super Bowls, one audience with the Pope at the Vatican, one lady of the night who was paid for a service she had never performed previously and a million happy memories. Covering sport, and in particular football, for a living certainly beats work. In fact I often threatened to leave the press box to take a well-earned job, but never got round to it.

It may appear unusual that journalists from rival newspapers working in a highly competitive industry can get on so well. We do – some of my best friends are rivals. I hope this book gives you an insight into the world of football writing, the highs and lows … a glimpse behind the scenes of covering major tournaments and events.

To outsiders it must appear wonderful to be paid to do what so many people pay to do. I'll let you into a well-kept secret – it is, with interest. But it is not all a bed of roses – or even sometimes a bed big enough to sleep in as you will discover. Like all jobs, sports reporting has its pitfalls and downsides; trying to understand what on earth Jack Charlton is on about, being under KGB surveillance, negotiating with a prostitute…

Then there's the tools of the trade. Mobile telephones and laptops occasionally (or in the Far East, seemingly always) malfunction, but when it prevents a humble hack from filing his/her copy then new technology is treated to some old-fashioned expletives.

I hope this book gives you an insight into the world of sports writing, the highs and lows, the hilarious and the sad … and gives you a glimpse behind the headlines created by those of us who cover major tournaments and events.

THE EARLY DAYS
(PART 1 - MOSCOW, ALBANIA, EAST GERMANY, UKRAINE, GLASGOW)

A FOOTBALL WRITER'S priority is to be able to file his or her copy by that ever-demanding servant The Deadline. Forget the five star hotels, the haute cuisine, happy hour (or happy hour and a half as we managed to extend it to in one Dublin hotel, convincing the manager it was appropriate for football reporters) and whatever other perks come our way. Many is the time I have sat in a luxury hotel cursing whatever it is that has prevented me from filing and would willingly have swapped the sea view, king sized bed, power shower and the rest for an internet connection or telephone signal in a tiny room overlooking a concrete factory.

The era of hi-tech has made filing match reports relatively easy, but pre-laptop hacks can remember, with mixed emotions, the bad old days of land-lines and copy takers.

In the former Eastern Europe it was necessary to book a call to London, which could take up to two hours, unacceptable now when even the engaged tone can provoke phone rage. There is a much-told story on Planet Football Writer when, during the Seventies, a reporter sat in a less-than-luxurious hotel room in Moscow staring and swearing at the phone, which amazingly did not speed up the connection process.

Eventually the phone rang and he was transferred to the East Berlin exchange, to Budapest, somewhere else, Paris and finally to London where the familiar English ring tone was music to his ear.

"Sports desk please," he said to the switchboard girl. "Sport," said someone on the sports desk. The relieved reporter said his name. "Sorry, he's in Moscow," replied his so-called comrade and slammed down the receiver. The two-hour process started again.

Moscow 1973 was much different from its current incarnation. I was there with England for a friendly against the Soviet Union and in those days Big Brother and his brother were everywhere. We were told that our rooms were bugged, so I went in search of said listening device, overturning pillows, waste-bins, mirrors and chairs in the process. Then I noticed the brass bed-head. I had just started to unscrew a knob on the top when the phone rang.

"Mr Davies, please do not tamper with your furniture," said a man who I imagined worked for SMERSH. Tampering was immediately terminated.

The roads of Moscow, now crowded with cars, most of which seem to be held together by the dirt, were almost empty in those days. Any vehicle you spied was almost certainly a KGB company car and on one visit during the Seventies Her Majesty's press were invited to the British Embassy for drinks, our coach taking us along the near-deserted roads.

We were greeted on British soil by someone sporting a handlebar moustache who said: "Hello old boy, come and have a pint of Red Barrel." Very appropriate in Moscow.

The embassy was also apparently bugged and I was told that when a meeting of national importance was held those concerned would go to a nearby wood for talks.

"Trouble is," said one of the embassy officials. "The housing problem is so acute in Moscow there are often three generations living in some apartments. This presents obvious problems for the youngsters to have a bit of nookie, so they tend to go to woods for some how's your father. No worries really, but it can be a little awkward walking along discussing government matters when you are ankle deep in cheap Russian Johnnies."

In those days the poverty of Moscow was an eyeopener to visitors from the West. Women would queue for hours to buy the most basic of foods in Gum, a huge store near Red Square. Now, Gum is full of designer shops with prices that reflect the newfound wealth among some sections of society living in the Russian capital.

During the 1970s a fearsome looking woman would be stationed on each floor of hotels to ensure guests did not bring any outsiders to their rooms. These women may have struggled to pass a sex test and the impression was that it was in one's best interests not to upset them.

Three decades on, the contrast between the rich and the poor in modern Moscow is stark. There is no real middle class, with 20 per cent of the people living below the poverty line. Contrary to popular opinion in west London, not everyone in Russia is a billionaire, though the oligarchs pay the same 13 per cent income tax as a road sweeper, which is brilliant for the oligarchs but not so good for the guys who keep the roads clean.

Kiev, now recognised as the capital of Ukraine, was still part of the old Soviet Union in 1987/88 when Rangers played Dynamo in the European Cup. As with Moscow, the poverty was depressing. People were happy to eat our leftovers. When we finished dinner in the hotel some locals, who couldn't afford to eat in the restaurant, which was basic to Westerners, finished off our plates. Let them eat scraps. Very sad.

A taxi driver told me he often had his wife and baby in his vehicle all day because his cab was heated which their apartment was not.

Ukraine's greatest footballer at the time was Oleg Blokhin, who played for Dynamo Kiev and the USSR national team during the Seventies and Eighties. He was voted European Footballer of the Year in 1975 and I remember interviewing the striker when he was at his peak.

Well, I say interviewing "him" – players spoke no English in those days, so the visiting media effectively interviewed the official state translator. I asked Blokhin if he would like to play in the West – Soviet footballers were banned from moving abroad then. You can imagine him thinking, if not saying: "Would I like to move to the West and earn more money in a month than I will in my entire career here and give my family a lifestyle beyond their wildest dreams? Live in a house that has more than one bedroom? Are you sure?"

Blokhin's actual answer via the translator was: "No, I am happy here, I have everything I want here."

Albania is slowly but surely recovering from the Stalinist regime of Enver Hoxha who ruled, putting it mildly, with an iron fist from 1944 until his death in 1985, the country being liberated by a revolution in 1990.

During his dictatorship there were only 600 cars on Albania's roads and in 1992 Tirana, the capital, boasted just 50 vehicles. In 1993, when the Republic of Ireland played Albania, the first traffic light was unveiled in Tirana. It was like stepping back into a different era.

Under Hoxha books were burnt, foreign radio and music were banned, while priests were buried alive. Religion – apart from atheism, if indeed atheism can be called a religion, go discuss among yourselves – was also banned. Even fishing was banned to preserve the best supplies for party leaders. The punishment for anyone caught dangling their worm in the water (so to speak) was 15 years in a labour camp. In fact, most things were banned. When Hoxha dismissed a cabinet minister once he simply shot him dead. Eat your heart out Sir Alan Sugar.

When I was there in 1993 policemen would wear balaclavas while making arrests for fear of avenging families. The Hotel Tirana was the best in the city and thank goodness we weren't in the second best. We had been told we may have to share a room, though I did not realise my roommate would be a rat.

There was no running water. At 8am a chambermaid knocked at the door and offered me a bowl of brown/grey water to wash in. We were there only one night, so we cleaned our teeth and splashed our faces with bottled water we had brought with us. The toilet, which did not flush, was indescribably filthy and smelly. Not exactly a super bowl. However, it was still better than the toilet facilities in the Ireland dressing-room at the stadium in Tirana. Any player suffering from prematch nerves had to squat over a hole in full view of his teammates.

The Albanians did not waste the opportunity of making a nice little earner from the visiting press. Journalists were charged a £50 'facility fee' for the use of the telephones that had been booked by our sports desk. No facility fee, no phone.

When Albania had played in Dublin a few months before the tie in Tirana the Football Association of Ireland took the visiting delegation for lunch on the day of the game to one of the city's top restaurants. The steak, potatoes and vegetables were a rare treat for the Albanians, but it was still something of a surprise when asked what they would like for dessert the guests replied: "Same again, please."

Ten years later I returned to Tirana with Ireland and the progress the country had made was incredible. We stayed in the same hotel, which had been rebuilt to the standard of a motorway stopover – perfectly acceptable for one or two nights. There were no rats in my room (or hopefully the kitchen) and Albania now boasted the highest ratio of Mercedes per capita anywhere in the world, even if nearly all of them were stolen and imported. Restaurants and bars had sprung up, while there was a shop that sold only Viagra – obviously a growing concern. Another sold stolen mobile phones.

Remarkable as it may seem, it is not an exaggeration to say the most popular person in Albania is Norman Wisdom. Seriously. Even Hoxha liked Wisdom, believing the Norman Pitkin character he played in his films represented workers struggling against capitalism, not a line I remember from too many reviews in England. When he visited the country, Wisdom – known in Albania simply as Pitkin – was treated like royalty. I think the Hotel Tirana is the only hotel in the world where I have seen a Norman Wisdom movie.

Bucharest is certainly the only place I have ever been mugged by the police. I was covering Romania v the Republic of Ireland and three of us were in a taxi going back to the hotel after dinner. I noticed we had taken a different route to the one the different driver used to take us to the restaurant but thought nothing of this.

Suddenly, police standing by a car on the side of the road waved us down. No problems, we all had our passports for identity purposes. Trouble was, a few minutes later what we didn't have was our money. There is something intimidating about an armed Romanian policeman who says "money", so we didn't argue or mention things like human rights, how wrong this was or particularly how they would be in trouble if the police found out. By coincidence we were left with just enough cash for the taxi fare. Perhaps significantly, the cab driver wasn't subjected to the Romanian robbery.

Passports can be a lucrative business in Moscow. The average monthly wage in the Russian capital is about £350 (twice the national average), but some, including policemen or perhaps those impersonating police officers, earn well above average. A tourist can be asked by a couple of 'policemen' for his passport, which he has probably left at the hotel. "Oh dear sir," they would say. "Sorry, you'll have to come to the police station and fill in the necessary forms. Alternatively you can pay an on-the-spot $50 fine."

Nervous of Newcastle is likely to opt for handing over 50 bucks rather than go to Moscow's Sun Hill. Let's say the Red Square passport 'police' manage to 'fine' five tourists in a day, they would then be $250 or £125 better off. In five days that would amount to £625 or just over £300 each. To pick up roughly your monthly salary in cash every week is a nice little bonus.

Food in the old Eastern Europe was basic at best, though when Nottingham Forest played Lokomotiv Leipzig, manager Brian Clough still believed his chairman should have his favoured York ham for breakfast.

"Young man," said Cloughie in his much-imitated manner to the East German waiter who spoke no English. "Chairman wants 'am. Not just 'am, York 'am. OK? Gottit? York f*****g 'am. For chairman. On your way, lad."

Cloughie was genuinely surprised when the waiter returned with a bowl of cereal.

Given his drinking habits Cloughie lived longer than most thought he would. One evening about six of us were in the hotel bar when Cloughie came in.

"So who's gonna buy me a drink then?" He asked. Without waiting for an answer, he continued: "No worries, I'll help myself." He proceeded to consume the contents of all our glasses and as he left, Cloughie said: "Hey, I bet you'll all claim for entertaining me on your expenses, won't you?" A magnificent performance. I think.

Eating in 'new' Eastern Europe can still mean a trip into the unknown. Covering Rotor Volgograd versus Manchester United in 1995 we were relieved when the waiter offered us an English menu. Our relief was short-lived when the menu simply said 'meat' and 'fish'. Not a good place to be a vegetarian.

There have been some memorable menu misprints. BBC Radio 5Live's John Murray tells of a "bag of sand" on a menu once. I've seen a roast virgin, a cowboy leg, a slippery chicken, a strange fish and the unforgettable – and untried – steamed crap.

There is also a belief that some things can taste better when you don't know what they really are. In a Moscow restaurant a few of us were eating steak which was a little on the tough side but nicely spiced. "How is the steak?" Asked the waiter halfway through the meal.

"Excellent, thank you."

"Good – so you like the bear...?"

Once aware of the origin of the steak our collective appetite disappeared.

Moscow provided the coldest setting I experienced for a game – Spartak Moscow versus Arsenal in November 2000. It was minus 13 degrees and my laptop decided it was too cold to work, ditto my Biro. So it was back to the good old pencil and paper, phoning the copy through over the landline.

When covering a game a football writer will generally file two reports. The first, called the runner, will be written during the match and the rewrite usually within an hour or so of the final whistle, including the managers' reactions.

The runner, usually 750 words for a big game, is filed in two or three chunks, as we call them – 450 at half-time, 150 more after 70 minutes with the 150-word intro on the whistle, the reporters praying for no late goal or incidents that affect the intro. We are selfish in that respect.

In Moscow I filed my half-time chunk of copy over the telephone to the *Daily Telegraph* copy taker. Now a good copy taker is worth his/her weight in gold. It took most of the interval to dictate my 450 words and team line-ups (oh those halcyon days of Smith, Jones, Brown…).

As I removed the phone from my ear, I discovered it was so cold that the skin of my ear had stuck to the perimeter of the earpiece. It took the ice station zebra Russian air a split second to hit my now exposed and skinless ear – the pain was sudden and severe.

Needless to say, there are many classic copy-taking errors that have somehow found their way into newspapers. Probably the best was the reporter filing a report on Wales when Ian Rush and Mark Hughes were at their peak. He told the copy taker: "The best strikers in Europe must be Rush and Hughes." Unfortunately it was taken down and printed as: "The best strikers in Europe must be Russian Jews."

When I was covering a Liverpool home game a copy taker once ticked me off by saying: "No, it isn't Anfield … it is a field …"

Another beauty saw it reported that England fans in France were met by a coach load of "John Barnes" instead of "gendarmes."

Reporting games in Europe means working nights and in October 2000 I engaged the services of a lady of the night for what she called "the most unusual thing I have ever been asked to do" – and the impression I was left with was that the list of what she had been asked to do was fairly extensive.

It was a night on which I had covered Celtic's UEFA Cup second round first leg victory over Blackburn Rovers and as I left Parkhead at around 11.30pm I asked a girl on reception if she could phone for a taxi.

She came back and said: "It'll be an hour and a half." I hadn't realised it was Hallowe'en. Deciding it would be easier to start walking towards Glasgow's city centre and hailing a taxi driving along or finding a minicab firm I set off on foot.

Five minutes later it started to rain. There was not an empty cab to be seen for love nor money. After more than an hour's trudge I arrived in the city centre wet and miserable. The queue in Central Station was never-ending, so I telephoned my hotel in Govan to see if they could arrange for a taxi to pick me up. They couldn't.

Whilst I was standing in the street contemplating the possibility of having to check in to another hotel because I couldn't get back to my original hotel a lady of the night approached me.

"Anything I can do for you darling?" she said.

"Yes. How much do you charge for a trick?" I asked – all those episodes of *Cracker* had finally paid off.

"Twenty five pounds."

"Do you have a car?"

"Aye."

"Here's £30," I said handing over three rather sodden tenners. "I want you to do something you have almost certainly never been asked to do before."

"Oh, I doubt that darling."

"I am tired, miserable, wet, my computer bag is the heaviest object in the world ... I just want you to drive me to my hotel in Govan."

"You're right darling, I've never been asked that."

To add an element of realism to the scenario, my hotel was called the Swallow. We drove in near silence, the passenger unable to think of anything to say to the unlikely cab driver. Something like "how's business?" did not seem appropriate.

We arrived at the hotel and as I climbed out she asked: "Sure there's nothing else I can do?"

Emboldened by my success in getting this far, I ventured: "Well yes there is one thing..."

"I knew it," she said with the confidence of a girl who probably knew MOST things.

In keeping with press tradition I had acquired a spare taxi bill from the driver (a proper cab driver) who had taken me to the game. "Could you fill in this bill for £15 so I can get some of my money back, please?"

"You really are a weird one," she said – and by her standards I probably was. "What shall I put?"

"Just today's date, city centre to Govan, £15."

"What shall I sign it?"

"Oh anything, it doesn't matter."

She performed her second unusual act of the night and handed me the receipt, which I put in my pocket. I made my excuses and left, arriving exhausted in my hotel room. After drying off I placed the receipt on a table and noticed that she had in fact signed it "Celtic 1, Blackburn 0."

Unable to submit the bill, I ... er ... swallowed the £15 and upon returning home framed the receipt as a memory of the only time I have ever paid a prostitute.

And yet a similar scenario presented itself to me during a trip to cover the Super Bowl in San Diego when, minutes after arriving in my hotel room complete with an eight-hour jet-lag, there was a knock on the door. Standing there was a stunning American-Chinese girl with a figure and face to kill for if not to pay for.

"Hi," she said as I stepped down from heaven. "The agency sent me. You have paid $1,000 and I am going to make sure you get every penny's-worth."

It was time for some quick thinking. Obviously there had been a monumental mixup, so I was left with two options. Either to explain to the breath-takingly beautiful girl in a dress that gave the appearance of having been sprayed on her hourglass figure that she had the wrong room – or to thank the Lord for working in strange ways and seize the moment.

There was no time to phone a friend and no audience to ask. What did I do? I did the right thing, of course.

THE EARLY DAYS
(PART 2 – TUNISIA, NEW ORLEANS, MALAYSIA, COLOMBIA, ARGENTINA, NIGERIA)

TUNISIA VERSUS EGYPT in December, 1977, presented problems I have never encountered elsewhere. The two countries were playing in the winner-takes-all decider in the 1978 World Cup African play-offs final round. I flew with Andy Cowie, Colorsport's award-winning photographer, to Tunisia ahead of the game.

Arab rivalry is always intense, but on this occasion the atmosphere was cranked up a few notches given what was at stake, and Egypt were keeping their headquarters a secret as they landed in Tunis. Andy and I set out from our Hammamet hotel in search of the Egyptians, which meant travelling on local buses.

What we hadn't bargained for was the local tradition of male passengers. Well, one of them. We were sitting near the rear of the coach … guy gets up … walks down to the back of the bus two rows from us … and takes a leak. He took out his thingy and weed on the floor. Just when you think you've seen it all … My remark that "if you do that again urine trouble" did not register with the Tunisian tinkler.

Andy and I tried various hotels to locate the Egyptians, but finally had to concede defeat and returned to our base in Hammamet in the early evening exhausted and frustrated. Imagine our delight when upon entering our hotel we discovered that the Egypt squad had checked in an hour or two earlier. Thank you God.

As Andy set about taking photographs of the Egypt players who lolled round the swimming pool, I chose one who looked every inch a centre-forward to interview (don't ask what an Egyptian centre-forward looks like, please). After introducing ourselves I asked if he could spare us ten minutes to chat about what it would mean for his country to play in the World Cup finals.

"Sure," he said sounding a little surprised, something I put down to meeting an English journalist and photographer in Tunisia.

Andy snapped away as I chatted to Egypt's finest. Or so I thought. When Andy had the photographs developed we asked the Egypt coach for the names and correct spelling of his players and he duly obliged. Except for one, the player I had interviewed. "Don't know him, sorry."

Unsure what was happening, I asked the hotel manager, who solved the mystery. "He's one of our waiters, he was on a day off," he said. I had not interviewed Egypt's star striker. I had interviewed a Tunisian waiter. Sob.

I went from feeling a mug to almost being mugged that day. I was the planned victim of two locals who, I later discovered, had broken into several rooms in the hotel and robbed a German woman of her passport. Andy was enjoying a last glass of sparkling water (ahem) in the bar and would be five minutes – I said I was heading upstairs to our shared room.

I left the door on the latch and climbed into bed. A few minutes later I heard the door open and to my horror it was not Andy but two men dressed in traditional Arab clothing. Presumably believing I was asleep, they started to look around the room.

For reasons I will never know, my instinct was to suddenly jump up and down and start waving my hands and legs around while making the sound of a dog barking (that one should keep the psychologists going for a while). Adding to this mad Englishman's midnight dog scenario, I was also naked – with apologies to anyone of a nervous disposition.

Quite what the two locals made of this I don't know, but unsurprisingly the sight of a naked foreigner jumping up and down on his bed doing a passable impersonation of Rin Tin Tin had the desired effect. They left without making any excuses and more importantly without any of our possessions.

My impromptu Poop Doggy imitation would have been unlikely to make me the lead (sorry) in any rap group, but when it comes to music nobody does it better than Bourbon Street in New Orleans. At the Super Bowl in 1997 I was with three of Her Majesty's working press doing research into jazz clubs when an American guy heard my accent as I ordered some drinks.

"English eh?" he said. "I worked there once…"

"Oh, where?"

"London … Birmingham … Manchester … Newcastle …"

"Did you enjoy it?"

"Man, yeh. I had a wonderful time…"

"What do you do?"

"I play in a group…"

"Well, if you are ever going to make it, Bourbon Street is the place to start, it's the university of music."

How smug was I thinking of the fabulous "university of music" line?

"Tell me the name of your group and I'll keep an eye, or even an ear, out for you."

"ZZ Top."

They were playing the half-time show at the Super Bowl. He was the one WITHOUT a beard. Called Frank Beard but, ironically I thought, sported only a moustache.

The beardless Mr Beard thought it was hilarious, a sentiment not shared by the graduate from the University of being a Clever Bastard. Perhaps I got the sympathy vote as he took the four of us into a private room where the more recognisable ZZs were enjoying the company of some girls so young they were still on their first breast transplants.

And yes, he told the story again. "I loved the university of music line," he said with delight that was matched only by my embarrassment.

It was embarrassment of a different kind when I underwent an involuntary name-change in Malaysia at the 1997 World Youth Championship. The computer could not fit "Christopher Davies" in the space allocated on the ID badge so self-corrected and came up with "Christ Davies".

For two weeks I walked around with a media accreditation that named me as "Christ". My parents were hugely impressed and wondered what it made them. Rather important, I suggested.

Questions like "is that really your name?" and "table for one for the last supper then?" soon wore thin.

It was also in Malaysia where one reporter perhaps proved that sometimes in life you can't always get what you want, but perhaps you do get what you deserve. We were in the night club, called Daniels, in the hotel and the manager said: "Gentlemen ... if you would like any of our ladies to do anything, just ask them and I'm sure they will oblige ... it costs just $25."

The Daniels dollies were stunning. First out of the traps was, let's call him Peter, who went over to one of the girls ... sat down ... drinks appeared ... a few minutes later the pair left the table, Peter disappearing in one direction and the girl in another.

Strange, we thought, no need for such subtlety.

Even stranger, about five minutes later Peter returned. Every guy has the occasional bad game (pause for collective male nodding – well, probably female too) but you would surely walk around the block for half an hour for street cred purposes.

"That was quick," it was swiftly pointed out.

Peter told us his tale of woe. "Sat down ... introduced myself ... bit of chitchat ... gave her $25 AND a $10 tip ... said that the manager had told us the girls would do anything we liked ... at which point she asked: 'Yes, what would you like me to sing?'"

Karaoke.

I Can't Get No Satisfaction was suggested.

Peter and the Daniels dolly did not spend the night together, though a trip to Colombia in 1998 saw something fade away from my pocket (a seamless link). After checking into my hotel in Bogota I decided to take a stroll round the block just to sample the atmosphere. Life can be far from normal in a country where a large coke is something to be sniffed rather than drunk and it was certainly out of the ordinary to see two Rambostyle armed guards outside a fast food restaurant.

Aware that pick-pocketing was rife, my hands were kept firmly in my pockets, not least because it was obvious I was not from this neck of the woods. Anyway, my money was inside a sock so I would have needed to be sock-pocketed (or should it be pick-socketed?) to be relieved of the $50 in my Marks and Spencer specials. As I took in the sights of Bogota I had cause to scratch the back of my head and that was all the encouragement my shadow needed.

In a flash a kid, no more than 12, thrust his hand deep in my pocket and ran off with the contents. There was almost a dark admiration for his sense of timing and after all, he hadn't taken any money ... just my Heathrow long-term car park ticket. If anyone has ever tried to leave an airport car-park without a ticket you will appreciate why I would willingly have swapped the useless (to the bandit of Bogota) piece of paper he had taken for the contents of my left sock.

If my welcome to the Colombian capital was unusual, my departure from Bogota airport was also unlike any other. As I checked in I was asked if I had paid the tax on what I had bought during my stay. "I haven't bought anything," I said. That was apparently irrelevant. I still had to pay $30 departure tax on goods I had not bought.

I changed flights at Miami and when the plane doors opened at the USA stopover there was a greeting party comprising countless drugs officers and sniffer dogs who checked everyone and everything as they disembarked. Frightening.

When I covered Colombia versus Yugoslavia – Colombia were among England's opponents at the 1998 World Cup finals – it was helpful that I could get by in Spanish. During my first World Cup in West Germany, 1974, I somehow managed to survive a month knowing only "ein grosse bier bitte" in the native language. When I went to Argentina four years later I promised I would be able to order more than one large beer. For example, two large beers.

Day college and night school gave me the basics in Spanish where my profesora impressed on me that when I spoke her language I only sounded "funny" to English people not Spanish speakers. This was put to the test in the lobby of the Plaza Hotel, Buenos Aires when a girl working for the World Cup host committee asked if she could help me.

"Si, quiero coger un taxi," I said Yes, I want a taxi.

"I am sorry?" she said.

Louder (the second language of the English abroad) I repeated: "Quiero coger un taxi."

"It is good that you have learnt some Spanish senor Davies," said the girl from Buenos Aires with a BA in beauty. "But we say 'tomar', not 'coger'. Like in England and the United States they use different words sometimes. Was your teacher from Spain?"

"Si."

"Okay."

"So what have I said?" I asked and braced myself for the worst. It was worse than the worst I had imagined.

"Well, you have just announced to the lobby of the Plaza hotel that you want to f**k a taxi."

In every sense it was 'taxi for Davies'.

My attempt at Portuguese 25 years after my Spanish inquisition in Buenos Aires was little better. At a pre-2004 European Championship function in Lisbon I asked a girl on the UEFA reception desk if I could leave my bag there.

"Of course."

"Obrigado, Janos," thank you Janos I replied after seeing 'JANOS' on her name tag.

"I'm sorry, my name is Patricia," she said.

"Oh, it says JANOS," I pointed out to the senhorita who didn't seem to know who she was. The girl occasionally known as Janos checked her 'name' and said: "That is my security badge expiry date – JAN 05."

But printed JANO5. An easy mistake – wasn't it?

There was no such language problem in Nigeria when I was made an offer I certainly did refuse. I understood it clearly even if I could hardly believe my ears. It remains the most unlikely and remarkable if apparently well-meant proposal ever put to me.

The people of Kano in northern Nigeria were among the most friendly and hospitable I have ever met – even if those in power are top of the corruption league – but one reporter took this to unprecedented extremes.

The background to this incredible proposal lies in the strange ticketing arrangements for the tournament. To watch a game spectators had to buy a ticket, but then also bribe their way into the stadium.

By the third match the fans had worked out that there was little point in buying a ticket – they just paid a bribe at the gate. The stadium, where the capacity was around 20,000, was jam-packed, yet the official attendance was only around 3,000, the number of tickets that had been officially sold.

Abu, a journalist who worked for a local paper, befriended me because he believed I was close to the Queen. He interviewed me and asked how Kanu would feel if he became the first Nigerian to win the FA Cup with Arsenal.

"He would be the happiest Nigerian in the world," I said, thinking I had given Abu the quote he wanted. It was printed as: "His eyes would shine like a million stars." Abu informed me that quote was better than the one I had given him. He had a glint in his eye as he told me.

Over the two weeks I was in Kano, I saw Abu regularly at training grounds and games and he was typical of the humble, friendly Nigerians I met while covering a tournament I thoroughly enjoyed. On the last day I said: "Abu, I am going home tomorrow. I want to say how much of a privilege it has been working alongside you out here."

"Mr Chris," he replied. "It has been an honour for me and it would be an even bigger honour if you would sleep with my wife."

It was one of the few occasions in my career when I was speechless. Eventually I found the words to tell Abu that where I come from, a man would not sleep with a friend's wife, fervently hoping he had never read the *News of the World*.

If Abu was friendliness personified, the hotel management's approach to their staff was less amiable. The hotel staff slept in the grounds – literally. They slept under a bush or tree and given this scenario it was no surprise the management treated them poorly in other respects. During the tournament, an England player reported that $100 had been stolen from his room. The security officer with the Football Association, a former commander in the Metropolitan Police, interviewed the staff and was satisfied none was guilty. The hotel management, however, decided the culprit must be the person who cleaned the players' rooms, so punished him accordingly. When I next saw this man, his face was swollen and teeth were missing.

A few hours later the player found the missing $100 in a sock. The management's view was that the swelling would go and it was "only" two or three teeth missing. So that's alright then.

THE REPUBLIC OF IRELAND

JACK CHARLTON is the most intriguing, charismatic and unfathomable manager I ever worked with.

When Charlton became manager of the underachieving Republic of Ireland national team in 1986 football trailed behind the Gaelic sports, rugby and horse racing in public interest. Lansdowne Road was often less than half full as Ireland became serial non-qualifiers for major finals.

Ten years later football had assumed a new status not just in Irish sport, but in the country's culture as Charlton's inspired leadership gave Ireland worldwide publicity through achievements on the pitch. Lansdowne Road was sold out for almost every game and the Green Army, who followed the national team abroad, became the most popular and well-behaved of visiting supporters.

The miner's son became a multi-millionaire, but he claimed his life had not really changed. He told me: "You might think my life is different from the way I grew up, but really it's basically the same. I've never been hungry in my life. It's just we live in a better house, have a few spare ones and eat different stuff. When I was a lad you'd buy a loaf of bread, rip it in six and share it with your pals. Now you get them round and eat salmon you caught yourself and drink decent wine. But it's the same thing."

At times I wondered if, during his 10 years in charge of Ireland, Charlton was like the monkey in the cage – laughing at the people laughing at him.

Once when Ireland played Romania, Charlton kept calling them Bulgaria even to a totally baffled Romanian press.

He would regularly read his team out from the back of a packet of cigarettes on which he had scrawled the names. "Packie [Bonner] ... Doings [someone whose name had temporarily escaped him] ... the Ice Cream Man [Cascarino, in reference to the striker's long-hidden Italian roots] ... John [Paul McGrath who he called John] ..."

Once when naming his team he read out only 10 players, ending with: "you know who the other bugger is, you don't need me to tell you."

From one under the 11, Charlton once named a team with 12 players. One player mentioned this to the manager who enquired: "Who told you this?"

"Tony Cascarino."

"Clever sod. Tell him he's not playing ... we'll have 11 then."

Charlton is famous for getting people's names wrong, not just Paul McGrath's. Like McGrath, QPR midfielder Gary Waddock was always John. More worrying, Arsenal's Liam Brady would be Ian. Charlton once told a television interviewer: "The centre-half will be the bloke I signed last week. What's his name?" When asked by a Swedish journalist which Sweden player could cause Ireland most problems, Charlton said it was "the blond feller." Charlton claimed his names-game was a joke and in his defence said: "It's possible that I may have called Liam Brady 'Ian' on a couple of occasions. I was stuck with this reputation for forgetfulness. It became a bit of a party piece with me.

"Announcing the Irish team to the press after training, I'd go 'Bonner, Morris, Hughton, Moran – and that big lad, what d'you call him?' and someone would prompt me – 'McCarthy' – without realising that I was taking the mickey yet again."

Flying back from Cork to Dublin after a B international I noticed Charlton had a bag of duty free drinks.

"What's that Jack?" I asked.

"Dooty frees," he said in his Geordie accent.

"But Jack, we are flying from Cork to Dublin..."

"No one said anything to me."

Four years before the 1990 World Cup finals in Italy when Ireland made their debut on football's biggest stage, Jack Charlton had promised physiotherapist Mick Byrne that if the team ever got to Rome he would arrange for him to meet the Pope. With a little help from Monsignor Liam O'Boyle a visit to the Vatican for the entire squad was organised during Italia 90 with Tony Stenson of the *Daily Mirror* and I the only journalists who managed to be part of the audience. Displaying our media credentials and saying "Her Majesty's press" to anyone who looked remotely like a security guard we managed to bluff our way in. The squad were on the 'stage' with His Holiness on the other side.

Charlton's concentration levels occasionally leave something to be desired, and after half an hour or so of listening to pilgrims from Paraguay and bishops from Brazil the Ireland manager nodded off. Upon hearing the first snore Byrne nudged Charlton in the ribs. At the moment Charlton opened his eyes the Pontiff was waving an acknowledgment to a group of nuns from Nicaragua, but the Ireland manager thought the Pope was waving to HIM. So Charlton duly waved back to the amazement of everyone, not least John Paul. This was to prove an integral part of his after dinner speech routines in the future (Charlton that is, not the Pope).

On Ireland away trips the sponsors, Opel and then eircom, have taken the travelling media out for dinner where we literally have to sing for our supper. Journalists either sing a song – the Irish usually sing because *Dublin In The Rare Old Times* is better than *Knees Up Mother Brown* – while the Brits tell a joke. Perhaps the finest act at these gatherings was Philip Quinn of the *Irish Independent* whose impersonation of Peter O'Sullevan doing a commentary on the Grand National never failed to earn a standing ovation. Quinn was so convincing that those cheering for Greasepaint were searching for their betting slips at the end.

On one trip Charlton came along to one of the soirées and treated us to a rendition of Blaydon Races – imagine Sven-Göran Eriksson singing Mama Mia or Fabio Capello stunning the journos who cover England with Just One Cornetto.

John Bean, formerly of the *Daily Express*, lived up to his Mr Bean name when he decided to sing a specially adapted version of the Kenny Rogers classic *You've Picked A Fine Time To Leave Me Lucille*. Beano, as he was inevitably called, rewrote the lyrics as a tribute to Fran Fields, the president of the Football Association of Ireland, who was stepping down.

So the chorus line became: "You've picked a fine time to leave us Fran Fields" with John even handing out song-sheets to ensure everyone joined in. Very clever and well intended. The problem was, John seemed the only person unaware that Fields was retiring because he had cancer.

Oh dear.

CRAIG JOHNSTON, best known for his time with Liverpool, tells a classic Charlton tale from his days as a young hopeful at Middlesbrough when Jack was in charge of a trial match. Johnston, who was brought up in Australia, said: "We were getting beat 3-0 at half-time. Jack came into the dressing room and he had a go at all the Middlesbrough trialists. He turned to me and said: 'You – kangaroo – you are the worst footballer I have ever seen in my life. You can hop it back home to Australia immediately.'

"That was my introduction to English football, Big Jack saying I was the worst player he'd ever seen. I was extremely upset and I wanted to go home. The problem was, my parents had sold the house in Australia to finance my trip to England. So I got on the phone and mum asked: 'How was your trial in front of Jack Charlton?' I said: 'Big Jack loves me, so much he's asked me to stay for a year.' And for a year I spent all my time hiding from Jack Charlton in the car park practising my skills."

After Charlton left Johnston's Boro career blossomed.

There are some legendary tales of Irish fans during this era. One arrived in Malta to watch Ireland secure their place at Italia 90 in November 1989 by winning their final qualifier – it would be the first time they had reached the World Cup finals – with a lunch-box complete with sandwiches. He hadn't told his wife where he was going, only that he would be working late.

It was claimed by a Maltese bar owner that the estimated 7,000 Irish fans in Valetta drank more in one night after Ireland qualified for the World Cup than they had served in the previous year. It's such a great statistic it seems wrong to dispute it.

In Italy, hotel rooms on Sardinia and Sicily, where Ireland were based for the group stage of their World Cup debut, were at a premium, so some Irish fans took to the sea. One group hired a boat that slept eight, having advertised for a 'captain' to ensure everything ran smoothly, with the added incentive of match tickets for 'il capitano.' Unfortunately the boat hit a rock, which caused severe damage to the vessel – in the room of the 'captain' a book entitled *Sailing For Beginners* was found. The Irish will do anything for match tickets...

Because of potential trouble involving England supporters there was an alcohol ban in Cagliari on match days, though we did not expect this to extend to the media hotel. It did. Imagine the horror of thirsty hacks returning to their hotel and finding (a) no booze available in the bar and (b) any bottles of alcohol in rooms confiscated.

For the second match some subtle tricks were used. Wine was placed inside pillow cases, beers were hidden in bushes and trees (some not hidden well enough), while it was rumoured one photographer removed two tiles from the side of the bath, hid his thirst-quenchers and replaced the tiles.

WHEN IRELAND played in Tbilisi, the capital of Georgia (twinned with Bristol, honest – and yes we did the full range of two Bristols jokes) in March 2003, among the local traditions was robbing tourists. Well, visiting journalists anyway. Three Irish journos had their money removed when a taxi was stopped by some locals who had more than Georgia on their minds.

We were advised to hire a 'security' driver which three of us did as we went on a trip around Tbilisi to take in the atmosphere of a city that was once beautiful, but had suffered over a decade of decay in the wake of independence from the Soviet Union in 1991. Our driver certainly knew his way around the potholes, while when we were stopped by a roadside police check he showed his ID and we were waved through.

"Very impressive." I remarked. "What does your ID say?"

As he showed us it, he told us his card was issued by the all-embracing Ministry Of Information. On it, in English, was written "licensed to store, carry and use firearms." To prove this he reached across to the glove compartment, opened it and produced a gun. A loaded gun.

This was not a guy to be messed with and we were relieved he was driving us rather than stopping us. He was almost too friendly and took us to a restaurant owned by some friends where he urged us to sample the local speciality which was some sort of meat dish. For Jon Brodkin of the *Guardian*, a vegan, this presented a problem. While keen to remain faithful to his beliefs, he was similarly eager not to upset the man from the ministry of guns. Jon tried the "not hungry" and "allergic to meat" lines, but the Georgian gunslinger was having none of it. To be honest the local delicacy did not look too inviting even to the non-vegans and eventually we made our excuses and left with Jon's stomach still free of meat. Close call though.

I shall share two pieces of amazingly interesting information with you to ensure full value for money. Georgians pronounce Tbilisi with a barely-spoken 't' so that it almost sounds like "BillEEsee." However, English speakers mispronounce it "TibLEEsee." The correct pronunciation is T*bilisi. There is no voiced sound between the 't' and 'b' and before you say this is boring it was on a piece of paper T*bilisi's John Wayne gave me, so I thanked him and said how interesting it was. And please put your g*un away.

The second? There is also a George W Bush Street on the way to the airport. One can only assume they ran out of street names.

I love Dublin and the Irish whose capacity to enjoy themselves is surely unsurpassed. Like their humour. The first time I arrived in Dublin I took a taxi from the airport to the city centre and some rather pleasant music was being played in the cab.

"That's nice – who is it?" I asked the driver.

"I don't know sir, I only work weekends," he answered.

"Oh. OK...sorry," I replied accepting his reply. I have yet to fathom out what he really meant.

Similarly, the guy from Cork who claimed the city's population "must be about two million," his estimate being based on the fact that "there are three cinemas here, you know."

Even the locals can be bemused by the language. Peter Byrne, for many years the football correspondent of the *Irish Times*, tells the story about a visit to a Dublin bar which tested his knowledge of slang. A guy asked for two Guinnesses "and a Shirley Bassey". Peter worked out every rhyme imaginable but "a Shirley Bassey" remained a mystery. He had to ask the barman.

"A Shirley Bassey? It's a Black Bush, sir."

A sad movie anorak once told me the word 'mafia' is not mentioned in classic mob movie *The Godfather*. During the 1994 World Cup finals four of us were made an offer we could not refuse and we, too, didn't mention the M-word. After the Republic of Ireland had beaten Italy 1-0 at Giants Stadium we were chatting to some New York Italians who seemed amused by four English hacks talking to them about soccer.

"You guys like Italian food?" asked a Robert De Niro sound-alike.

"Of course."

"We would like you to be our guests at our uncle's restaurant in Little Italy." Pronounced as one word Liddleidaly.

BEHIND THE BACK PAGE

Size may not matter, but a free Italian meal does.

Two nights later we made our way to their uncle's restaurant. What we were unaware of was the identity of the uncle, who actually was the head of a Mafia family. A real life Tony Soprano. When the uncle lost his battle against cancer a few years later (in jail) some believed he was the only member of the family to die of natural causes. This was not the usual family dinner. Or even a usual family.

However, the nephews were wonderful hosts. "Have any table you like..."

It was a warm June evening so we chose a table near the window.

"We prefer our special guests not to sit by the window..."

We were given a table near the kitchen. Dinner chat was like shadow boxing, testing each other.

"So what does your uncle do apart from the restaurant?"

"Import and export."

They knew that we knew that...

The food, company and dinner talk were excellent and at their suggestion we went on to a nearby blues club.

No doubt encouraged by some of his uncle's vino, one of the family was on the dance floor when his piece dropped out of his pocket. As a man of peace I retrieved it and handed him his handgun with the delicacy of a surgeon performing a heart transplant. Mine stopped for a few seconds while I handed him what appeared a tool of his trade.

TWO OF THE most memorable trips with Ireland were to Macedonia in October 1999 for a Euro 2000 qualifying tie and to Iran in November 2001 for a 2002 World Cup playoff tie.

Skopje, the capital of Macedonia, is close to the Kosovo border, which was still in a state of high alert following killings and atrocities by Serbian forces on Kosovan Albanians that year. Frank Stapleton, the former Ireland captain, was going to Kosovo with a television unit to talk to the Irish soldiers in the K-For peacekeeping force. I had the chance to travel with them in a K-For jeep and Kosovo provided the most gruesome sights I have ever witnessed.

Crossing the border was frightening, with young soldiers high on nerves and emotion with hair-triggers. Once through, as we drove towards the camp where the Irish troops were stationed, I saw hundreds, maybe thousands, of body-bags containing those killed in a massacre.

The television news teams which had covered the atrocities had left Kosovo by then, but outside the camp one soldier pointed to a wall and said: "That's where Kate Adie slept." At least I always had a hotel room (rat optional) – Kate and the other TV reporters who had covered the war had slept under the night sky in tents.

Over breakfast the K-For troops told harrowing tales of rape, torture and murder carried out by Serbians. We were taken to a house where a Kosovo Albanian and his two sons lived – their mother had been shot in front of them and one of the boys was so badly traumatised he had not spoken since. They both had to share the single top bunk of a bed because of the floodwater in the house and it causes me no embarrassment to say tears were shed as I looked at their living conditions and learned what had happened to the family.

Returning to Skopje later that day Frank and I told the Irish and British reporters on the trip what we had seen. An impromptu collection raised enough money for the soldiers to buy better sleeping facilities for the family.

Tehran was equally unforgettable in a more positive way. Obtaining a visa for Iran is not easy, but under FIFA rules a country must allow the visiting press entry. My visa always caused panic when entering the USA subsequently.

"Why were you in Iran sir?"

"To cover the 2002 soccer World Cup playoff tie between Iran and the Republic of Ireland."

I can almost hear the customs official saying to himself: "What the hell does he mean...?"

Needless to say it was a dry trip and there is something unreal about a group of football writers in a hotel bar drinking orange juice or Coke. A trip to the centre of Tehran revealed the new address of the British Embassy, which had to be changed after the Iran government renamed the street where the entrance was as Bobby Sands Street. Sands was the IRA hunger-striker who had starved himself to death in 1981 in Maze prison where he was serving a sentence for possession of arms. To Iranians he was a freedom fighter, so they named a street in his honour, which by coincidence happened to be where the British Embassy was based.

Aware that the address 'British Embassy, Bobby Sands Street' was not exactly politically correct, the embassy moved its entrance round the other side to a different street. Not that Iran is totally anti-West – there is a restaurant called McHamburger.

The Saadbad Palace, the summer palace of the last Shah of Iran, redefined the meaning of ostentatious. Shah Mohammed Raza Pahlevi fled to France in 1979 after months of protest against his regime as Ayatollah Khomeni made the reverse journey. What was a lap of expensive, lavish luxury is now a tourist attraction, displayed as a warning of Western decadence. The last guest to dine there with the Shah was US President Jimmy Carter and not a lot of people know that.

The Shah liked to spoil himself – his bedroom was fitted with the finest quality Persian carpet (yes, it cost a pile...) on which, the guide told us, he preferred to sleep rather than in his bed. Each to their own, I guess. The chandeliers inevitably brought back memories of the classic *Only Fools And Horses* sketch, though when one reporter said to the guide: "If you need these cleaned my uncle Derek will do you a good rate" it was met with the blankest of looks.

George Best Tells Me I'm The Expert

A QUESTION I am frequently asked is: How do I become a football writer?

There is no easy route to what most still call Fleet Street. It is the same as it ever was ... local papers, sports agencies ... waiting for the break. As much as the ability to write, work ethic is also a skill. Those who go that extra yard, make that extra call ... they are the ones who go farthest.

Neil Ashton of the *Daily Mail* is a good example to any would-be football writer. When he was with the *People*, Neil would go to midweek reserve games to make contact with young players just starting their professional career. He'd chat to them, not necessarily for interviews or articles, but just to get to know them, to start a friendship that would serve him well if that player made the grade. Ash is now as good a football news reporter as there is and I know he looks back on those cold, lonely nights at games nobody gave a toss about as a significant part of his learning curve.

It was different as I made my way up the Fleet Street ladder in the Seventies and Eighties. Journalists could drink and socialise with players and managers who knew confidences would not be made public. In these days of circulation wars and a growing intrusion by news desks into sport when Ashley and Cheryl or Harry Redknapp can make front page news it is difficult going on impossible to have that type of friendship with football folk.

These days press conferences are organised (some better than others) and once the manager or player has spoken to the media, that's it. Arsène

Wenger having a metaphorical pint with a journalist is something no-one will ever see. I used to have the home number of just about every London-based player and manager. I could – and did – phone them for fitness checks or to see what else was going on. These days, journalists' contacts books are less prolific. We tend to know the people who know the people now.

I became friends with George Best when he was a columnist for *Shoot* magazine, where I worked from 1969 to 1982. It might be a hard point to sell, but despite his image as a womaniser, Bestie was happiest – okay, happy – having fish and chips with some mates, picking a World XI to play the moon.

At a time when Best was having problems with his marriage to Angie I flew back from the United States with him. He had written a poem for her and said to me: "You're the expert. Let me know what you think."

George Best, the finest footballer the United Kingdom has ever produced, was telling ME that I was the expert … the poem wasn't bad actually.

There are many anecdotes about Bestie, but I love this one told to me by my late father who knew the taxi driver concerned. George had told the cabbie: "Heathrow please," and chatted away about the weather and other non-football events. As the driver pulled off the M4 he said: "Okay … I give up … tell me …"

"George Best," said George, no doubt bemused by the question, not least as the journey was coming to an end.

"I meant which terminal…"

The driver had had no idea who his passenger was as they chatted.

AFTER THE Republic of Ireland beat England 1-0 in the first match of the 1988 European Championships in Germany, that night three or four English-based hacks who covered the Republic celebrated with some of the Ireland players in Stuttgart. It would be impossible to enjoy such celebrations with international players in the modern era, when a footballer seen drinking alcohol can lead to a front page 'booze shame' story. Life moves on, though not always in a positive way.

Players earning more in a week than most of us earn in a year are prime targets for what some people perceive as easy money. Kiss-and-tell is a nice little earner. Sleep with a famous, or even not particularly famous, player and a girl can sell her story that "love rat soandso broke my heart" for a grand or two. It's little more than prostitution in print, but it works.

One well-known footballer was having a regular away fixture with "a leggy blonde" who eventually felt the arrangement was coming to an end, so she did the decent thing and contacted a tabloid. Proof was needed and the honey trap was set, a video recorder the size of a lipstick secreted in a hotel room's television. In the next room a journalist of said tabloid monitored the goings on (and takings off) of said footballer and the leggy blonde. Having done what they usually did, the leggy blonde went to powder her nose (or whatever), so the footballer decided to surf the television channels. To his horror on channel 13 he appeared to see himself.

Thinking on her feet, the journalist in the next room immediately 'pulled the plug' and channel 13 went dead. One can only imagine what was going through his mind, but full marks to the journo for the quickest of thinking. She then telephoned next door and when the footballer answered the phone she said: "Good afternoon sir, hotel manager here ... just wanted to check that everything was okay and you were enjoying your stay."

The footballer mentioned the mystery of spying himself for a second or two on his TV. "Ah, that was probably channel 13 which is our dedicated babysitting channel," explained the journalist. "If you and your wife or partner wanted to have dinner in our restaurant, all you have to do is turn on the television to channel 13 and our staff can monitor your son or daughter."

It worked. He bought it. And two days later the leggy blonde was able to go on a shopping spree with the 'reward' from the tabloid as they told how "love rat *** broke my heart."

Sometimes scoops go wrong though. When Terry Venables was coach of Barcelona a tabloid received a tip he was 'playing away'. They sent a reporter and photographer over to Barcelona who set up camp in a bush with the camera lens trained on El Tel's apartment. After a less than comfortable night with no sighting of Venables, at about 8am he appeared on his balcony wearing shorts and a T-shirt. A minute later he was joined not by a leggy blonde but a 'busty brunette'. Venables kissed her on the cheek and put his arm round her waist, his affection obvious – she was at least 30 years younger than him too. What a story. Click click click. The camera burst into belated life.

The pair returned to London with their scoop, the reporter given the awkward task of confronting Mrs Venables with the photographs of her husband and Miss BB.

Under such circumstances the wife normally says nothing or tells the reporter to go forth and multiply. To his amazement she asked him in for a cup of tea.

"I am sorry Mrs Venables, but I have to ask you for your reaction to the photos."

"On or off the record?"

"On, please."

"OK. They are some of the nicest photographs of my husband and daughter I have seen."

Own goal. Massive own goal.

Despite the lurid stories that can be all too common, we must not lose sight of the fact that the majority of players are decent guys, many giving much of their time to help promote the game at grass roots level in the local community or charity work. The bad apples are very much in the minority even if they make the majority of the headlines.

A puzzling development is the insistence of negativity in football reporting. A player or manager signs for a club and too many sports desks demand a former team-mate or someone who played under the new man puts the boot in.

A journalist can present a balanced article but invariably any praise will be cut out. This pre-supposes readers (i.e. fans) only want to read negatives about the club they support, the players and the manager. Really? While supporters can be more critical of their club than any reporter, the passion they have for it is far greater than any faultfinding. However, there has been a trend towards only printing 'blasts' or 'launched an amazing attack' type interviews. no-one is allowed to be nice any more. Good news is bad news and bad news is good news.

I have mixed views about the influx of those involved in football – or those from other walks of life – becoming journalists. If they are to work alongside those who have come through the learning process of local papers or agencies to earn a job on a national newspaper they must tell readers what reporters cannot. They should take us into the dressing room or the board room, using their firsthand experience to compare with current incidents which reporters cannot.

Journalists can and do write whatever they believe, but some football folk who join Fleet Street are reluctant to talk too deeply about those they played alongside or managed. There are some notable exceptions. Graham Taylor was able to write more freely when he quit management. Taylor could then put forward views he would have been reluctant to offer while Aston Villa manager – not least about his chairman Doug Ellis. His *Daily Telegraph* columns are always informative, reflecting his vast insider's knowledge of the game.

Taylor has recollections the more traditional reporter cannot possess and he shares anecdotes with readers while not afraid to upset those still involved in the sport with his opinions.

Former referee Graham Poll writes a Saturday column in the Daily Mail and no-one could ever accuse him of sitting on the fence. Poll will criticise his former colleagues if he believes they have made mistakes, writing with the knowledge and authority no journalist could on refereeing matters. He also does his best to explain why decisions were or were not made which commentators are often unable to do.

Maybe big names sell newspapers regardless of what they say, often in ghosted columns or exclusives, but that downgrades the art of journalism. It is saying anyone can be a football reporter and I believe sports writing is an art, one which I value.

If footballers, managers or referees are to take the space and place of a rank-and-file reporter they should offer more than writing the sort of articles a journalist can produce, not just being in print because they are who they are. A so-called star's opinions or ideas are often far less valid than those of someone who has been round the block many times and reported on 1,000 Premier League games.

When football writers appear on Sky Sports' *Sunday Supplement* we hear intelligent, honest views of experienced observers. The likes of Paul Hayward, Joe Lovejoy, Henry Winter, Martin Samuel, Shaun Custis, Oliver Holt, Matt Lawton, Patrick Collins, Matt Dickinson, Mick Dennis, Patrick Barclay and Ian Ridley, to name but a few, invariably give more of an insight than a former England international or a manager filling in time on TV in between jobs.

Yet for all its ills football remains a sport that raises passions like no other and reaches parts other aspects of life can't touch. The sheer joy of seeing your team score or the abject misery of conceding a late decisive goal – "to THAT mob of all people" – provides a wonderful roller-coaster of emotions. Watching all this from the press box has been a privilege.

So has knowing some of the truly great characters of Fleet Street such as the late Frank Clough of the *Sun* who was capable of making someone who had lost his lottery-winning ticket laugh, such was his infectious sense of humour. On one occasion at a charity function some journalists were chatting to Dame Kiri Te Kanawa, the New Zealand-born opera singer who performed at the wedding of Prince Charles and Princess Diana. Cloughie joined the group and, taking his trademark cigarette from his mouth, introduced himself to one of the world's finest sopranos.

"Frank Clough of the *Sun*, love," he said.

"Please to meet you. Kiri Te Kanawa."

"And what do you do?" asked Cloughie.

"I'm a singer."

"I do a bit of karaoke myself," said Cloughie unaware that the 'singer' performed at slightly bigger places than the Dog and Duck – Royal Weddings for example – but fair play to her, she found it hilarious.

COVERING MAJOR tournaments, internationals, Champions League ties and the Super Bowl isn't always fun, but it can still be funny.

Just as whoever invented the wheel probably regrets not having the idea sooner, I wish I had started to keep a daily diary – I don't think 'blog' was in the English language then – of foreign trips before the 2002 World Cup finals in Japan and South Korea.

Better late than never. Enjoy.

2002 WORLD CUP JAPAN/SOUTH KOREA

SATURDAY SEPTEMBER 1, 2001

An unforgettable day – and night. Holland had to beat the Republic of Ireland at Lansdowne Road to qualify for the 2002 World Cup finals. A draw would suit Ireland. The Dutch arrived in Dublin with their usual array of household stars, some even spoke of retiring from international football after the finals. Whoa – hold on lads, you're not there yet.

Louis van Gaal, the Holland coach who could be described as many things, though with modest not high on the list, had been speaking about Ireland possibly sacking their manager Mick McCarthy if they lost. Unsurprisingly McCarthy was not amused and his last words to his players before the game were: "Just give me the chance to shake his hand afterwards and say 'unlucky'." That is the family audience version of Mick's sentiments, by the way.

The atmosphere was incredible and the noise level rose a few more notches when, in the opening minute, Roy Keane clattered into Marc Overmars with such a ferocity that it probably still gives the Holland winger nightmares. The old adage of not being cautioned for your first foul worked and Keane's challenge set the tone for Ireland's display.

Holland, who in football parlance 'didn't like it up 'em', struggled against a spirited Ireland, but in the 58th minute the home side were reduced to 10 men when Gary Kelly was sent-off for a second yellow card offence.

McCarthy took off striker Robbie Keane and replaced him with Steve Finnan, a full-back – the manager obviously going for the draw which should see Ireland through to the finals.

Van Gaal's response was to bring on substitutes Jimmy Floyd Hasselbaink and Pierre van Hooijdonk and play with four strikers, lumping the ball upfield to them, which Ireland handled comfortably. Then in the 67th minute Finnan, on the right, found Jason McAteer, who scored with a half-volley. Lansdowne Road erupted as the ball beat Edwin van der Sar.

McAteer, nicknamed Trigger after the *Only Fools And Horses* character, was one of the most endearing of Ireland players. Filling in a form for a credit card (he was 25 at the time) under the heading 'position within company' McAteer wrote 'midfielder'.

He once managed to lock himself out of his car and stopped a passing police car for assistance. The officers recognised McAteer and apparently were not surprised at what had happened. "Can you help me at all?" asked McAteer. While aware that they should not really do it but wanting to help a tormented Trigger, one policeman asked: "Do you have a coat-hanger?" A few minutes later McAteer returned with ... a wooden coat hanger.

There is also the story of McAteer in a Dublin disco where he noticed Jimmy 'Whirlwind' White, one of the leading snooker players in the world. McAteer wanted to chat to White, but his team-mates suggested the Whirlwind was with pals so maybe best not. A whirl, sorry, while later McAteer spotted his chance as White went to the bar.

"Hey Jimmy," said McAteer. And as White turned round McAteer said: "One hundred and eighty..."

McAteer's finishing against Holland was more accurate than his choice of sports and the remaining 23 minutes were probably the longest in the lives of most at Lansdowne Road. At the final whistle McCarthy got his wish and went up to van Gaal and said: "Unlucky Louis" before joining his jubilant players.

Later that night I watched Germany versus England and, after the professional satisfaction of Ireland's success, much Guinness was taken on board as a Michael Owen hat-trick helped the visitors to an unforgettable 5-1 win in Munich.

I was so happy I didn't even care about the inevitable hangover.

WEDNESDAY MAY 22, 2002

THE 2002 WORLD CUP starts here. The weather is warm and cloudy – rather like a Ben Johnson dope test. Arrived in Dublin 10pm. The other lads are scoffing in the airport hotel's Chinese restaurant. I was knackered, so decided to have early night.

My room is the furthest from the reception desk that is possible on the third (top) floor. No lift and a case weighing 25kg, which seemed like 250kg when I finally made it to my room that was so far away from the lobby it needed its own post code.

THURSDAY MAY 23

Woke up at 6am – well, to be precise, as a journalist must be, of course, the alarm woke me up – and switched on the TV to discover Republic of Ireland captain Roy Keane has said he will retire from international football after the World Cup. Thanks Roy. Watched all Irish news programmes, listened to Irish radio and wrote 800 words on Keane's pending international retirement.

I also had to rewrite my Friday for Saturday piece, which because of travelling all day Thursday I'd had to leave (filed early) with the sports desk. So instead of a nice relaxing start to the day I ended up frantically writing and rewriting 1,500 words while the rest of the country slept. I hope the World Cup gets a little easier.

Colin Young of the *Daily Mail* just made the airport bus because like me he was hurriedly rewriting all he had originally written. Having checked in at the airport, Colin then had to make a swift return to the hotel as he hadn't paid his bill.

It was apparently my fault, though reasons were not given. Somewhere on the return journey Colin dropped his passport, which was also my fault. For 15 minutes it was blind panic – hot and cold sweats – but when he checked with security at the airport he discovered that someone had handed in his passport. I had nothing to do with this, however.

Roy Keane had given a long interview to Tom Humphries in the *Irish Times*, which amounted to pressing the self-destruct button on his international career. I read it while having a heart-attack-on-a-plate Full Monty vein-clogging artery-busting breakfast in the airport to the soothing sound of a faulty alarm bell which rang throughout the 10 million calorie intake, predictably stopping as I left the table.

Youngy is 32 today and I told the Aer Lingus crew this historical statistic which was announced on the plane. They gave him two miniatures of champagne and wine to commemorate making it to 32 not out. The short flight to Amsterdam (the first leg of the long journey to Japan) was unsurprisingly full of Keano chat. Upon arriving at Schipol airport we discovered Mick McCarthy, the Ireland manager, had sent Keane home after a blazing row in front of the other players in their training base in Saipan, an island near Japan. So the 800-word piece I had written in Dublin plus the 700-word rewritten piece (Friday for Saturday's article) were both scrapped, overtaken by subsequent events. I had 90 minutes to rewrite and re-rewrite them after Brendan Menton, chief executive of the Football Association of Ireland, gave all the Keaned-off travelling journo's some background to what was going on in Saipan.

Managed to get hold of former Ireland manager Jack Charlton for his views, the *Daily Telegraph* office fed me some McCarthy quotes from the news wires, and I was writing almost literally as I was walking to the plane for Japan. When I attempted to file the copy my laptop would not work.

There is a rule on Planet Laptop that when you really really REALLY want it to work it doesn't. Swearing does not do justice to my language. I had to dictate to a copy-taker while walking along, hand-baggage in one hand, laptop in the other, reading off the screen, mobile phone under chin (okay, one of them). I received some strange looks from other passengers. In fact, I even gave myself a strange look.

The flight to Tokyo was a nightmare. Our preassigned seats were all over the place with nobody next to anyone they knew. I sat next to a priest, resisting any remarks about Judas.

The two movies showing were *Ocean's 11* and *Beautiful Mind* – the last two films I saw at the cinema. Why does that always happen? Do they somehow know? Who are the 'they' we keep referring to?

Flying over Siberia was amazing, hours and hours of nothing. Bit like *Big Brother*. The pilots have to be specially trained to deal with the problems of flying over such terrain for long periods. This is one of the many interesting things I know that make me such a fun person, first on the list for any dinner party – "hey, put that Christopher Davies down for the next soiree – he can tell us the Siberia story..." No, I'm saving that one for Parky.

Arrived in Tokyo 8.30am local time feeling like death Siberia'd up. A sniffer dog checked our baggage. I checked the sniffer dog, which didn't go down too well with its owner, though the dog didn't seem to mind.

We sat on the coach due to take us to the other airport in Tokyo for an hour-long internal flight. This is what football journalists do. We sit on coaches. On our passports under occupation we could justifiably write 'coach sitters'. We had long enough for Colin Young to estimate that the average football hack spends two and a half years of his career sitting on coaches waiting to leave for somewhere.

After the usual 30-minute wait on the coach for no apparent reason we eventually arrived at Haneda airport and discovered we could not check in our bags as the flight to wherever we are going does not leave until 6.30pm.

The journey to our final destination will take longer than the World Cup at this rate.

Wasn't sure what time it was by my body, so played safe and had a beer. Food was spaghetti with basil. When in Japan, don't do as. A call of nature was required and it was unsettling to discover the Japanese loo was an air raid shelter affair. Standing up was necessary whatever the order of the day (or morning, afternoon, maybe even night – I've lost track). No paper, so napkins had to be used. It was a memorable first experience of this side (or back side) of life in Japan.

The Ireland squad have landed in Izumo from their pre-World Cup base of Saipan, a tiny Pacific island which one Irish paper managed to call Spain. The players have given a press conference, but most of the Irish and British media are still with me in Tokyo ... hmmm. More like a lack of press conference.

Later in the day I had a pot noodle eaten with chopsticks, which was an interesting challenge. Bad jokes about it being a Pol Pot Noodle or even a Graham Poll Pot Noodle were an indication of how our normally sharp wit had been affected by jet lag. Tried to grab some shuteye at Tokyo airport, but needed a shutear too as the place was bedlam and I succeeded only in getting cramp, not sleep.

Everyone agrees this was the worst, longest most never-ending journey ever. Bad moods were obligatory. We finally arrived at Izumo at about 9pm, tired to the extent that my eyes were not focusing properly. Thankfully I only had to write 1,300 words.

The hotel room – well, I say 'room' but I have seen bigger cupboards, maybe even drawers – was so small there was not even space to unpack. Had to pay £45(!) for a phone card, accounts will love that. They don't like me spending that amount on a room.

Inevitably the laptop would not work for love or money (even £45) or even swearing. The hotel has a bar on all free-phone numbers and to say the troops are not happy is an understatement.

My Japanese mobile arrived, but needed a special code before it could be activated. Again, for some unknown reason, swearing at it failed to make a difference. I finished writing at 1am and had to dictate all my copy. Almost fell asleep dictating it and not for the usual reason. I am tired and hungry as I write this; just to round the perfect day off there was no food available in the hotel.

I found two Kit Kats in a bag somewhere, bugger the eat-by date. I barely bothered to unwrap them I was so hungry.

The final indignity came when I discovered the pillows were so hard – and I mean seriously hard – they could not be used as pillows. I somehow made the duvet into a pillow and slept with just a sheet over me. The end of one (or maybe two) of the most demanding days of my career.

SATURDAY MAY 25
A day lost somewhere travelling. Awakened by Clive White of the *Sunday Telegraph* at 10.30am. "Hey Chrissie … how are you?" Well, asleep for starters. Can't remember when I last slept for so long – and it would have been longer without Clive. Almost broke my ankle getting to the phone because of bits and pieces everywhere. Why do people who wake you up always sound so cheerful? Probably because they haven't been awakened. Only makes the whole thing worse.

The hotel loo is rather different from the air-raid shelter previously encountered. Again there is no paper, but pressing one button saw a spray of warm water do the job normally reserved for Mr Delsey. A second button sent warm air towards the wet part to dry. This is wonderful and a stomach upset suddenly seems appealing.

Found a nice croissant shop by the station – four croissants and an orange juice cost a bargain £12. Went to see Ireland play a local side in the afternoon. The evening was spent in a karaoke bar where I did a Mick

McCarthy version of *I Will Survive* ... "Once I was afraid, I was petrified, by that lousy f****** captain who has left my side..."

Climbed into my pit at 1am.

SUNDAY MAY 26

God knows how much it cost in the karaoke bar last night. Even affording a round of drinks is worrying. I may have blown my entire trip's allowance being Gloria Gaynor. I really am afraid and petrified by the size of the bill that is by my side.

Went to Ireland's training session, but there was no press conference. Eventually we talked to Brendan McKenna, the Football Association of Ireland press officer and an incredibly nice man.

Also spoke to eircom, possibly the best sponsors in the world, who play a more hands-on media role than most sponsors, to ensure three players are put up at 5.30pm with Mick giving his views on the Cameroon v England friendly (Cameroon are in Ireland's group) at nine o'clock.

Did very little in the afternoon apart from sitting in front of my laptop reading on line what the Sunday papers are saying about Roy Keane. Izumo dead on a Sunday and not particularly alive the other days.

The techno side seems to be looking up. The hotel loaned me a lead that connects to their computer system, which costs 3,000 yen a day, about £15. But it means I will have unlimited access to the net as well as being able to send emails though not receive them.

No idea why, but at least I don't have to dictate my copy over a phone. Hiring a cable at £15 a day is still cheaper than dictating copy. Accounts may not quite see it that way though.

For lunch one of the Irish journos had a pot noodle called – honestly – UFO. He produced the empty pot as proof, which wasn't the only empty thing it seems. "It had the desired effect," he said with a self-satisfied look, thankfully not going into details.

Probably the best decision I made pre-World Cup was to bring a huge jar of Marmite out here. It is my saviour. Marmite sandwiches are becoming a major part of my diet. Also, talking to the other lads my idea of making the duvet into a pillow seems to have spread (Spread? Bed spread? Oh never mind). Two outstanding decisions of the 2002 World Cup and my worry is that I have peaked too early.

Went to the 5.30pm press conference and Roy Keane's team-mates (or rather, former team-mates) are clearly not best pleased with him, particularly the critical remarks he said to force his departure. Got back to my cupboard at about half past seven and wrote two pieces, finishing about half past 10.

Some of the other lads are still writing, but there is nowhere open anyway so nowhere to go to eat. Pot noodle and a Marmite sandwich for dinner washed down with a lemon sports drink that tastes nothing how I think a lemon sports drink should taste. Not the most exciting of days but workwise can't complain. Whatever the rights and wrong of Keano's antics he's ensured big licks for those covering the story.

As it turned out he's done a deal with the *Daily Mail*, being paid handsomely no doubt for two pieces. That's the Roy Keane who refused to attend the media party in Saipan because we are all scumbags or whatever. For abusing his manager and slagging off his team-mates Keano looks like pocketing a six-figure sum. Probably more than the Irish players at the finals.

MONDAY MAY 27
Made it to breakfast in the hotel for the first time. Horrified to see some of the lads eating sushi at 9am. They should be sent home, like Roy Keane.

Training (the players, not me) was at 10am, Mick McCarthy press conference at noon, back to the hotel by one. Went to the bread shop and bought some more bread plus croissants. Marmite sandwiches are seriously losing their attraction.

The TV in the hotel is crap. Six Japanese channels. No CNN, nothing to link us to the outside world in a language we are vaguely familiar with. There is the *Daily Tribune*, an English language newspaper whose back page lead today was about Japanese baseball. Hardly any of the lads ate last night. Everyone worked late as filling a sports section in the run up to a major tournament is far more demanding than when the action has started. An allegedly decent Italian restaurant has been spotted and is favourite for tonight.

There is a footy match between the hacks at 4.30pm, which I may watch because the alternative is four walls or six Japanese TV channels.

I have been attempting to roll up the blind in my room/cupboard since I arrived because I am fed up living in permanent darkness. Today I managed to do this, but I have a horrible suspicion that in getting the blind up I may be unable to perform the reverse action.

The day develops into a night with no sleep. Having filed a nicey-nice piece about nothing in particular word reaches us at the Italian restaurant (where the starter and main course were served together) that Keano is to apologise on Irish TV at 10pm Guinness time in an effort to get back into the fold.

That is 6am sushi time and the best possible argument that time-differences should be abolished. The assembled Irish and British hacks somehow stayed up and Jonathan Overend of BBC Radio 5Live was a star, using the Beeb's facilities (don't know what facilities but my licence fee suddenly seemed incredibly worthwhile) to find out what Keane said.

Rumours were rife about what he MIGHT say, but in the end he stopped short of saying sorry. Few of us got to bed and are now in a sorry state. At just after 7am, unshaven, unhappy and uneverything Ireland-covering hacks walked to the squad's hotel to wait for Mick McCarthy to emerge, which he did at 8.30am.

Tell us Mick, what did you think about Roy's appearance on TV last night – or this morning? He gave us a short non-statement (saying something but in effect saying nothing) which I filed for the *Daily Telegraph's* last edition. It was strange filing copy on the day the piece would effectively be published.

Back to our hotel for breakfast – toast and jam for me. Someone had an egg and regretted it later. So did the rest of us. Then to training to discover all press conferences had been cancelled. Fiasco turned to farce. Back to the hotel and wrote a piece about the shambles out here. Was just about to file when a call came through to say there was going to be a 5pm press conference. Article on hold.

Back to the training ground where we were told Niall Quinn would appear at 6pm and Mick at 8pm. So, only a three-hour wait in all. Never has a player dominated my life so much but also producing so many back-page leads as Roy Keane has.

We are all tired through sleep deprivation. I am suffering from living in a Marmite world. A man needs more than beef extract to survive. Well, this man does. Press conferences finished at 9pm, then it was back to the hotel to start writing. Another night without food in the accepted sense of the word.

The pot noodle machine in the hotel is probably the most lucrative piece of machinery in Japan. Dinner was three slices of bread and Marmite – washed down with a beer, as you do.

Nothing open anywhere in Izumo, the hotel doesn't have a bar or a restaurant. However, Roy Keane is the best story of this World Cup by a mile, knocking England off the back page and despite the lack of sleep I wouldn't have missed this for the world. It's what a football journalist dreams of, being on the inside of the biggest story at the biggest football event. However, he does not dream of living on a diet of Marmite sandwiches.

WEDNESDAY MAY 29

I seem to have lost a day again because of interrupted sleep patterns and time-difference. Where was yesterday? Where did it go? Maybe I should offer a reward? I remember when Spike Milligan's dog went missing he placed a full page advertisement in his local paper which just said: "HERE BOY." Brilliant.

Monday night/Tuesday morning was another Roy Keane interrupted affair. Computer decided not to work at 5.30am. Thanks laptop. After waking up twice for reasons I cannot remember I awoke properly at 1pm, but in my cave life is timeless (and yes, I did get the blind down again).

The Keano soap opera just won't go away. Rarely has a football story had such legs, as we say (one Irish hack also said the same about one of the translation girls). It dominates all conversation. "Hi – how's things? What you heard about Keano...?" It's almost becoming a chat-up line. "Hi babe...want a drink? By the way, you heard anything on Keano?"

Went to Ireland training, ate Japanese pancakes for breakfast/lunch. Received my millionth nod since arriving here. Came back to the cave, wrote my piece and the computer worked. Yesss!

The Italian was again the venue for dinner because it was the only place open in Izumo, maybe even the whole of Japan. I dined with the BBC boys and was so hungry I had two of everything – two cheese and mozzarella salads and two penne arrabiatas.

The irregular sleep/eating patterns are catching up on me. I have barely thought about Ireland v Cameroon, the Republic's opening game, because everything here has been so Keane-dominated. The front page of the *Times of India* today was Roy Keane and not the possibility of nuclear war in the region. Madness.

THURSDAY MAY 30

Slept until 8.40am, but couldn't remember what time I went to bed so don't know how long I was asleep. God knows why, but I actually feel worse after what was almost certainly a good night's sleep, probably not used to it. I'll set the alarm for 4am tomorrow so my sleep can be interrupted, that way I'll feel a million yen.

Had breakfast and went to the Izumu Shrine with Colin Young who forgot his bung, so I had to pay for the taxis. The Shrine was incredibly peaceful. Colin and I had our fortunes told by virtue of picking a piece of paper from a wooden box. We had the messages translated, the girl looking at Colin before saying: "Good man, happy, good family." Good Man Colin had the smug look of someone who knew it was borrocks, but had got away with it. Then she opened mine. She shook her head. "Not good..." Japanese custom dictated I had to fold the piece of paper and tie it to a tree in the Shrine before going to a special area to pray for forgiveness. "I'll see you Tuesday week then," said Colin as I started to pray for forgiveness and for his wallet to appear.

Mick McCarthy's press conference went well. He was asked if he'd had any good luck messages. "Yeh, one from the missus. Not sure how she got my number ... didn't tell her where I was going."

Then the players came in. Damien Duff knocked the backdrop of sponsors' names over as he climbed on to the podium. Matt Holland, an eloquent, intelligent player, was asked by a local journo what he thought of Izumo water. Matt, being Matt, replied: "Excellent. After training we all need water to stave off dehydration and the water here is superb ... clear, clean and cold. Perfect." It was the ideal politically-correct answer.

The same question was asked of Clinton Morrison, a smashing guy, but not the friend you would ring if a million quid was on the line. Or even 10 yen. "I think the same as Matty," was his reply.

I remember sharing a long-term car park bus with Clinton at Gatwick after a trip. As the bus entered the car park I told the driver which stop I needed.

"Hey man, how you know that?" asked Clinton.

I showed him my ticket on which I had written the bus stop number and the lane where my car was.

"They never did that for me," he said. I looked at him for a smile but there was none.

Talking of Matt Holland ... one English newspaper has a house style that is checked by the sub editor pressing a certain button on his keyboard. So if, say, the reporter has filed 'judgment' and the paper's style is 'judgement' (both are acceptably correct) it is automatically altered before going into the system. The paper's style sheet dictates that Holland is in fact the Netherlands so in one article Matt Holland's name became Matt Netherlands throughout.

Which reminds me ... I remember once chatting to Neil Harman of the *Times*, who swapped football for the demands of the tennis circuit, about newspaper styles and he said the *Daily Mail*, where he worked at the time, would not use the word 'nevertheless,' which gave him one of his funniest moments in sport.

Neil was at Madison Square Gardens for a National Basketball Association play-off game and after welcoming the fans the announcer said: "And tonight the national anthem will be sung by Janet Chakowski from Milwaukee."

As silence fell and the spectators stood a guy shouted: "Janet Chakowski once sucked my dick."

The crowd stood in stunned embarrassment before the announcer said: "Nevertheless…"

"No other word would have been more appropriate," said Neil.

Back to the cave to pack for Niigata, 7.50am departure. It'll be good to see some football after a week of Keano.

FRIDAY MAY 31

Our last night in Izumo was spent in a Chinese restaurant. The language problem is becoming expensive, five of us asked for a spring roll each and 25 came up. Bed at midnight, up at 7 bells for a bit of breakfast (can't remember which bit I ate) before leaving for the airport. A few of the Irish journos ate gizzard last night. They are now (a) asking exactly what a gizzard is and (b) wishing they hadn't eaten whatever it was.

The Japanese friendship is touching. Yesterday Colin Young went to a supermarket where the owner had a four-year-old daughter. Colin showed her a photo of his son Tom who is also four and the woman became very excited as he has blond hair, unusual to say the least in Japan. On the way back from wherever we also went the woman came running out and gave Colin a box of crayons and a picture book, his initial joy partially diminished when he realised they were for Tom. Another example of incredible friendship from the locals though.

At the airport a Japanese band played the Irish national anthem and there were hundreds of locals to wave goodbye to the players. As the plane was taking off a lone Japanese fan was standing in a field alongside the runway waving an Irish flag, probably my defining memory of the warmth of the people of Izumo.

Upon arriving in Niigata we went straight to the press centre to be accredited. To the delight of the other lads I was given ticket number 69 in the queue. Little things… It was a slow process and at 3.30pm, having collected my credentials, I was hungry, ordered a pizza and paid £8 for the privilege. What I didn't have was the privilege of eating it because suddenly there was a shout "coach leaving" and I had to scoot. It was the most expensive pizza I never had. Can I claim for it on my expenses as technically I didn't eat it? There is no section on the form for not-eaten subsistence.

A 30-minute drive to the hotel and the difference between small town Izumo and big city Niigata was startling. However, the hotel was awful. Basic doesn't do it justice. Basically (very basically) there is literally just enough room for my suitcase in the room plus the owner. The room is smaller than my office at home, which doesn't have a bed in it. It makes the room in Izumo seem like a penthouse suite. Ronnie Corbett would have complained the bed was too small. I could almost have had a pee while lying in bed if my aim was truer and I was into that sort of thing. Thank God we are here for only one night.

Needless to say the laptop doesn't work. Until I can operate this it is impossible to enjoy the World Cup. My Japanese mobile buzzes but doesn't ring. When someone says "I'll give you a buzz" it has a literal meaning. There are no instructions and the writing on the bits IN the mobile are in Japanese. I can make calls, but have to keep the phone hung round my neck so I can 'hear' it if it rings. It's more Niigata bling than Niigata ring.

Spent 30 minutes on the phone to our technical support – how much did THAT cost? Not being able to use my laptop means I am totally isolated from the rest of the world, can't read anything on line and have to file everything by mobile to a copy-taker. I am becoming Victor Meldrew. And yes you can believe it.

The bathroom is not really a bathroom as it doesn't have a bath and anyway, there is not enough room for a bath. So it is really a bathless room. There is a toilet and a shower, but no bath, I would go crazy if I was here for longer.

We're told the hotel in Chiba, our next port of all, is bigger with smaller rooms. They cannot possibly be smaller than this. They could not even be called rooms if they were.

There is a sign in the lobby of dos and don'ts. You cannot bring anything with "an offensive odour" into your room, so we are all sockless. Inevitable gag about a bit of the odour was made. One radio guy is 6ft 4ins and not only is his bed way too small so that his feet touch the wall, but he will have to sleep with his legs bent. At least his computer works. Still, the view is nice. Niigata station looks beautiful.

The good news is the World Cup starts tonight and someone has discovered a sports bar with big screens where we can watch France v Senegal. The screens will probably be bigger than my room. So will the ball.

I saw the game in the sports bar, which was in a nearby hotel. Sat next to *Sky Sports*' Andy Gray – I ghosted a column for him on *Shoot* magazine in the Seventies and I have always found him a friendly, good guy. He said:

"Hey, listen to this." His mobile ring tone was *Dancing Queen* by ABBA. I have silence and vibration. I hid my envy. And my phone.

The sports bar had John Motson's commentary. The BBC boys joked they would prefer the Japanese commentary. Ate sausages and chips and drank Budweiser as Senegal beat France. Very Japanese. The bill certainly was – £31.

SATURDAY JUNE 1

This is the worst hotel anyone can ever remember and one we'll never forget. Someone who had stayed in the hotel in Chiba said it was okay and we watched his face for any suppressed laughter.

Went for a stroll to get some polluted fresh air and saw a great flag some Ireland fans had made. It had two (albeit not very well drawn) pictures of Mick McCarthy and Roy Keane with "It's Good To Talk" above them ... below was every foul term of abuse imaginable.

We depart for the stadium at noon. An hour after the game between Ireland and Cameroon we MUST leave for the airport to fly to Tokyo and then we have a 30-minute drive to Makuhari. Some of the Irish reporters will have to stay another night in Niigata because they won't have finished their work by an hour after the final whistle. So they have an extra night in Niigata and then have to make their own way to Chiba in a country where the language is impenetrable. Bon voyage chaps.

To the stadium where I saw former England manager Graham Taylor being interviewed by Cameroonian TV. Chatted to him (after the interview, not during it) and the TV guy said to me: "Are you the world famous BBC commentator?"

I said no, I was not Barry Davies, but he replied that "it doesn't matter, you'll do," and interviewed me about the upcoming FIFA presidential election. Following my 'give 'em what they want to hear' theory wherever I am in the world, I said that Issa Hayatou of Cameroon would be a much better president than the present incumbent Sepp Blatter ... how the people in Britain are behind Hayatou's candidacy ... it flowed like Cameroonian concrete.

Surprise surprise, could not get my laptop to work at the press centre. Called it worse than Keano called Mick. no-one seems to know why it won't work. The World Cup organisers have a special IT help-desk, but they couldn't help me. God knows when I'll manage to send this, probably in August. Spent an hour trying to get the thing to work while watching every other journo filing merrily.

Ireland had the better of the 1-1 draw with Cameroon. I was pleased for Mick who is one of football's good guys and as honest as the day is long. And there have been plenty of long days here, honest.

Security scare at the airport when my jar of Marmite showed up. I had to open my suitcase and show them what it was.

"What is it?" asked a Japanese security official who spoke three words of English.

How do you explain what Marmite is to a Japanese guy who speaks only three words of English?

"It's like English jam," I answered.

Mr Three Words took off the top and smelled the aforementioned 'jam'. I have never, ever seen a human being reel back so quickly. Given his ex-pression, I was amazed I wasn't arrested for carrying chemical warfare, a jar of mass destruction. The Marmite was returned swiftly by the security offi-cial, who can probably still smell the contents in his nightmares even now.

To the hotel in Makuhari near Chiba where Japan's Disneyland is located. Maybe I'll get Goofy to check out my laptop. At 50 storeys (the number I have been unable to file) it is apparently the biggest hotel in Japan. Big hotel, but small rooms. The radio and TV guys have particular problems with all their gear.

There is barely room in my lack of room for my suitcase let alone any TV and radio equipment, not that I have any thank goodness. And, yep, my laptop won't work. All I can get is 'no dial tone' which is never a good sign. Spent 30 minutes on the phone to our technical department (making 50 in all today) which is incredibly wearing. It is taking over my life. Is this really the techno-capital of the world?

It is now 12.30am. Everywhere is closed, including my laptop. No room service, probably because they realise the rooms aren't big enough to get a tray in. My dinner was a box of Jaffa cakes and a glass of water from the tap. I cannot believe anyone back home is tucking into that fare tonight.

This is some country. Wonderful friendly people, but they roll up the streets at 9.30pm. Tomorrow I will have to go through all this again no doubt. I will have to read 850 words over on copy, which means I can't file until at least 6pm Japan time which is 10am in Blighty when the copy takers start. This is Christopher Davies, pissed off, very bored, very frustrated and very hungry saying goodnight.

SUNDAY JUNE 2

Tried to photocopy something. An act of naïve optimism. Guess what? Machine broken. Does any technology work here? I asked reception if anyone might be able to help me with a computer problem and was told: "Er ... maybe the housekeeper." No need for a follow-up question.

Western breakfast was very welcome after no dinner last night (or most nights). Five glasses of orange juice, industrial strength and size omelette, French fries and pancakes. And for the main course...

Breakfast talk was of poo, not the best topic over a mountain of choles-terol granted, but we are Keaned-out. Given the air raid shelter style public loos that demand deadly accuracy (the previous occupant's aim is rarely true) this is an important issue. The general opinion was that there is a morning poo and an evening poo – but it was the wild card poo sometime during the day you have to beware of.

We decided to call it the Martini poo – it can strike any time, any place, anywhere. If you happen to be in your room, fine. No problems. One guy's Martini poo apparently arrived full steam ahead when he was booking a train ticket at the station, which was not ideal. The matter was closed suddenly when two guys had to dash off for their morning constitutional, leaving them to worry when the next one would strike.

Perhaps the best poo story I ever heard – a dubious honour I agree – was told by golfer Bernard Gallagher. One of his friends had a business meeting and on his way to the station 'followed through,' the previous night's curry returning with devastating effects.

Luckily he was outside a Marks & Spencer, so dashed – maybe pebble-dashed is more appropriate – in to buy some new underwear and trousers. Inevitably when you are in a rush there's a delay and the till wouldn't work … girl had to go to another till … he went with her to pay … came back … picked up the bag – "don't worry about the receipt" – and just made it to the train.

He went straight to the loo, cleaned himself up … didn't know what to do with the soiled underwear and trousers … sorry environment … he opened the window and threw them out. He then opened the Marks & Spencer bag and to his horror there was a jumper inside. Wrong bag. Maybe the environment had its swift revenge.

There is also the story told by someone within the BBC about a guy who was unaware that the temporary loos where he was working were unisex. He sat down to do what comes naturally and started with the sort of ripsnorter that many males pride themselves on.

From the next cubicle a female voice said: "Is that you Maureen?"

The job was completed in silence.

Back to the World Cup and things were getting worse. The business centre is closed today. Even when it is open it shuts just as Europe is starting work at 5.30pm local time, or so it says, no one has ever actually seen it open. Before a business centre can be shut it surely has to be open at some stage? Farcical. A hotel with 1,000 rooms (should have been 500, each double the size) has no internet, no photocopying, no business centre (okay, no business centre that is OPEN, but it amounts to the same thing).

Of all my pre-World Cup worries technology was not on the list as I prepared for Japan, but it has come in straight at number one (ahead of the Martini poo). Estonia was far better in this respect, I kid you not. The journos are not a happy bunch.

The collective mood improved when the city of Makuhari gave the Ireland squad a tremendous welcome in an Irish village set up in the grounds of their hotel. Even Guinness was available for members of the Ireland media with hundreds of Japanese kids in green Ireland jerseys adding a really nice touch to proceedings.

Back to reality at the training ground and – just when you think it can't get any worse – the media centre has only ISDN lines. Great for radio and TV, but no good for the written press with their laptops (well, those whose laptops work). The local organisers say the Football Association of Ireland requested the ISDN lines, which I found surprising.

Needless to say as something has gone wrong no one is claiming responsibility. It is said they will convert some lines to analogue, while a BBC technician is searching for somewhere that sells ISDN cards. The words 'breath' and 'hold' spring to mind. So, in a country famed for being world leaders in technology, hardly any hack can use his or her laptop in the media hotel or the media centre. Desperate.

Returned to the cave, wrote 1,000 words on Ireland v Cameroon and dictated it while watching a very disappointing England struggle to draw their first group stage match against Sweden. Why can't we beat Sweden? Not since 1968 have we put one over them. Not even Svennis the Swede can break the stranglehold. The copy taker told me she had drawn Saudi Arabia in the sweep. I said I hoped she was luckier in love.

Had dinner on the 50th floor of the hotel; fried camembert, chicken (hopefully) and chips plus some Canadian wine – a new one on me. A bargain £45, my entire day's food allowance for breakfast, lunch and dinner.

MONDAY JUNE 3

Groundhog Day opens with a visit to the business centre. As it is the first Monday in June or there is a 'y' in the day it was closed. But! I have found a special phone jack that allows me to use the internet. A bargain 5,000 yen (£25). The laptop god has belatedly smiled on me.

We were told Mick McCarthy's press conference would be at 11am, so my second act of misplaced optimism (after seeing whether the business centre was open) was to be there by 11.

In fact it was 1pm when the press conference finally started and, would you believe it, nobody seems responsible for the change of time or failing to tell the media it had been altered. The assembled hacks spent two hours telling each other how pissed off we were to be at the press centre for two hours where no-one could use a laptop.

Back (eventually) to the hotel where I wrote an Ireland piece and attempted to watch Croatia v Mexico followed by Brazil v Turkey. Unfortunately in Japan these ties were not televised to all and sundry.

Brazil, four-times world champions, could not be seen on the joint-hosts' terrestrial television channels, only a cable company's. Nothing is easy or straightforward here.

However, ITV and BBC are sharing the Irish team's hotel and part of the agreement is that all the players' rooms have feeds to English television – they can watch *Far East-Enders* then. Having charmed our way into a room where there was a BBC feed, the picture quality of Croatia v Mexico was so poor we had to switch to the Japanese cable broadcast – and commentary.

Tomorrow, after writing my Germany v Ireland preview, I must take a train to Chiba to buy my tickets for trips later in the week. Chiba is an hour each way, so I will spend two hours on a train to buy tickets in order to spend even more time on a train. Come back British Rail, all (well, some) is forgiven. However bad our trains are at least you can book your usually delayed journey easily.

Changing money is another major hassle. It is not a question of signing a few travellers cheques and getting the money from the hotel. Oh no sir, sorry. It requires a 15-minute walk to the bank and enough paperwork for Sting to do a concert for some Amazonian rain forest ... all told an hour's job. So to buy some train tickets and cash travellers cheques is a four-hour operation. Heart surgery is quicker. Italy has had two prime ministers in less time. While the people are incredibly friendly I doubt if many hacks will be coming back to Japan in a hurry – not that you can do anything in a hurry here.

While drinking a cup of brown liquid (aka coffee) in the hotel I was asked if I would like some HäagenDazs ice cream by a sponsor. I said yes and wished I had said no. It was green tea flavour and yes, it tasted as bad as it sounds. We found a Tony Romas for dinner where a burger and chips, mud pie and a couple of Budweisers cost £35. Mud is not cheap here. Spotted the Maharajii Indian restaurant on the way back, so some good old home cooking may be on the agenda tomorrow night.

Turned on the television and there was Arsenal manager Arsène Wenger, who used to coach a J-League club out here, on a panel game with an Elvis Presley look-alike. Am losing all hope of sanity.

TUESDAY JUNE 4

It has now become a personal challenge to find the business centre open, but I fear I must live to be at least 100 to achieve this. I asked why it was closed. "Yes sir, business centre closed today."

I did a Basil Fawlty. "Yes I know the business centre is closed. How do I know this? Because it has 'closed' on it like it has every other time I have tried to use it. It should be called 'business centre closed today' not just 'business centre.' In fact the words 'business centre closed today' give the impression it could possibly be open at some stage, even if maybe for only five minutes. Or even five seconds.

"Imagine if the hospitals were like the business centre. Guy scraped off the road, multiple injuries – 'operating theatre closed today.' I suppose we must be grateful hospitals do not operate – no pun intended
– like your business centre."

The guy at reception smiled, nodded, probably wondering what the hell I was going on about and went about his business, but, of course, not in the business centre because it was closed.

Ireland players will be available for interview at noon, Mick McCarthy at four, which we all agree is masterly scheduling, just the four hours between the two press conferences. Japan couldn't organise a drink up in a brewery and certainly not in a business centre.

Mick turned up sharp at 5.30pm, which meant we had been at the media centre for almost six hours. No food or drink available, only bad moods and there were plenty of bad moods rising.

Back to the hotel, wrote 1,600 words – 800 for the front page of the sports supplement and 800 for inside. With the press conference delays I finished writing at around 10.30pm, so going to Tokyo for a meal was a non-starter. And a non-main courser.

We went to the 50th floor restaurant again where I had fried something and two beers – a snip at the usual £35. Seems a standard price.

"Just a glass of water please."

"Okay sir, £35."

When the waiter presented us with the bill we asked him for five copies and he came back with five coffees. So it cost us another £15 NOT to get individual bills.

WEDNESDAY JUNE 5

Awakened by English referee Graham Poll at 7.20am. "Did I wake you?" he asked in a mission-accomplished tone. Refused to give him the pleasure of confirming what he already knew.

Went to Tokyo station to book a seat on the bullet train for Sweden v Nigeria in Kobe on Friday. The station is so big it probably has its own national anthem and flag. It was a 20-minute walk from entering the station to the booking centre.

I am confirmed on the 0818 bullet train to Kobe and you know, apart from death and taxes (and the business centre being closed), the other certainty of life in Japan is that the 0818 will leave at 0818.

Big game today, Ireland v Germany in Ibaraki. The coach is leaving at 4pm, probably home about 1am, but that is only 5pm in Blighty. Gives more time to write the match report.

I was sought out at the stadium by someone from the IT department, the main man, el chiefy. The people in Niigata had phoned ahead about 'the guy from the *Daily Telegraph* whose laptop won't work.' El chiefy had apparently never been beaten by a laptop connection problem before. But history was made.

He had my computer for an hour and returned a broken man. With a still broken computer.

Away from laptop torture, a last minute equaliser by Robbie Keane saw Ireland draw 1-1 with Germany, a terrific result for the Republic. The journos had a fiver-a-head sweep with £150 in yen for the winner (should buy him a coffee and a small croissant). I had the correct score, but was five minutes out with the time of the Irish goal, which was the tie-break.

Coach left the stadium at 11.30pm, so wrote on the journey home, finishing when I returned to my hotel cupboard. Business centre still closed. So was everything else, which meant dinner was four slices of bread from a loaf I had bought spread with the inevitable Marmite plus a Diet Coke.

Cannot find my English mobile, which is worrying. I haven't taken it anywhere but it has gone AWOL. Go to bed concerned.

THURSDAY JUNE 6

Another search, no mobile. The room is so small it should be oh so easy to find.

Today is Cameroon v Saudi Arabia in Saitama and I have managed to arrange for a coach to take the Irish and British journos to the game. No official transport had been laid on, but the Saudis are Ireland's last group opponents, so the match is of interest.

I had investigated the train journey to Saitama, but it was complicated, to put it mildly. It started with a 10-minute walk to the station ... 30-minute journey into Tokyo ... connecting train and change again ... with a 15-minute coach journey from the station to the stadium.

It was not easy to arrange the coach. I certainly didn't attempt to do it through the business centre. The Japanese don't like anything not on the schedule. One travel agency offered me a coach, but I would have to drive it. I don't think so. Anyway, I secured a coach (plus driver) for 25 people, which will cost around 60,000 yen each (£15).

From our hotel to the stadium should be 65 minutes by Doyen Travel (Doyen being the nickname I was given by the Irish journos because of my longevity), so I am everyone's favourite at the moment. It won't last. How can I get the boys receipts?

We had a full coach of 25 going out – and an even fuller coach coming back. All 25 seats taken, plus the jump-seat with five sitting on the floor. Doyen Travel is a victim of its own success. The bonus was that the TV on the coach going home showed France v Uruguay, which I told the boys I had arranged. Nope, no-one believed me.

We arrived back at the hotel and realised we had left Clive White of the *Sunday Telegraph* behind. It had to be Clive, the latest person in the world (apart from the occasional early morning telephone call). He phoned me later to say he wasn't aware the bus wouldn't be leaving from the same spot at which we'd arrived – a fact which had been announced upon arriving. He said he would probably have taken the train back anyway, but the option was taken from him. By himself.

Still can't find my English mobile. I would get the worry beads out, but there isn't enough room for them in the cave.

FRIDAY JUNE 7

Got to sleep about 1.30am last night. Up horrendously early to get to Kobe for Sweden v Nigeria. Business centre closed.

The train ride to Tokyo was an education. The Japanese are the most polite race in the world, but on trains they become hooligans. The pushing and shoving to board a crowded train is an effective if dubious art. Everyone was squashed so tightly and the breath god decided I would have the high prince of halitosis polluting my space (or lack of it).

Had time for breakfast at Tokyo station at a sort of bakery called – honestly – Let The Good Times Roll. Pointed to the bottle of orange juice I wanted, the girl poured it out and I then I pointed to a croissant, which she put on a plate. I got my obligatory £15 in yen out.

But what's this? A mere £7. The orange juice was cold, but made me yearn for Marks & Spencer's freshly squeezed OJ. Still thirsty and hungry, I had the same again.

I felt queasy after my second orange juice, so asked the girl in sign language if I could look at the bottle, hoping she wasn't the only Japanese girl who understood Cockney rhyming slang. Upon turning it round I saw in English "Screwdriver – double vodka included."

So at 8am I had knocked back two double vodka and oranges. I did a Paula Abdul-type walk to the bullet train, two steps forward, one step back. It has also cost me £14 to be tipsy – my first car cost less than that, I think.

The bullet train is wonderful, not least because I had somehow been given a first class ticket. It is so smooth a ride that the top of your coffee – or screwdriver – barely moves. Reclining seats … it is a journey to take your breath away. Pity the guy on the earlier train had not been on one.

At the stadium the subject of the wild card poo was brought up again because an Irish photographer had been forced to ask the taxi driver to pull over so he could have a squattie – or Martini. How he got the message across to the driver heaven only knows. The loos at the stadium are spotless. You could eat your dinner off the floor except of course I don't have dinners, so in my case it would be – you could eat a Marmite sandwich off the floor.

Thankfully the English habit of blocking the troughs with a mountain of dog ends and chewing gum ensuring a yellow river in the loo hasn't reached Japan. Unfortunately, neither has the concept of an open business centre.

Inevitable laptop problems. The IT people saw I was having trouble with it – the torrent of abuse hurled at the useless piece of machinery and me jumping up and down on it giving them a vital clue. They said they would take the laptop away and fix it. I said yes, they could take it away but no, they wouldn't be able to fix it. They did – and they couldn't. Whatever job it is that you do, take away the most crucial piece of equipment and you'll know how frustrating this all is.

SATURDAY JUNE 8

An unforgettable night in room 2410 of the Shin-Kobe Oriental watching England beat Argentina 1-0 complete with Japanese commentary. I had witnessed Germany 1 England 5 in the Hibernian Hotel in Dublin, so obviously me watching David Beckham and the boys in hotels abroad is the secret behind their biggest successes in recent years. Yet how much credit will I be given? Yup – zip.

I was knackered last night. Finished writing 1,500 words at 12.30am, my eyes stinging. I know half twelve is only just past pumpkin hour, but there have been too many late nights plus a crap diet ... it's overtaking me now. One of the Irish journos was simply too tired to work yesterday. "I've hit the wall," he said and for once there were no jokes. I can sympathise with him.

The eight-hour time difference means we are often working until two or three in the morning because of the schedules back home and then it's an early start because of the schedules here. Oh the glamour! The weather is humid and though the World Cup is just getting underway those who have covered the Roy Keane story – by now I had worked out that at one point in that saga I went 44 hours without sleep – need our batteries recharged. I haven't had a day off since arriving. Colin Young of the *Daily Mail*, Danny Taylor of the *Guardian* and George Caulkin of the *Times* are on a day off today and have gone to Tokyo.

Me? I'm at Italy v Croatia. My travelling time from Kobe to Ibaraki and then back to Makuhari will be eight or nine hours with a game thrown in somewhere along the line. I'll be back in my cupboard about midnight. So another day without decent grub, but at least my jar of Marmite will be there waiting for my return. I've missed it.

You can get snacks on the trains, but not proper food like muffins with so many additives you may never sit still again. The canteens at the media centres are awful, no hot food, mainly crisps and stuff and something that looks like seaweed. I would pay 50 bucks for beans on toast. In this country I'd probably have to.

The day turned into a nightmare – in fact not just a nightmare, but an official nightmare. The train I was assured I needed arrived at Ibaraki station at 5.23pm – for a 6pm kickoff. I reached the stadium at 5.40pm to be told that I should have notified them if I was arriving less that an hour before kick-off. I did not know that, I said.

"It was in your press kit with your accreditation," said Mr Unhelpful of Ibaraki. "There were no press kits with my accreditation," I replied. "That is not my fault," said he, confirming my punishment for being unaware of what to do was not to be issued with my original press ticket for the game.

I had to sit in a room with other journalists who had not applied for a ticket, and so had been also wait-listed. I missed the first 15 minutes of Italy v Croatia while in effect waiting for my own ticket to come round again. The press box had 120 empty seats, which didn't help my frustration. The Japanese are immovable in whatever system is in place.

Left the stadium at 9pm, boarded a train full of happy Mexicans, who had been to the game even though their team wasn't playing, for the 20-minute journey which for some reason took an hour. Changed trains, another hour to Chiba ... Chiba to Makuhari another 40 minutes.

To rub salt in my wounds my Japanese mobile has, it seems, stopped accepting calls, so now I have a phone that I can only use for outgoing calls and a computer that doesn't compute. We can put a man on the moon (if not on Martina Navratilova), but Mr Moon couldn't phone me and I couldn't send him an email.

Since scrambled eggs on toast at 9am I'd had a bar of plain chocolate, two croissants and three Diet Cokes. When people say how lucky I am to be at the World Cup I know what they mean, but...

SUNDAY JUNE 9

It's supposed to be the rainy season out here, which is why this World Cup started a week earlier than most World Cup finals. Ten days into the World Cup I have not seen a drop of rain – plenty of Marmite but no rain.

It is very hot during the day. The sun rises at 4am (so I am told) and the temperature reaches 80 degrees during the day with warm nights. Some of the boys are getting a nice tan. I have spent so much time in my cave I will need a week in the sun just to get white.

The Ireland press conference descended into a farce. We are rightly asked to turn off our mobiles before it starts, though as mine doesn't really work it makes little difference. I could receive 26 calls during the press conference and no-one would be any the wiser.

A photographer forgot to turn his phone off. How you can forget after someone on a podium has said "please turn off your mobile phones" I do not know. Suddenly, *Dancing Queen* starts playing from his bag. Sod's Law dictates he can find everything in his bag except ABBA.

Managed lunch today. Two portions of lasagne and two chocolate ice cream bombs, which cost ... yes, a bomb.

The *Daily Telegraph* have signed Eoin Hand, the former Ireland manager and an incredibly nice person, to do some World Cup columns. I am his ghostwriter so an extra workload. This means by the end of today I will have written 800 words on Italy v Croatia, a 350-word follow-up on Nigeria, 600 words on Irish news, probably 800 on the Japan v Russia game – over 3,000 words. What are the chances of my laptop working?

Answer: none. The stadium in Yokohama for Japan v Russia became the latest place where my computer wouldn't function. Got back to my cupboard at 1am. Had a slap up meal of three Milky Ways and a Diet Coke as I wrote my match report and spent God knows how long dictating everything over on copy.

MONDAY JUNE 10
While the World Cup is, professionally, the biggest and best competition to cover, the routine is prison-like (no, no first-hand comparison). I get up, turn on the air conditioning which I have to turn off at night because of the noise. Turn on CNN to find out what the boy Arafat is up to. Ask myself for the millionth time – doesn't he look like Ringo Starr? And, when asked if he was her child, did his mother reply: "Yasser, that's my baby."

Decided which was the least creased T-shirt, down to breakfast. Pay the £12 to the same guy. Wait for him to print the receipt. He says something to me in Japanese and smiles. Head straight to the orange juice, then to the cereal, which is Corn Flakes or Corn Flakes. Cup of black liquid from a machine that claims it is coffee, but would not stand up to forensic tests. Two omelettes, croissant ... but today I rebelled and sat in a different seat.

The journos who opt for the Japanese breakfast of raw fish are banished to their own fishy table. I am sure someone said: "Go to your own plaice." I'm equally sure it would have been me.

There is a rumour that if Ireland beat Saudi Arabia and move to South Korea we will have to share rooms in Seoul. Trouble is, there is no-one here who wants to share with anyone else. While we all get on famously we like our own space, or rather lack of it given the amount of square inches per room. If the rooms in Seoul are the same size as they are here sharing with a fly would be impossible. I hope the rumour is just that.

Thankfully Seoul rumours were unfounded. We have a 5star hotel apparently. Must wind down my Japanese money, only two more days here, assuming Ireland beat Saudi Arabia.

The boys are talking about going to a baseball game tonight, but I would rather risk the [home] runs at the Golden Sari or whatever the Indian restaurant I spotted is called, than watch the ball game. I can't remember when I last had a beer. I am in danger of becoming healthy. But the good news is my British mobile has been found. It was ... somewhere.

Went to the Indian restaurant and devoured a chicken (please God) jalfrezi, saffron rice and a naan. It was probably the best meal (pro rata) I have ever had. I have immediately been installed as the early favourite for the Martini wildcard.

I made an official complaint about my Japanese mobile phone. The company who arranged it on behalf of the Daily Telegraph are called, I kid you not, Enable. I was given a mobile number for a girl at Enable, which is always on answer-phone and there is no point in leaving a message for her about my phone not receiving incoming calls as ... my phone doesn't receive incoming calls. So basically I have a phone with no instructions that doesn't work and no-one can fix it. In Japan. The techno capital of the world.

TUESDAY JUNE 11

Today Ireland play Saudi Arabia at 8.30pm. They need to win by at least two goals and Ireland have never scored twice in 11 previous ties at World Cup finals. It'll be tough, but I am confident history will be made tonight.

Breakfast chat was of ex's. Not wives, but expenses. I am doing my ex's on a daily basis and any journo who doesn't will regret it. Arriving home with a bag of receipts in Japanese and, hopefully, Korean with no record of when, where or why the money was spent is financial suicide. And entertaining Harry Kari is unlikely to be accepted by accounts departments.

Did some shopping. Even the cheap things are expensive. Not sure if I will come back to Japan later in the tournament. The office may ask (tell) me to stay in Korea. I'm sorry I won't have seen Tokyo. I've only seen the station where I inadvertently got legless at breakfast.

Japanese timetables are impenetrable. You can see what time the trains leave, but it's impossible to understand where they are going. You know you'll leave and arrive on time, but have no idea of your destination.

The mobile phone saga has reached new heights/depths depending on your viewpoint. I emailed another girl at Enable, but had no reply from her. I was given two help-desk numbers. The first had a message only in Japanese which wasn't much help and the second is a number that cannot be accessed from my mobile which was similarly unhelpful. I tried dialling it from a landline and it was unobtainable. Help!

But! On the coach to the game my phone suddenly rang. Frightened the life out of me. It was a girl from the Enable help-desk. She didn't speak too much English, so explaining to her that the problem I had was that my phone didn't ring when in fact she had just got through to me was not easy.

"So Mr Davies, you cannot receive calls on this phone but we are talking..."

"Yes but you are the first..."

After we finished speaking it was business as usual with the mobile, messages that someone had tried to contact me came through, but had failed to speak to me.

Unlike the phone, Ireland did the business against the Saudis, winning 3-0. When we arrived back at the hotel – at 2.30am to be precise – the staff stood in a guard of honour while the Irish and British journos climbed off the coach, waving Tricolors and shaking hands with all and sundry as if it was our triumph. The manager said everyone could have a free beer. We all liked the manager.

However, no dinner again. Four doughnuts and a Diet Coke. Seoul must be better ... surely?

WEDNESDAY JUNE 12
Up at 7am, said goodbye to the Closed Business Centre, paid my extras – a £150 phone bill which didn't include the internet. That was for filing copy on what I thought was a free-phone number. They don't do free here – or open business centres. Mixture of moods as we headed for the airport. Everyone is delighted Ireland have reached the second round, but the sleep deprivation is apparent in the group.

A lack of sleep maybe but no shortage of hospitality. The Japanese people had been amazing. For all the techno problems their friendliness and warmth were incredible ... overwhelming . There may be no such thing as perfect hosts (or co-hosts), but the Japanese have run this close. They could not have made us more welcome.

The flight to Seoul was the most turbulent I have ever experienced. It was as if there were sleeping policemen on the clouds. To add to our discomfort the travel agent did us like sushi'd kippers. When we were all on board it was announced our baggage was being flown to Seoul on another flight, the general feeling that this was done to save getting a bigger and presumably more expensive plane.

Our baggage arrived a few hours after we did, which was particularly frustrating for the photographers, radio and TV boys, who found it rather difficult to carry out their work without cameras and microphones.

The welcome in South Korea was very different to our farewell in Japan, with armed soldiers resembling Ninja Turtles at the airport in Seoul. The hotel, thank you hotel god, is excellent ... big rooms and plenty of space to hang my clothes. Except my clothes haven't arrived yet. My Korean mobile does not seem to be working – well, it ISN'T working – and with instructions in Korean (perhaps not too surprising, granted) I am unlikely to work out how to make it work. Another row, another memo.

The centre of Seoul looks very lively compared to Makuhari, but then the Gobi Desert would be lively in comparison to our Japan headquarters. All dog jokes have inevitably been told and we have even stopped calling each other chum.

THURSDAY JUNE 13

Hotel very busy and business centre is open. Had to queue for breakfast and because it was so chaotic I think I may have got away with the £20 they charge for what, it must be said, is a splendid spread. The only slight problem is that whenever I sign for anything I have to sign 'C Cavies' as that is how I am registered. Just what I need – I am now someone else. I hope the new me has better luck than the old one. Also the telephone in my room doesn't work properly. If I want to retrieve messages I have to dial laundry. For laundry I dial alarm clock etc. I have made a note of what I need to dial for whichever service I need. Just when you think the madness cannot become madder...

Went for a walk and Seoul is very impressive. Lots to see, do, buy, eat and drink, though some smells from the market did not encourage anyone to guess their origin. Had to go to the press centre to gain accreditation for Sunday's Ireland game against Spain.

What a place, or rather what a palace. It had everything including a sports massage facility. Only for necks before you ask. It has a bank, business centre (open), post office, travel agency and more monitors than a TV store.

Bumped into Charlie Sale of the *Daily Mail,* who writes the best sports diary in the country. Charlie is a legend, a truly professional operator. He usually has skin of armadillo proportions, but had been upset by something Paul Newman, the Football Association's media head honcho, had said. Before a press conference a cockroach was spotted scuttling (or whatever cockroaches do) across the floor and Paul said: "Oh look, there's Charlie Sale." I probably didn't help Charlie's mood by laughing uproariously at the telling of this tale and he didn't seem to believe me when I said I was laughing at something else I had just remembered. I said the anecdote would make a nice diary item and took a step back.

Seoul has made a really big effort to create World Cup fever. Posters are on every building, banners are everywhere – so different to Japan, though in fairness in Japan we were staying in a city where no games were being played. Got to say it, sorry – it wasn't big in Japan.

Mick McCarthy's press conference was at 5.30pm. Came back to my hotel room to write it up while watching Mexico v Italy. In Seoul we can eat later and I hope we do.

In the hotel bar beer was £5 a glass and potato skins a giveaway £20 a plate. The music was so loud you had to lipread. You couldn't hear yourself think – but thinking about it, how can you EVER hear yourself think? I had one beer before wandering out to the downtown area where I met up with some Irish journos in a bar (no, not in an Irish bar) where we sat outside eating, drinking and watching the world go by. A very pleasant evening.

FRIDAY JUNE 14 and SATURDAY JUNE 15

Too busy to write the diary yesterday. Did Mick McCarthy's press conference on Wednesday ... gave the office a check call when I returned from watching the world go by. It was about 6pm in London.

"Oh, someone wants to have a word with you," I was told.

They are the words that send shivers of fear down a journalist's spine. There are other words like "Give me all your money," from some guy with a gun that would have equal effect, but in office terms... "someone wants a word with you" is squeaky bum time. Those words are never "hey, just wanted to say what a brilliant piece you filed today." In this case it was: "Can we also have an 800-word player piece please?"

I had to start writing an 800-word player piece at two in the morning with matchsticks keeping my eyes open. Matt Holland (or Matt Netherlands) had appeared at the press conference, so I tried to read my notes, which I could probably have taken to Boots to be made up for a prescription they were so badly, doctorlike scrawled.

Two hours later, having written about Matt Holland/Netherlands and filed via copy-taker my head hit the pillow and there it stayed until about an hour later – 5am my time – when the hotel phone burst into life.

Someone on the sports desk: "Thought you were doing Matt Holland?"

"You mean Matt Netherlands."

"Sorry?"

"Never mind. I filed it an hour ago."

"Oh yes, here it is, sorry. Bye."

Two hours later I was up to catch the early coach to the DMZ – the demilitarised zone by the border with North Korea. Naturally I was delighted that we sat on the coach (as journalists/coach sitters do) for 40 minutes waiting for latecomers.

There is a certain latecomers' expression of fake guilt, the shrug of the shoulders and half-smile, which demands painful removal from the face as they say "sorry...", while they run the gauntlet of the bad mood on-timers in the coach.

It was a day off for most of us, but very few journos could be bothered to go to the 38th parallel, which has divided North and South Korea since 1953. It is apparently the most heavily-armed border in the world – even more so than the border between the writers and sub-editors in newspaper offices.

In the Seventies, tunnels – one a mile long and 246 feet below the surface (yes, I took notes) – were dug from the North, who initially claimed they were for coal-mining purposes. The weakness in this argument is that there was no coal in the tunnels, which we were able to go through on a sort of pulley-carriage.

Another reason the cynical South believed the tunnels were not for coal purposes is that they were large enough to permit the passage of an entire military division in an hour as opposed to a team of North Korean coal-miners. The North, we were told, later denied they had dug the tunnels. As denials go that one rates up there alongside some of Richard Nixon's.

Looking from the South into the North we saw a 'typical' North Korean village, which was in fact more of a typical North Korean film set (though I have little knowledge of the North Korean film industry or even if it exists). The 'houses' have no rooms inside and the 'inhabitants' mowing the lawn, hanging out the washing, turning lights on and off and doing everyday chores are in effect actors and actresses hoping to give the impression of what a swell place North Korea is.

The South call it Propaganda Village and what it is NOT is a proper village. no-one ever cleans the windows in Propaganda Village as high-powered binoculars reveal there is no glass in the windows. The inhabitants of Propaganda Village rarely stray far from their 'homes', which may have something to do with the thousands of landmines in the area.

The 2.5 by 151-mile border is patrolled by one million North Korean soldiers (it's a tough job but...), and 600,000 on the South side, with around

40,000 American troops helping their friends in the South and ensuring everyone has a nice peaceful day.

It was a fascinating, if at times frightening, day, but an experience I would not have missed. Incredibly only a handful of the world's sporting journos (just John Cross of the *Daily Mirror* and myself from the Brits) made the effort to travel the hour or so from Seoul to the border.

Back to reality and my Korean mobile (about the fourth I have had) is faulty. The battery runs down in half an hour even if it isn't used. The good news is that my complaints about the silly phone in my hotel where I have to dial laundry to retrieve messages have paid dividends – I have been moved to a bigger, better room.

The bad news is that at 2.45am the air conditioning went on the blink, making a hissing sound a viper would have been proud of to awaken me. I telephoned maintenance and asked if someone could "come and take the hiss", which I thought was quite funny for Mr Grumpy in the middle of the night – even if it got zero laughter.

At just before 3am someone was taping over the air conditioning outlets, which of course meant no a/c, but at least the room was quiet.

SUNDAY JUNE 16

Awakened by a girl from the J and J Corporation at 8am who told me the reason my mobile battery was running down so quickly was that I was using it for my laptop. I said no, this was not the case because I did not have the relevant software to use the mobile with my laptop.

Yes, she said, you mustn't use it with your computer. I repeated I was not doing this and, realising we could be saying the same things for goodness knows how long, signed off with "this is a bad line ... lot of interference ... hope we don't get cut off" and hung up. I might still have been talking to her now otherwise. I nodded off again and was awakened a second time by another girl who said: "I hear you are having trouble with your mobile because you are using it with your laptop." I did my denial routine and this time we were cut off because the phone's battery, rather poetically, I thought, went dead.

She rang me back on the hotel phone and promised I would have "a new Korean phone delivered today, sir." But by the time I left for the stadium nothing had arrived, so I went to the ground phoneless.

I am not alone in having communication problems. Emmett Malone of the *Irish Times* is a reluctant member of the Techno Trouble Club, too. Emmett needed an AOL card for his laptop, so his newspaper arranged for one to be delivered to Saipan, Ireland's pre-World Cup base, by DHL. Unfortunately it arrived the day after he left, so the hotel in Saipan kindly forwarded it to the hotel in Izumo. You are probably ahead of me here, but as I've started I'll finish. Yes, this, too, arrived the day after he left for Makuhari.

The hotel in Izumo didn't know where Emmett was heading for next, so they sent the AOL card back to the *Irish Times* in Dublin. When it arrived in Dublin it was immediately sent megafast speed-of-sound post to Makuhari but ... yes, it arrived after Emmett had left for Seoul. Makuhari sent it to Seoul and now Emmett was proudly announcing that he had just been to collect it.

High fives all round because we all love a happy ending.

We saw Emmett an hour later looking like a guy who had won the lottery and lost his ticket. "It doesn't work," he said with the air of a man as broken as his laptop.

Tony Roma's for lunch and I decided a pig-out was needed. I ordered a burger and French fries ... no relish, nothing ... just a bare burger please. "If anyone has the urge to put anything on the burger please tell them to resist it," I told a bemused Korean waitress. My plea was generally successful. The virgin burger arrived with all the relish on a side plate "as you've paid for it, sir."

Left on the official coach for Ireland v Spain at 4pm, in the stadium by

5pm – kick-off 8.30pm. no-one knows why we left so early. Air conditioning in the press centre not working, but thankfully it was only 88 degrees.

A terrific display by Ireland saw them push Spain all the way in a game they could have won. Spain took the lead after only seven minutes through Fernando Morientes. Ian Harte, Ireland's most reliable dead-ball kicker, had a 63rd minute penalty saved by Iker Casillas, the rebound striking Kevin Kilbane's shin and bouncing for a goal-kick.

In the final minute Ireland were awarded another penalty, a superb decision by Swedish referee Anders Frisk, who spotted Fernando Hierro trying to remove Niall Quinn's jersey when they challenged for a high ball. As Spain argued, Robbie Keane picked up the ball and looked calmness personified for the biggest moment of his career. He sent Casillas the wrong way and equalised – extra-time.

Ireland had the better of the extra 30 minutes, but there was no sudden death golden goal winner. The lottery of a penalty shootout would decide the victors. The tension, as Motty was no doubt telling the British TV audience, was palpable as the shootout began.

Matt Holland, David Connolly and Kilbane failed to convert their penalties and Spain won the shootout 32. Plucky, unlucky Ireland will go home undefeated as a shootout goes into the record books as a draw. Small consolation. Having covered Ireland since 1986/87 I refer to them as 'us' in a professional way and my adopted country had done the Republic proud. They have entertained, been a personality team of the finals, provided tension and fun with players such as Damien Duff establishing themselves on the world stage.

Ireland were left to reflect on what might have been while I returned to my hotel about 2am and reflected on what wasn't there – the new mobile. Dinner was a chocolate slice and croissant I 'borrowed' from the media centre. Wrote my match report and got to sleep about 3.30am.

MONDAY JUNE 17

A bad day. Awakened at 8am by the front desk. "Someone from the J and J Corporation is in the lobby to see you," I was informed, information I did not need at 8am after four and a half hours' sleep. Mr JJ's English was so poor a girl from the front desk translated. He handed me my new Korean mobile and told me the reason my previous one did not work properly was because I was using it with my laptop.

I asked the girl to tell Mr JJ that not only was this not the situation, it was impossible as I did not have the relevant software.

She said: "He said 'yes'." Suicide flashed through my mind. His suicide.

Mr JJ then started to fiddle with my laptop to make it compatible with my new mobile. "Please tell him to stop that," I pleaded with the translator. Her words fell on deaf ears and I almost had to pull him away from my computer. The damage had been done. Mr JJ had overridden all the existing modems in an effort to hook it up to the mobile, so now it was in effect an electronic typewriter.

I spent an hour on the phone to our technical desk who couldn't correct it. I told the sports editor and when he spoke to J and J in London they said a girl in their London office had made a complaint that I had sworn at her. Thankfully the sports editor knew I would not (and did not) do that and he told J and J that I would not act in such a manner.

I had said I was bored, frustrated, fed up and angry at 'this farce', but I never swore. I spent another 50 minutes on the phone to a different guy in our technical support who managed to help me reboot the laptop. I was in my room from 8am until 11pm, the morning spent getting the laptop to work, the afternoon writing my Ireland obit and a preview to Italy v South Korea. At least I could watch Mexico v USA and Brazil v Belgium on TV.

But ... I still couldn't file via the laptop, so almost 2,000 words were put over to a copy taker. I went out to eat alone because by the time I had finished filing everything the other journos were out on the town.

When I returned to the hotel I went to the bar to say goodbye in the traditional manner to the Irish journos who were going home the next day.

TUESDAY JUNE 18

The world is against me. I received an alarm call from the front desk at 7am, who thought that I was one of the Ireland journalists returning home and needed a wake-up call. Did not have the energy to reply. Managed to get back to sleep. Up at 10am for some breakfast and on the road to Daejeon for Italy v South Korea.

Five of us had hired a people carrier, even though we had initially paid £12 each for return train tickets. But the taxi driver taking us to the station said he would drive us to Daejeon, wait and drive us home for £30 per head. As the station in Daejeon was quite a way from the stadium and the return train was a late one we agreed this was a better deal. So did Mr Kim the driver, who we hilariously called Mr Quim.

Upon arriving at the stadium Mr Kim announced he would now be sleeping as he had been working all night and was just going home when he picked us up. Hmmm.

Watched Turkey beat Japan on television in the press centre where only cold food was available. We were there for 10 hours in all, our diet consisting of croissants, mini-wafers and a slice of cake. At least smoking is banned.

A highlight of the day was seeing a journo from Colombia eating a Snickers ice cream with half of it dropping down the front of his black T-shirt. He looked up in the naive hope no-one had seen this. Sorry amigo.

The South Korea v Italy game was incredible. The passion from the home crowd was almost tangible and must have had such a positive effect on the South Korean players. Astonishingly they beat Italy with a golden goal, Korean journalists openly crying in the press box. I was tempted to ask one if he had a J and J Corporation mobile.

The five English hacks were almost in tears as none of us could get a line, dialling tone, connection ... you name it, we couldn't get it ... at the stadium. So the five of us had to file to copy from the people carrier. Five journos all on to copy-takers in a confined space is an interesting scenario. We were convinced parts of our reports would appear in each other's papers.

The news desk phoned me and wanted a 750-word colour piece for the front page. I wrote that when we arrived back at the hotel as my laptop ran out of power (as did I), getting to bed about 4am.

WEDNESDAY JUNE 19

The day started with a good bit of tittle-tattle, though for legal purposes the identities of those involved cannot be revealed. A recently sacked manager had apparently been invited to his chairman's holiday home to discuss his payoff. They went out on the chairman's yacht, as you do, to talk. The manager was a weak swimmer which the chairman was aware of and, as the talks got going, the chairman suddenly pushed the manager overboard and yelled: "So you agree to my settlement then?"

The chairman helped his panicking manager back into the yacht, claiming it was just a joke, but getting the desired agreement. Oh yes, hilarious.

Italy are staying in this hotel. I went down in the lift with Paolo Maldini and it has to be said, the Italians are the style champions of the world. The men, the bastards, are so handsome – give the rest of us a chance will you? And even the ugly Italian women are pretty.

You take any Englishman, put him in a Savile Row suit and an Italian wearing jeans and a T-shirt and the Italian will look better than us. They all have great sweptback black hair, no grey bits, you look for some salt to go with the pepper but there is none – must be using dye then. Even their names are better than ours.

Imagine the scene in a club ... smooth as hell Italian guy goes up to a girl and says in his heartbreaking Meg Ryan orgasm-inducing accent: "Hi, my name isa Paolo ... I woulda be honoured to buy you a drink..." If it isn't Paolo it's Gianfranco, Pierluigi, Pepe, Gianni, Luca ... what girl is going to say no to a guy who has just walked off a film set, eight per cent body fat, six pack, teeth like piano keys and even a name to make her heart flutter?

Now it's England's turn. "Ello darling ... Trevor's the name ... fancy a lager?" He probably lets off a silent fart as he says it. If it isn't Trevor it's Bert, Dick, Brian ... beer gut ... minimum of two buttons – that have given up because of gut pressure – undone ... no two teeth the same colour or size ... probably a bit of spinach of *Antiques Roadshow* vintage stuck between a couple of them ... adidas hair (three strands combed over) ... it's a no-contest.

While the Italian would be something in fashion, public relations or some other trendy as hell profession, Trevor (waist size 46) would be a brickie. "Hey they say I'm the brick with the prick," he delivers as his hilariously witty chat-up opener whilst wondering how on earth the girl isn't telephoning a hotel to book a room for two instead of a taxi for one.

Having briefly contemplated changing my name to Luca, I did some work and went for a meal at a restaurant where I sampled Korean wine for the first time. And the last. A blind tasting would have you wondering if it was in fact wine. I have drunk tastier medicine. How anything could taste so bad was beyond comprehension.

THURSDAY JUNE 20
I was awakened at 7.30am by a call from Korean TV who said a camera crew was on its way to the hotel to do an interview with me "if that's ok?" Jumped in the shower, made myself as presentable as is possible at such an hour and the reporter and cameraman duly arrived. The reporter was stun-ning – a minor detail, of course – and she wanted me to compare North

Korea's win over Italy at Middlesbrough in 1966 to South Korea's victory over the Italians a few days ago.

We chatted for 10 minutes. I said that the noise level at Ayresome Park was nothing like that which I had experienced in Daejeon ... compared the respective teams, their preparation and what have you. I didn't like to tell her I hadn't been at Middlesbrough 36 years earlier, but she was pleased with her interview and, as ever, give 'em what they want to hear.

This is my 30th night away from home. I think. You begin to lose track of time after a while. Journos know days by which matches they are covering. Life at a finals can be timeless. Because of the time-difference we are working what amounts to two days ahead in newspaper terms so to me tomorrow is more Saturday than Friday. The real Saturday will be a long day.

The train for Gwanju leaves Seoul at 10.25am and arrives at 2.18pm. John Cross of the *Daily Mirror* was late in booking his ticket and had to stand all the way, which he didn't find anywhere near as funny as the rest of us did. Standing for eight hours will no doubt rank as a memorable experience for Crossie, who didn't think my "I've stood for you for years" remark was particularly witty.

The troops are spread far and wide and I am the only one of the Seoul pack in town tonight. Went out about 10pm by myself after I had finished writing, almost aching with hunger. Found what looked a decent restaurant and ordered smoked salmon on what amounted to a crusty pizza base and pasta.

When the drinks arrived I thought I'd won the wine lottery – Villa Maria Sauvignon Blanc (my favourite sauvignon blanc) and at £6 a glass one of the cheapest on the list. When it came up I looked at it longingly for at least a second before taking a well-learned, long overdue mouthful. And almost spat it out.

It was more Aston Villa or Ricky Villa than Villa Maria. I told the Korean waiter as subtlely as I could that he had inadvertently brought me something other than Villa Maria (ox's urine sprang to mind). Shocked of Seoul brought me the bottle to prove it was Villa Maria. It was a fake. Well, the bottle was real, but the label was totally different to every other Villa Maria label I had seen. And I've seen quite a few.

I stood my ground, if you can do that whilst seated. The manager became involved in the wine whine and basically asked me if I felt he was a crook who was selling imitation sauvignon blanc. "I am sure you would never knowingly do anything like that," I said looking at the first dan black belt taekwando waiters waiting to pounce.

"There appears to have been a mix-up," I said. "Can I pay for the mouthful of wine and leave?"

My humour/sarcasm was not appreciated for some reason and the manager said something to me in Korean, which was probably not complimentary before saying: "Go."

I went to a noodles bar and had … guess … noodles and chicken with a glass of Millers, the beer a bargain four quid.

FRIDAY JUNE 21
England 1 Brazil 2. Diary in mourning.

SATURDAY JUNE 22 and SUNDAY JUNE 23
My last weekend at the finals.

Today was a long day even if it only lasted the regulation 24 hours. Gwangu is four and a half hours from Seoul, though Korean trains are excellent and the second-class fare for the 300-mile journey was £12. The seats reclined like first-class on a plane, while mobile phones are banned (so no-one could ring their mum and say they are approaching Pyeongjeon station and should be there in five minutes). Arrived on time and took a taxi to the stadium which was 45 minutes away. Trains may be cheap, but taxi's aren't.

Korea beat Spain on penalties courtesy of some very dodgy decisions by the match officials, which result in the Spanish somehow not scoring a goal in the 120 minutes. I had been scheduled to return on Monday, but because of the controversies and Korea's progress the desk want me to stay until the semi-final on Wednesday. After 30-odd days on the road (and in the air and on trains) I was ready for Blighty, but, having experienced the incredible Korean celebrations, two more days here are not exactly going to be torture.

Getting away from the stadium in Gwangu was a challenge. The last train departed at 8pm and three English journos, me among them, virtually threw a local out of the cab he was in, waved loads-a-money at the driver and said in our best Korean: "Station guv and move it."

We made the train by 30 seconds and sat opposite a Spanish fan. "I don't like this Korean food," he said as he ate, er … Korean food. "Very hot. Burns my ass something terrible." He'd had seven poos yesterday, he said (which by my reckoning is five Martinis). How nice that a stranger should share such personal details.

They showed Senegal v Turkey on the train (all trains have TVs in each carriage with an earpiece by your seat). There was a crowd of Germans in our compartment cheering for Senegal because they don't like the Turks, so we cheered for Turkey because we eat them at Christmas.

Arrived back at the hotel at midnight, another night without food. Couldn't sleep, so wrote for an hour. My body seems to be craving working until 3am. I hope I can quickly become unused to this when I am home. Not eating properly is boring and no doubt unhealthy.

In all the time I have been here I have not had what I would class as a decent sitdown meal in a restaurant – a combination of late kick-offs, late returns, a lack of food outlets and in this hotel refusing to pay £20 for a plate of pasta. Tony Roma's is as good as it's been.

Sunday proved another longie. Up early, went to breakfast because I needed some hot food and wrote a 900-word piece on refereeing and linesmen. Went to the media centre 40 minutes away, did some research for the next match and three of us jumped in a cab to go to the Korean team's press conference, a 45-minute journey. After the presser we stood in the rain and hail trying to hail a taxi. A Korean journalist, spotting some international colleagues in distress, kindly took us back to our hotel. Because of the weather/traffic this took 90 minutes, so we didn't arrive 'home' until gone 9pm. He refused to accept a penny (mind you, that was all we offered).

Wrote a 750-word report on Korea/Spain, a 750-word colour piece for the front. And yes, no dinner again. A packet of Korean Jaffa cakes and a Gatorade was my midnight feast.

MONDAY JUNE 24

Awakened at 3am by the office. "Chris? Paul here. Don't seem to have your Korea report ... oh yes, here it is ... sorry, bye..." Have they never heard of time-difference?

Couldn't get back to sleep, so turned on the TV where there was a documentary with English subtitles on the 1966 North Korea side that beat Italy 1-0. I liked the remark by Pak Doo Ik who scored North Korea's winner: "If I make a traffic offence, when they see my name is Pak Doo Ik I get let off." I was under the impression there were next to no private vehicles in North Korea. Shows the importance of scoring the winner against Italy.

In October 1989 I was in Singapore to cover the Asia World Cup final qualifying round and South Korea were one of the six countries involved. I saw them play Qatar and when handed the Korean team-sheet noticed with schoolboy delight that their team manager was called – honest, hand on jar of Marmite – Oh Wan Kon.

There have been other marvellous sporting names over the years. The most appropriate by far was Wolfgang Wolff who was the coach of Bundesliga side FC Wolfsburg. If ever a player was born to be a quarterback it was surely Chuck Long of, amongst others, the Detroit Lions.

When the Washington Redskins played in Super Bowl XXII there was a Rusty Nails in their front office (I thought it was a cocktail). Panathinaikos once had Joonas Kolkka and Blendar Kola, a partnership worth raising a glass to. There was a New Zealand cricketer called Cunis, whom the late John Arlott unforgettably described as being "neither one thing nor the other..." There was also a Dutchman called Ruud Bugga, honestly ... while I am still trying to work out how to react when an American introduces himself by saying: "Hi, I'm Randy."

I digress. Eventually got back to sleep about 4am. Up at nine and felt like I had a hangover. I don't mind feeling that way as long as I've had the fun to make it worthwhile. I hadn't.

Went to the media centre to see what was happening. There were loads of journos who were also there to see what was happening. So what was happening was that there were lots of reporters at the media centre asking each other what was happening.

Peeing down again. The rainy season has well and truly arrived. Did some work and went to the canteen at the media centre for mushroom soup, orange juice, spaghetti with tomato sauce, garlic bread and a coffee. It was probably the best meal I've had since arriving here. Seriously.

Tried to get a taxi back to the Lotte Hotel. It was still bucketing down and I had my arm in the air for so long trying to get a taxi cramp set it. Then ... a car pulled over. YES! Another lift from a guardian angel ... thank you car god. The electric window went down, a woman's hand came out and handed me an umbrella ... she flatteringly said something to me in Korean as if I was fluent in her language ... and the car sped away. Holy thanks withdrawn.

It was also a ladies' pink umbrella.

I had the chance to go out for dinner tonight, but none of the other journos is around. They are all at the Korean press conference (which Henry Winter is covering for the *Telegraph*).

Did some shopping at the duty free store in the hotel only to be told – no word of a lie – "Oh no, sir. You can't actually BUY anything here." The process is that I choose what I want to buy, pay for it and then collect it in the duty free store at Seoul airport as I go home. So, no chance of anything going wrong then.

TUESDAY JUNE 25

Strictly speaking it is now tomorrow – Wednesday morning 1.30am – and I am drinking a bottle of champagne alone in my room. The toast is … the Lonely Journo's Hearts Club Band. Germany ended Korea's dream in the semi-final, but the people of Seoul are still celebrating 31 floors below. Singing, chanting and dancing … they have been the lifeblood of an unforgettable World Cup – for many reasons. Hopefully when I look back I will remember the warmth and friendliness of the Japanese and Korean people rather than the techno nightmares.

When I left the press box after Korea's defeat there was a little girl, aged about seven, face painted, wearing a 'Be The Reds' T-shirt, crying her eyes out. The Korean people didn't expect their team to reach the semi-finals, but they deserved it and maybe more.

EURO 2004
PORTUGAL

THURSDAY JUNE 10

A positive start to the trip. On the plane out I sat behind Gary Lineker, which made me feel safe because in the event of a crash his ears would cushion the impact. I took a taxi from Oporto airport to the accreditation centre.

Bumped into *ITV's* Peter Drury, who had just completed his accreditation process. "They're pretty well organised there," he said, but Peter no doubt had an up-to-date photo of himself in the Euro 2004 system.

Not me. For some reason the *Daily Telegraph* didn't send a photo of me taken a year or so ago. Instead an eight-year-old photo was emailed to the Euro 2004 media accreditation centre and they reckoned I bore so little resemblance to how I looked in 1996 I had to have a new one taken. It's been a tough if enjoyable eight years, though.

The press pack contained lots of goodies, including a model of a Hyundai car (official supplier to Euro 2004) and a McDonald's book of vouchers for cake, coffee and water, but not a god-knows-what burger. Literally let them eat cake (incidentally, why do we say you can't have your cake and eat it? What's the point of anyone having cake if they are not going to eat it?).

The hotel is okay, though not quite as good as the brochure made out. They have put a block on all free-phone numbers (along with, it seems, other hotels in Portugal), so instead of connecting to the internet 'free' we have to pay to use the landline number. This costs a quid a minute, so I'll be using the mobile (lovely fast connection).

My colleague on the DT, Jim White, is in the next room while Phil 'Plat Du' Shaw (think about it…) is opposite. We went to a local gaff for dinner and Phil ordered a "really nice bottle of white I had a couple of days ago." It was sparkling white and he sensed from my expression that something was wrong.

"Doesn't it stay on the tongue?"

"What tongue?"

It should have been good – it cost 5 euro. The sole was, however, splendid.

FRIDAY JUNE 11

Woke up at 0507, but as the clock on the TV is seven minutes fast (do I have my own time zone?) it was really earlier. Room very hot. Trouble is the a/c is too loud to have on at night. Well, too loud for me.

At Euro 2000 in Belgium my hotel room in Brussels was so hot (air conditioning hadn't reached the Belgian capital, well not the bit where I was) that I used to write in my car. I would turn on the engine, sit in the back with the a/c on, tapping away at my laptop. And yes, I did get some strange looks.

Breakfast was poor. Cereals and cake/bread and stuff you only get abroad, like unusual cheese. Still, having a bowl of corn flakes and looking at the Atlantic is something I rarely do in Bromley. The hotel seems to be almost empty apart from a plethora of honeymoon couples.

Myself and Plat Du managed to go through breakfast without (a) talking about football or (b) moaning about our papers, an almost impossible scenario for two or more journalists. No doubt we'll make up for this later.

The nearest we came to work-based chitchat was when I told Phil about a question Graham Beekroft asked Kit Symons, the Crystal Palace coach, on talkSPORT. It was a kind of broadcasting Russian roulette with absolutely no room for error. Making a reference to Palace chairman Simon Jordan's reputation for not throwing the dosh around, Beeky said: "Does he still run a tight ship, Kit?" Say it five times to yourself and you'll realise how brave/foolish Beeky was.

Plat Du, who works for the *Independent*, is a serious music buff, the only journalist I can talk to about Carter USM. He's a really nice guy and I'll even forgive him that he's a Leeds fan. His current malady is that his 17-year-old daughter Ellie has become a Kevin. "Huh ... why do you nag me about tidying my room ... there are people dying in the world and all you can do is moan about my knickers on the floor."

He asked my advice. I told him to leave home.

My room has a sort of balcony, almost a conservatory, but not quite. Maybe a conserve, but not really a conservatory. It was foggy when I got up which I hoped was a heat haze, but Mr Sun is elsewhere. Today I have to write previews for Portugal v Greece (the opening game), Spain v Russia and Croatia v Switzerland. I have a feeling Greece could hold Portugal to a draw.

The hotel won't cash travellers cheques. The nearest bank is one and a half kilometres away, but "sorry sir, they're closed as it's gone three o'clock – they'll be open again on Monday."

Okay, that's fine then. I won't spend any money over the weekend. Strange official media hotel this – they have blocked free-phone numbers and you can't change t/c's, two of the services journos need when abroad for a month. We are very isolated here. To one side there is the Atlantic and to other ... well, very little.

Spent the day writing my previews and Mr Sun burst through about 4pm. Plat Du says he had "a bit too much to drink last night" (my thirst was barely quenched), so he is having an early night. His idea of a late one is 10pm though. He probably doesn't know who Trevor McDonald is.

Jim White drove off in his car after breakfast and hasn't been seen since. Hopefully I can meet up with a few of the hacks who are staying in the

BEHIND THE BACK PAGE

centre of Oporto. Even *Sky News* is boring, the local elections dominating. I wonder how the Monster Raving Loony Party did at Croydon? They had their Minister of Chocolate standing.

This is not at all as I imagined/hoped/expected. It is the dead end of Portugal. The hotel was described as 3km from the centre of Oporto – in fact it's about 25 minutes by cab. There is, literally, nowhere to eat a decent meal anywhere in the area. With Jim having a car, we drove for around 25 minutes. We didn't go into the centre of Oporto, naively believing that a holiday resort on the Portuguese coast in the summer while there is a major football tournament being played would have a restaurant or two. We checked out five places, but they were no more than ice cream parlours and we were after more than dessert. We ended up at this place that LOOKED like a restaurant and indeed displayed the word 'restaurant' outside. Weak with hunger we ventured in. The menu was in Portuguese, so decided to play it safe – Sopa de Legumes. Three sausages arrived. So much for safety first.

I opted for beefsteak and something resembling a beefsteak arrived topped with mushrooms and sauté spuds on the side, nudge nudge know what I mean. I could not cut the steak with the knife, though that may have said as much about the knife as the steak. I ended up eating as many mushrooms and spuds as I could. Plat Du and Jim had a fish that was so salty it was impossible to eat. You could smell the salt.

The waiter was most unhappy that my entire steak and most of the fish was left. The only consolation was that the red wine was good. My tongue was particularly grateful. We each had chocolate mousse for dessert to fill us up.

But what a hole, what a place we are staying in. This is seriously bereft of any culinary outlets. Still, only another two and a half weeks.

Had a call from the office at 10pm. "Er, I have a query about your Portugal preview."

"What's the problem?"

"We (changed from 'I' for safety reasons) think you have a semi-colon in the team in the wrong place."

So, nothing trivial then. "What do you mean?"

"Well, you have the back four and a colon, no problem, and then you have Maniche and Costinha and a semicolon, then Figo and Rui Costa and another semi-colon."

"That's because Maniche and Costinha play as two defensive midfielders with Figo and Rui Costa the attacking midfielders…"

"Oh…" Roll on tomorrow when the action starts.

SATURDAY JUNE 12

Not much action over breakfast. Or of any kind in the Germany camp it seems. The German doctor has, according to reports, encouraged the players not to have sex before games, but to drink plenty of water instead.

"I regard sex a few hours before a game as a problem," said the doctor, talking about the players not himself. The players' wives and partners are staying in the hotel next door. I shall resist the obvious joke about saving the scoring until the kick-off. Suffice to say, from the Germany players' viewpoint, a WAG definitely is out of the question.

To Portugal versus Greece at the Dragao Stadium in Oporto and the Greeks had obviously not read the script, beating the hosts 2-1. Portuguese errors enabled Greece to score twice before Cristiano Ronaldo's last minute header. "The next game will almost be a matter of life and death," said Luiz Felipe Scolari, the Portugal coach keeping football fully in perspective.

SUNDAY JUNE 13

Hardly slept last night in anticipation of Switzerland versus Croatia in Leiria today. Not. I could write the report now. I am sure it will be goalless because Switzerland are almost allergic to scoring. Both teams know that, bar a major upset, neither will qualify from Group B where England and France are favourites to go through to the next round.

Security at the stadium meant a 30-minute wait in temperatures touching 80 degrees. Then someone asks you to open your bag, they take a look and wave you through. Farcical. I'd complain about it not being done properly, but we'd probably have to wait for an hour in the heat then which wouldn't make me the most popular journalist at Euro 2004 (not that I am anyway).

Yes, Switzerland 0, Croatia 0. The only thing I missed in my prediction was Johann Vogel's sending-off. Apologies, must do better. No goals, one red card and seven yellows. Colourful, but still desperately dull.

Back to Oporto for a slap up meal of a Mars bar and a Coke which was more enjoyable than the match.

MONDAY JUNE 14

Had as big a breakfast as is possible in Portugal where a good fry up tends to mean being sunburnt. I allowed myself a fifth croissant as I chatted to some Danish fans about England's 2-1 defeat by France at the Stadium of Light a couple of nights earlier.

They felt England were unlucky, which will be a massive relief to Sven-Göran Eriksson whose name is now Sven-Göran Eriksson Must Go in the tabloids.

Denmark 0 Italy 0 was much better than Switzzzzzerland versus Croatia even if the scoreline was the same. As someone once said, there are goalless draws and goalless draws, but this wasn't really a goalless draw.

Italy look as if they could flatter to deceive again after going home early from the 2002 World Cup finals. They have great players, but they aren't doing it for the national team and coach Giovanni Trapattoni.

Back at the hotel we took in Sweden 5, Bulgaria 0. I started to watch the game in the hotel bar on the big – well, biggish – screen, but was driven to my room by the smokers. A takeaway pizza and a bottle of wine represented a banquet by recent culinary standards.

TUESDAY JUNE 15:
Bumped into former Republic of Ireland manager Mick McCarthy today. Mick's here working for the BBC, but was at the England/France game as a spectator. To avoid the crush he left a couple of minutes from the end, so he missed the two Zinedine Zidane goals – a free-kick in the 89th minute and a stoppage time penalty after Gerrard's suicidal back-pass – that gave France a 2-1 victory.

The hotel has been taken over by Dutch fans, so the present, if not the future, is orange. Ruud van Nistelrooy upset a few, well, quite a lot, okay probably everyone, in Germany by saying Holland want to win "for soccer history and other history." Former Dutch international Ronald Koeman added to the "don't mention" scenario when he said that at Euro 88 he exchanged shirts with a German opponent "but I only use the shirt to wipe my arse." This is incredible. Koeman must have made a lot of money as a player and a coach and yet he cannot afford a roll of toilet paper.

If Germany beat Holland tonight it will be a case of "don't mention the score..." in the hotel. I think it will be a narrow win to the Germans because even their bad sides are good.

Emmett Malone of the *Irish Times* is due to be kipping in my other bed tonight, my debt to the Irish repaid in that single gesture, slate wiped clean (like Koeman's arse with the German shirt). Emmett is based in Lisbon for the tournament and has struggled to find a hotel in Oporto, so kindhearted me offered to put him up. I hope there are no problems with snoring, belching, coughing or farting – still, if he doesn't like it, tough.

In fact, as it turned out, Emmett managed to find a hotel in Oporto, so I slept alone, no doubt to his relief. The 1-1 draw (van Nistelrooy equalised) was better than I expected, very intense, with an obvious anti-German feeling in the stadium. Got back at 12.45am and raided the mini bar ... hadn't eaten since breakfast. The restaurant at the hotel was taken over by a 'private lunch' for the Dutch and the supermercado was closed for, I presume, a supersiesta. A fourstar hotel, but no lunch served unless you were Dutch. I asked for room service, but would probably have had better luck asking to sleep with Julia Roberts. In fact, today I might just try that. My luck, I'd probably get Graham Roberts.

Hungry as I was, I could not face a sandwich from the fridge at the stadium where I couldn't even buy chocolate. So my midnight snack was two Sprites, a small tube of Pringles and a Mars bar. Phil Shaw, the bastard, knocked on my door to tell me he'd found an orange in his room. He's a flash northerner. With an orange.

WEDNESDAY JUNE 16

I am sitting on the toilet writing this. Not doing what Popes, royalty and world leaders also have to do, but because it is the only available seat in a media centre with limited facilities at the Estadio do Bessas in Porto. The facilities could also be described as smokey. You can catch cancer from the air.

I also like the idea of having to walk up (and of course down) seven flights of stairs to the press box, honest I do. Much better than a lift. Nice to work up a good sweat. Pity there weren't more stairs really. Luckily it was only 90 degrees.

Gerry McDermott of the *Irish Independent* was breathalysed last night. You can't just go down a one-way street in Portugal the wrong way without (a) being caught by the Old Bill or (b) being breathalysed. Gerry is probably the only Irish journalist (ever, in the history of Irish journalists) who doesn't drink. Like, how unlucky can the Portuguese Old Bill be?

Some bastard has nicked my prescription sunglasses. They were on my desk next to another English journo (who shall remain nameless) and at half-time I said: "I'll get us a drink – are you staying here?" He said "yes", so I went to get us a drink and when I came back the sunglasses (in their case) were missing because he had gone to chat to a pal. Still, he said "sorry", so that's alright then. Pair of £100 prescription sunglasses half-inched, but he apologised so no problem.

I reported it to the media desk and they said I should contact them later. This is not easy. Well, when I say not easy, what I really mean is impossible. There is no method of telephoning the media centres, I kid you not. The desks don't have phones.

This is terrific for those working there as they don't get bothered by phone calls from journalists (who I believe the media centre is for). On the other hand, and forgive me if I am biased, there is a strong argument that a media centre SHOULD be contactable by the media. Maybe I'm just old fashioned. The media guide, in its useful contacts section, lists the town hall, police, firemen, Sao Joao hospital and the tourist office. But obviously it was not considered that 'useful' for the media centre to be included.

If I want to find out about the local council tax, report a mugging or fire, have an ingrowing toenail seen to or find out the tourist hotspots, then I know who to contact. But, despite being an accredited member of the media, I cannot telephone the media desk in the Estadio do Bessas.

Martin Samuel of the *News of the World* and *Times* was involved in an unusual car crash. Martin was driving along minding his own business when, without warning, the air bag deployed. It was, he told me, something of a surprise to be pootling along the motorway, listening to a bit of Half Man Half Biscuit, when suddenly a bloody great inflatable thing was in his face. Such was its force, Martin had burns on his arms. He did, however, confirm that it is probably the only 100 per cent guaranteed cure to constipation.

I think Martin's a very talented journalist. I have known him since he first came on the circuit and rarely have I seen such a hunger in a writer to search for a different angle to an obvious story-line. He invariably manages to find one and has deserved the awards that have come his way. Martin also invariably manages to find the most expensive restaurant in any city in any country. I have almost finished paying off a dinner in Barcelona, 2005.

Just watched Portugal 2 Russia 0. Looked a very generous red card decision in favour of Portugal to send off the Russian goalkeeper. I think the reason the referee showed the keeper the red card was that he couldn't be bothered to caution him and take his name – Ovchinnikov. The tournament needs Portugal to go through.

Interesting watching the game on Portuguese TV. During half-time they did not show any of the first-half action, just had two commentators talking while the camera panned round the crowd, which included a Russian girl with huge assets. At full-time they showed the goals by Maniche and Rui Costa over and over again. The red card given to the Russian keeper for what was deemed deliberate handball was not shown once. Nothing like nice unbiased news coverage.

Off to Leiria tomorrow for Croatia v France. Managed to blag a lift. Dreadful journey on the rattler. Three different trains including a wait of 70 minutes for one connection. It's about a two or two-and-a-half hour drive, but the train journey takes more than twice that long. Length matters. It means I will get back to Oporto that night, well, in the early hours of the morning. On the rattler I'd have to stay overnight.

THURSDAY JUNE 17

Just been trying to buy some new prescription sunglasses. They should take four days, but yer man Nuno cut some clip-on Raybans to the size of my 'ordinary' glasses and they are excellent, certainly ok until I get home.

The only problem was that when he clipped the originals over my glasses and was marking them accordingly he had, beyond any argument, the worst breath in the history of bad breath. Worse than that feller on the bullet train in Japan. Still, it doesn't make him a bad optician. Just one that you wouldn't want to breathe in your face. Unfortunately mine was that face.

Had breakfast with Plat Du, who said his daughter 'Kevin' is missing him. "Marvellous, when I'm at home she never speaks to me, only the occasional grunt. Now I'm in Portugal it's 'when are you coming home?'" I didn't say it but we're talking presents here, Plat Du.

Arrived in Leiria. The 'security' at this tournament consists of little more than a gratuitous peep in the computer bag, but this time I had an overnight bag to be inspected as well. The shaving foam, shampoo and sun tan lotion were confiscated as 'offensive weapons' that could be thrown as objects.

It gets better. Simon Mullock, who works for the *Sunday Mirror*, bought a small iron earlier today because there is no ironing service in his hotel. At the security gate there was the following conversation:

"What's this?"

"An iron."

"That's dangerous."

"I haven't plugged it in yet..."

[Bemused of Leiria] "Oh, okay then..."

So you can take an iron in, but not sun tan cream. Or shampoo – whether it's plugged in or not.

Still, no such security lapses down in Faro where a freelance writer is covering Euro 2004 for various national newspapers. Only one small problem, he doesn't have accreditation. He still got into Russia v Spain by wearing his African Nations Cup accreditation around his neck. Correction, it was someone else's accreditation. He was in the media overflow section, sitting 15 yards from the King of Spain. How lucky he didn't have any factor 6 with him or else El Rey would really have been in trouble.

Apparently Mr Freelance is moving hotels. "The guy in this one is ripping me off," he said.

"How much are you paying?"

"Forty five euro a night, but I've found somewhere for 25."

He must be the only non-Tunisian in the place. And I feel sorry for the Tunisians.

Croatia 2 France 2. Robert Prosniecki, former Croatian legend and now serial smoker, sat in front of me in the press box with a journalist who smoked even more heavily than Prosi (not the best of abbreviations, I accept). Between them they must have got through 100 fags during the game. Thank God there could be no extra-time as it was a group stage match.

There were no desk lights in the press box and by 9pm it was very difficult to see properly. Even so, many hacks – myself included – stayed there to do their last edition rewrite, preferring darkness to the smokey atmosphere in the media working area. It became something of a farce trying to type in the pitch black. Still, the night did end on a positive note when I had a half litre (which quickly became a low litre, the nearest to porn since I've been on this trip – think about it, it's there somewhere) of Carlsberg for one euro served by a girl from Lithuania called Graziana. She was so impressed when I told her I'd been to Vilnius, the capital of her country. Well, actually she didn't seem to give a toss, but I'm sure deep down she was mighty impressed. She just hid it well.

Got back to my hotel at 2.15am. A long day.

FRIDAY JUNE 18

Had five hours kip after a tiring day in Leiria. Went down to breakfast and discovered that the Swedes are in town in force for the game against Bulgaria tonight. Not a Bulgarian (or, thankfully, a Bulgarian umbrella) in sight.

Very hot here again. The next time I'll sweat like this is when I put my expenses through.

To Braga for Denmark v Bulgaria tonight, not one to get the enthusiasm juices flowing. At least it's a 5 o'clock kick-off.

Michael Walker of the *Guardian*, whose wit is not so much dry as arid, is having a mixed European Championship. Michael's office gave him American Express travellers cheques when he came out here. Apparently the only place in Oporto he can change them is the airport, about 30 miles away from where he's staying. Those familiar with Michael will know he took such information very philosophically, not swearing or threatening to rip the manhood from the guy who gave him the t/c's in the first place. Not Michael, oh no.

Michael is also attending Bulgaria v Denmark. "Your office obviously don't think very much of you then, do they?" I observed subtlely.

"Where are you going?" he asked me.

"Bulgaria v Denmark, too," I replied.

"My office don't think much of you either, then," he said.

Fair point well made. Denmark won 2-0, an enthusiasm-free game.

One of the perks of hotel life is watching CNN, invariably the only English language station available (though Sir Bobby Robson thinks it's Portuguese). There was an item on George W. Bush – the US president who once said he was in favour of a stronger death penalty, honest – welcoming Bill and Hilary Clinton for the official unveiling of Clinton's official portrait at the White House. I wonder if it'll be hung on a wall or placed under a desk.

There was also a piece on Michael Jackson at a fast food restaurant wearing a Spiderman mask. I may be wrong but people could start to think he's a weirdo if he's not careful.

SATURDAY JUNE 20
Not a good day. In fact, it could hardly have been worse. Woke up about 6.30am with a bit of a stomach ache. By half-eight it was a bad stomach ache and by about 10am it was excruciating pain. I have not felt so bad since I saw my perfectly crafted intro from an Arsenal match report rewritten earlier this year. It felt like there was an alien in the centre of my stomach trying to get out.

I was so bad Plat Du went downstairs to call a doctor (Phil has a very loud voice). Fortunately within half an hour one arrived. The doctor didn't speak English, so the guy from reception translated. The doc gave me various tests, including maths and English (I failed the latter).

Though I was baking hot, my temperature was normal. He said he thought I had a bug, literally, in my system. He gave me a pain-killing injection which took away most of the pain. I have to take pills before and after meals. "No alcohol, no fried food, no butter etc," he said.

There was only one thing for me to do. I changed my doctor.

The irony was on the Saturday night three of us, myself, Plat Du and Jim White (I must get a nickname for him, maybe Jaime Blanco) went for a ruby, at a place called the Real Indiana. We all had pretty much the same. We all dipped and dunked each other's meals, as you do, and I only ate chicken, not prawns or any salad.

I thought the only thing I may have had different was a yoghurt dip with my popadom, but Plat Du said he had some, too. I had a cheese roll at the press centre, which could have been handled by someone who didn't ... well, who knows?

Anyway, I made it through the night and feel about 80 per cent today (Monday as I write this). That's five per cent better than I usually feel. I'll go to France v Switzerland tonight. Felt so poorly yesterday I couldn't even write my report from Latvia v Germany, which I believe is the first time I have ever been too ill to file.

Been here for eight days now. Still far too many problems for it to be as enjoyable as one would like, but at least the tournament is starting to take shape. Spain v Portugal to decide which progresses will be a belter.

MONDAY JUNE 21:

Improving as the day goes on, but still not feeling 100 per cent. Miserable weather, drizzly and not exactly warm. Turned on the TV and it was raining at

Wimbledon, what a surprise. I heard a Brit had returned a serve this morning, so that will no doubt be the sports lead tomorrow.

The people on reception have been brilliant during my illness, more concerned about me than I am. While the organisation here is poor the people remain extremely friendly. Plat Du told me I reminded him of Sybil in the episode of *Fawlty Towers* when she pretended to be someone who was ill … that perked me up, being compared to Mrs Fawlty. Obrigado (that's Portuguese for 'Thank You') Plat Du.

An uneventful morning, unless you count sorting some clothes out for washing, shaving and having a shower as eventful and if you do you are indeed sad. Drove down to Coimbra with Oliver Kay of the Times and Michael Walker. Well, Oliver drove with Michael and I grateful passengers. Oliver is destined to be a football correspondent one day – or as we call it, a number one (not the best of phrases, is it really?). Oliver is the *Times'* north west-based correspondent and is an excellent writer who breaks a good number of stories, too. Like Michael, Oliver is also great company. And a great driver.

Coimbra's media centre was smogsville. UEFA ban smoking in the technical area because it sends out the wrong signal (smoke signal?), but they allow hacks to pollute the air in media centres. It is becoming a big issue. There will be a punch up soon, not necessarily involving me.

Opposite me a guy sat down next to someone who had just bought something to eat and lit up. The eater said something and the smoker replied thoughtfully: "There are no No Smoking signs" and carried on. UEFA don't care because the people who make such decisions aren't affected by them.

Up to the press box and it became England versus France II. My seat was next to David 'Disco' McDonnell of the *Daily Mirror*, who had just logged on. Next to me were two French guys who had been on line about 45 minutes and it was only when I plugged MY phone cable in to what, it turned out, was actually Disco's line, that he realised they had been using HIS line. This is a problem in the press boxes, the phone bandits. They find any vacant line and just plug in. Their excuse was "it was free". Disco said: "Available, yes, but not free, my old sunshine." The French became most upset with Disco whom I backed up in the phoney war.

One of them, who had the sort of face and attitude that demanded a thump on le hooter, kept saying "Ssshhh" putting his finger over his mouth. Disco said he would like their names so his office could bill THEIR office (which never happens, but it was worth a try). I called Mr Ssshhh a thief, which for some reason he took exception to. He called me a putain, which I think is French for something rude. I responded by calling him a wanker, which I think is the French for wanker. He understood because he called me a putain again.

He then said: "Let us talk French or can't you do that?"

I said: "Let's talk a neutral language" and started to insult him in Spanish. It was quite comical, French guy insulting me in French and me insulting him in Spanish. I said in English that it was unusual for a Frenchman to be so aggressive and I think he almost took it as a compliment rather than the less than complimentary remark it actually was.

A telephone guy came over and told the French pair to move to their own seats. which, surprise surprise, didn't have any phone lines. One of them was working for the French Football Federation and I said I would be reporting him. He gave me a sneer and said: "Go ahead."

He thought I was bullshitting, but he should have known better – the email has already gone off to the FFF about his fff***ing bad behaviour.

Back to the hotel 1.15am. Just as well I didn't feel like dinner.

WEDNESDAY JUNE 23

My last day in Oporto. Woke about 6.30am after what is becoming the regulation just over four hours kip. Foggy again. Down for breakfast and the room was full of Dutch who are in town for the Holland v Latvia match tonight in Braga where I shall be. One Dutch girl has a huge pair of clogs, which have transformed my toast and marmalade experience. Shared a table with a Dutch fan who started to relate a story (in English) about how he was once taken ill on a plane coming back from Liverpool. Appendicitis. Those listening who were still awake even got the flight number. My toast started to move away, it was so bored.

Wrote a piece on Italy during the morning. Had lunch with Plat Du and Jim White. Was hungry after my Kit Kat dinner last night and runaway breakfast. The manager came over to chat with us and said how fresh the sole was. Yes, he said, they would do it off the bone.

Waiter comes, sole off the bone please.

Sorry Senhor Davies, no sole.

Had the sea bass instead, which was full of bones. I felt like saying to the manager: "I have a bone to pick with you."

To Braga where the stadium is a 25-minute walk from car to media centre, the last 10 literally up a long and winding road. By the time you get to the top you are sweating like a pig, though hopefully any comparison stops there.

I tried to buy something at the official merchandise store. The helpful guy wrapped it up for me.

"How much?"

"16 euro"

Gave the guy 20 euro "Sorry sir, we don't have any change."

He said I would have to pay 20 euro.

I said why not 15 euro, preparing to hand him a 10 and a five euro note.

He laughed. I laughed at his laugh.

I went off having paid four euro over the odds.

Home at 12.45am. Alarm set for 5.45am for trip to Faro.

THURSDAY JUNE 24

To Faro on the southern Algarve coast. Woke up at 4.45am, an hour ahead of the alarm. Why does this always happen?

Cristiano Schumacher drove me to the airport, stopping occasionally at a red light. Incredibly there was nowhere at Oporto airport to change travellers cheques. Unbelievable.

There was one high spot and you have to be a guy to fully appreciate the enjoyment, indeed, necessity of this. Had a pee and in the trough was a piece of chewing gum. What is it that makes someone want to spit his gum out while he's taking a leak? Are the two, in any way, connected?

But, of course, it being there and me being a guy, I aimed for the ball of gum and drove it down the other end of the trough. It is an offer that cannot be refused by any self-respecting bloke under such circumstances. Gum, dog end ... the REAL challenge is a block of disinfectant. Anyone who can even MOVE that, let alone encourage its journey three, four, maybe even five feet along the trough, is a man to be reckoned with.

The hotel in Faro is very special, excellent. Weather is good, no fog and the Swedes are in the hotel next door. Saw England versus Portugal in the quarterfinal in the penthouse suite of *5Live's* Simon Brotherton, who, apart from being an excellent commentator, also has the knack of always seeming to be happy. A splendid place he has, his television able to pick up BBC1 with John Motson's commentary, which is quite remarkable. England didn't deserve to win and did anyone seriously think we'd triumph in the penalty shootout? We never win them. It's what England do, lose penalty shootouts. Back to hotel about midnight, streets packed by celebrating Portuguese with big horns. Which is nice.

SATURDAY JUNE 26

Very busy yesterday, he writes unconvincingly, so no diary. Not the best of starts to the day. Awakened about 4.30am by some noise. Thought it was the faulty air conditioning, tried to get back to sleep but it was impossible. At six I rang down to the front desk to say there was a noise "from above" and the guy said he'd investigate.

Ten minutes later, having heard nothing from reception, I went down to the front desk not in the best mood of my life (even the good moods are bad).

Guy on reception said: "My colleague has investigated and has been to room 401 [immediately above my room]. There is a couple making sex [smiles]. They checked in a couple of hours ago [bigger smile]."

"Well, I need another room to finish making my sleep [no smile]. I'll probably find it funny later but for now... [absolutely no smile]"

I was given a temporary transfer to room 204 and was just nodding off when, from the street, I (and probably half of Portugal) heard: "Ingerlund ... Ingerlund ... Ingerlund..." The great unwashed were returning from their MENSA meeting. Anyway I did eventually get back to sleep and woke up 9.15am.

Went down to reception en route to breakfast where a girl was now in charge. Ever the diplomat I told her: "There was an unfortunate incident a few hours ago. I had to change rooms because of the noise coming from 401..."

At that point the guy I'd seen originally came from the office and said: "Are they still banging away then? [smiles]" So much for diplomacy.

"They are a British couple, called McNamara."

I said: "Just tell me ... please tell me ... he's younger than me."

"Oh yes he is, Mr Davies."

But most people are.

Had breakfast, was tempted to order eggs McNamara [easy over], but didn't. Went downstairs later and by coincidence the McNamaras were sitting in the lounge, taking a well-deserved timeout from their shagfest. I always thought I would recognise her, big smile on her face, walking like

John Wayne. To make matters worse she was stunning, about 30, fit as a butcher's dog. He was – well, lucky.

Paddy Barclay of the *Sunday Telegraph* and Tony Banks of the *Daily Express* are now in the hotel. At least I'll have company when I go out for a Diet Coke. It's been six days since I had a drink [alcohol] and the dreadful thing is, I feel much better. This cannot be sustained. I shall join Alcoholics Unanimous – if you ever feel like NOT having a drink, ring them and they talk you out of it.

To the stadium for Holland v Sweden and Faro is like a furnace. It's too hot to watch, let alone play. Unfortunate incident in the media centre. Sat down to do a bit of work and someone from Holland sat next to me and lit up, which sadly he had every right to do. Fortunately or unfortunately, whichever way you look at it, someone [can't reveal who] let rip with a silent but violent. Divine retribution? Dutchie was not impressed.

"Is that you?"

"Yes," I lied, but flattered in a strange way.

"Do you have to do that here?"

"Listen – there are no No Smoking signs, so you are able to smoke. Tell me sir, where are the No Farting signs?"

"You should go to the toilet to do that."

"Why? Because you don't like the smell? I don't like the smell of your cigarette and I'll carry that home with me. You won't go home smelling of my [or whoever it was] fart."

I think I won the tactical battle. The Dutch gave the world Total Football in the Seventies. Thirty years later they experienced Total Farting.

The game was average, another shootout, Holland edging Sweden 5-4 on penalties after a 0-0 draw. The press conference in the mixed zone was a joke. No players were interested at all. Arsenal's Freddie Ljungberg, bless him, at least stopped to talk in English to the nation where he earns his living.

Edwin van der Sar of Manchester United, however, walked past us without even bothering to answer. I chased after him and asked if he has heard the request for two minutes of his time in English.

"No, sorry."

"But you earn your living in England..."

"Yes, but I am playing for Holland," he said in English and walked off. It has been noted.

Chaos and farce at the end. There were no buses or coaches to take anyone, punters or journos, anywhere from Portugal's purpose built stadium in the middle of nowhere. We had to wait for cabs, but thankfully one came along after only an hour and a half, so it wasn't as if we had to wait a long time.

This was my 13th game of the tournament. I think the maximum any journalist could have covered was 16. Most have done six or seven. Believe it or not it is knackering. OK, don't believe it. Got back to the hotel at 1.45am, a familiar tale. The organisation has been unacceptably chaotic for everyone. I'll be delighted to watch the remaining three games on TV from the People's Republic of Bromley.

SUNDAY JUNE 27

One day to go.

Woke up at 7.17am. Could've done with more than five hours' sleep, but such is life. Went down to breakfast at half eight and found a table by myself. Had the obligatory bowl of muesli with melon and pineapple and a double espresso to get things going double-quick, then sat down to read yesterday's *Daily Telegraph*.

No-one else in the hotel, not literally, but no other journos. Strange scenario ... fabulous hotel, superb weather ... but none of the chaps to socialise with. Well, I'm here to work not socialise, which is just as well.

Sat around the pool for an hour or so, got bored, also got very bloody hot. Can't get the Sunday papers, the guy who delivers them has gone AWOL. Maybe he's Mr McNamara's substitute.

It's the Czech Republic versus Denmark in the final quarter-final tonight. I'll probably wander down to the marina. Table for one please senhor.

I did indeed wander down there and found a place with 52inch plasma screen (size matters), and – final insult – "would you mind sitting here, sir?" The waiter ushered me to a table for two rather than the table for three I'd prematurely claimed. So clearly not having anyone join me. Am I that easy to read? Had a splendid tapas of exotic fruits with coriander and a huge 'tom and moz' salad to follow. Far too hot to eat anything else. It was 82 degrees when I sat down, not comfortable.

The Czechs gave the Danes a football lesson winning 3-0. I wandered back to the hotel managing to buy the *People*, *Sunday Telegraph* and *Sunday Times*. Wanted to sit on the balcony and read them, no light though.

Shared an elevator with the McNamaras, who were no doubt going to have an early start to their nuptials. He doesn't look like Superman. Must check out what he has for breakfast. Apart from sex.

MONDAY JUNE 28

My last day.

Woke up 6.20am. Hot as hell. The last time someone sweated like this was Bill Clinton when Hillary phoned to say she'd be home early.

Down to breakfast. With the finishing line in sight I broke loose and had baked beans on toast after the regulation muesli, melon and pineapple plus double espresso.

To Albufeira for the Holland press conference at the Sheraton Algarve prior to their semi-final against the hosts Portugal. What a place, it's so up-market even Roman Abramovich was thrown out. Fair do's to the Dutch, it was brilliantly organised, signposts everywhere to where the press conference was to be held … freshly squeezed orange juice with ice … PRs to hand out stats sheets ... sarnies, goodies, fresh fruit, cakes ... a magnificent spread.

Dick Advocaat, the Dutch coach, has been getting fearful stick back home to the extent that one TV pundit said he should be hanged or stoned. The idea of someone being stoned in Amsterdam does not seem to be unusual, though.

May eat in the hotel tonight after packing. Yet again sad bastard table for one please. I even said to a Russian waiter last night: "I'm working here, you know," in case he thought I was some kind of international sad bastard. Of course, Dimitri, at home, jeez, I have friends wait-listed to dine with me ... table for 38, maybe more. Take over the restaurant. Here? Well, table for one'll be okay my old comrade.

Checked out the menu, pleasantly inexpensive for a top-class hotel. Most expensive main course is, or maybe are, prawns – 25 euro. Most expensive steak is 15 euro, a tenner. It's too hot to eat a steak with sauce and all the trimmings. I'd love grilled chicken, fish or a pasta dish, but none such is on the menu.

Decided against the hotel restaurant, the fact that it was empty at 9pm a factor and instead found a place 100 yards down the road, choosing the soup and sole. Too hot to eat outside, so went inside where the a/c was welcome. Back to the hotel by a quarter after 10. Up at six tomorrow, so will try to have an early night.

Have I enjoyed Euro 2004? No, not really. That may be hard to sell to the folks back home, but the aggro has outweighed the pleasure. I speak only as a journalist and not a supporter, but UEFA must improve the media organisation for Euro 2008. I am not a lone siren voice, honest.

The Czechs have been a breath of fresh air (unlike the press centres), the Dutch are never boring, Portugal have given their supporters much to cheer about, the eventual winners Greece have shown that the little guys can have their day. Generally speaking Euro 2004 has been a victory for coaching over individualism; perhaps inferior players who for whatever reason haven't played so much having the advantage over those who have sweated blood for 50-odd matches in top league teams.

Super Bowl XXXIX, Jacksonville, Feb 2005

TUESDAY FEBRUARY 1

Good news for those envious of me in Jacksonville. This is building up to be a less-than-super Super Bowl. While the owners of the National Football League clubs who voted to bring the SB here probably didn't realise that Jacksonville would be Siberiaville, the organisors should have ensured that there is just the tiniest grain of Super Bowl fever in the city. There is, I'm sure, more SB fever in Gateshead. Nick Szczepanik of the *Times* and I are the only two English hacks in the Marriott, which, to be fair, is a nice hotel.

The rooms are spacious and quiet, the phones work and my maid comes from Bosnia – "I'm divorced … I haven't seen, how you say, that f****** bastard of a husband for seven years," she told me. Maybe not quite how I'd say it, but I got the drift. I also got the drift when I stepped outside because of the sleet.

Upon arriving at Jacksonville airport at about 11pm (or 4am by my body, what remained of it) last night I went to the airport's Media Center as instructed to arrange for the promised Media Bus to take me to my Media Hotel. Unfortunately the Media Centre was an ex-Media Center, closed, gone to its maker, bereft of personnel. Thankfully, the taxi ride was a mere 35 minutes and only cost $60. That's OK then.

The Super Bowl's official Media Center is nine miles from the Marriott (aka the Media Hotel). It is traditional at such global sporting events for the

Media Center to actually be placed in the Media Hotel or pretty well next door. This time it's a big door, so it's impossible to just 'pop' there.

Media Day today was the usual circus. It consisted mainly of ex-players and people I didn't know but who were obviously famous asking current players questions, with lots of palm-slapping.

From the circus we made our way to Lynch's Irish Bar on Jacksonville Beach. Simon Veness, who used to work in England for the *Sun* but now lives in Orlando, is here with his car and his American fiancée called Susan. Simon gave Nick and I a lift, sorry ride, to Lynch's.

The beach area is the centre of the alleged Super Bowl entertainment, but as it was willy-shrinking cold it was pretty well deserted, save for a few sad Brits en route to watch Arsenal versus Manchester United at a bar.

WEDNESDAY FEBRUARY 2

Last night the local Organising Committee arranged for the media to go to Sawgrass which was a 45-minute drive away. There, in temperatures hovering just above freezing, would-be Tiger Woodses stood under a restaurant-type heater trying to hit a golf ball on to the famous 17th green which is in effect an island in a lake.

The alternative entertainment was to stand in line for 20 minutes for food that you stood up to eat in a very crowded marquee. The third alternative – that we actually chose – was to go straight back because (a) we didn't want to play Tigers and (b) couldn't be arsed to wait 20 minutes for standup food.

Unfortunately the coaches didn't start the return journey until 9pm, so we had a 40-minute wait in temperatures hovering just above zero. When the 9pm coach arrived we sat on it for an hour (bringing back those memories from Japan) before it moved off. So we spent roughly four hours going to and from a golf club, eating nothing, doing nothing and, from my viewpoint, consuming two screwdrivers. The bartender who served me the drinks asked me: "From London, eh? Is Stringfellows still open?"

"Do I look like the kind of guy that would go to Stringfellows?"

"Yes, sir."

No further questions.

THURSDAY FEBRUARY 3

Yesterday saw the rain arrive, so now it is cold and wet as opposed to cold and dry. Keith Webster, editor of *First Down*, is in what amounts to a bed and breakfast God knows how far away from us. There is no bar in his place and Keith is not amused to be staying in the Bette Ford Clinic. Webby calls it the Dry Bowl.

Spent the morning writing and then Nick and I went to the Avenues Mall. I wanted to look at some iPods and he wanted some books. The Mall had many things to offer, but not, yup, you've guessed it, iPods and books not among them. I bought a cartridge for my printer because it was half the price I pay in England, but as it cost $25 to get to the Mall it worked out more expensive in the end. Nick phoned for a cab to take us back and 40 minutes later it arrived. Name of the cab company? Hurry Cabs. That, ladies and gentlemen, is irony.

The Marriott is in some sort of hotel complex. Trouble is, it is like staying at the Watford Gap. The complex is set just off the interstate with literally nothing but three or four other hotels within walking distance. No public transport in any form. As a cab into the centre of town is about $30 each way we decided to eat dinner in the Marriott. There we were, Nick and I, in the Marriott restaurant, four nights before the Super Bowl with not another customer in sight.

However, after the meal, I heard some music, so went to investigate and in the bar was the First Coast Shag Club ('Free lessons, partner not necessary'). About 30 people were shagging on the dance floor.

The Shag in the good old US of A, bless 'em, is a kind of line dance. Managing (just) to keep a straight face I asked a woman if she would show me how to shag. She responded by asking: "Do you shag like this in England?"

It was too good to be true. There was The Shag Basic, Female Turn. The Belly Roll. The Cuddle Pivot. And last, but by no means least, the Behind Sailor Shuffle.

God Bless America.

A tenuous link but perhaps the best music/shag story ever was told by a *Telegraph* colleague and concerned a mix-up on a girls' night out which his wife was part of. The Chinese restaurant where the party were due to eat had double-booked so one of the wives said: "No worries ... we'll get a takeaway ... we can all go back to my place."

The wife and seven of her friends complete with takeaways went back to her house where her husband was expecting a relaxing night alone. What he most certainly did not expect was his missus and her mates to come home early in the evening to interrupt his relaxing. To help him relax the hubby was watching an, er, adult movie and as he became aroused he got a grip of himself as he lay on the sofa, his enjoyment heightened by listening to his favourite record on his headphones. Because of this he did not hear the fugitives from the Great Wall of China restaurant open the door and come in the house. In turn they did not believe the sight that would greet them upon entering the front room – the husband watching two Swedish girls and a guy having lots of fun with the viewer joining in as best as he could.

Moving swiftly on. There is little evidence of the Super Bowl on Sunday. It doesn't help being in the Watford Gap, but it is not so much low key as underground. The American press are really putting the boot in on Jacksonvile (no misprint). The Super Bowl is normally not so much a game but a week when people come to town, party, see the sights, have a good time. With no sights to see (apart from a couple of hacks shagging for England) and the weather more suited to *Ski Sunday* than Super Sunday it is difficult to have a good time.

A plaintive headline in one paper summed it up: "Is it too late to switch to Miami?"

FRIDAY FEBRUARY 4

Paul Tagliabue, the commissioner of the NFL at his annual (obviously) Super Bowl press conference, said that Jacksonville "was already a success." A guy from Boston radio asked Tags whether it was practical to put the game on in a city that didn't have enough hotel rooms or taxis.

Tags replied: "What you are seeing is what you see when you have winter Olympics or summer Olympics in a smaller community like Atlanta. You see more private homes leased out and more people having to drive a greater distance to get to the game. But those inconveniences, in some cases they're not inconveniences."

So being housed in a business park just off the interstate where there is nothing for miles and it's a $60 round cab fare to the beach area, where most of the 'action' is … that isn't an inconvenience. At least now we know.

Still, we are here to work not have a good time, apart from the occasional shag.

SATURDAY FEBRUARY 5

One of the great perks of covering a Super Bowl is watching the ads on American TV. Today there was one for a brush that cleans "everything" in the kitchen. It was displayed in front of the camera by a rather attractive girl with the line 'Number One Scrubber' above her head. God Bless America II.

One commercial I remember from Spanish TV comprised a pretty girl advertising Victor Davis aftershave. Her payoff line was: "A man isn't a man unless he's got VD." God Bless Spain, too.

The Michael Jackson trial is getting megalicks here. Every day there are about 100 Jacko fans outside the court, though, correct me if I'm wrong here, maybe he should be concerned that the number of his supporters is outnumbered by the number of witnesses queuing up to give evidence against him.

There is plenty of culture here, not least the Wing Bowl, a competition to see who can eat the most chicken wings (rules: "most" of the meat has to be chewed off and swallowed). After two 14-minute periods, plus two minutes of overtime, it was level pegging (or level winging) so there was a 10-second eat-off with Bill 'El Wingador' Simmons beating defending champion Sonya 'The Black Widow' Thomas 162161. How heartbreaking to lose your title by one wing.

You occasionally meet people in America you suspect could not exist anywhere else, such as the young girl with a baby called Fallon who was just a few weeks old.

"That's an Irish name, yes?" I asked.

"Sure is," said Fallon's mother. "I'm an Irish-American. I have a son called Sean, too."

I remarked that she seemed very young to have two children and quickly wished I hadn't.

"I'm 21 and I have five," she said. "When I was younger I thought I had cancer so wanted to have children before it was too late. I got married at 13, had my first baby at 14 and now have five."

Fine upstanding member of society that I am, I said that I didn't think it was legal (outside of Iran maybe) to marry aged 13.

"Because of my circumstances I had to," she informed me. "I took my parents to court to get an order allowing me to marry. They allowed it because my husband [who is 14 years older than his child-bride] was self-sufficient. You can do that in South Carolina."

There was more: "My mammy is 41 and she has 11 grandchildren."

It reminded me of the old Groucho Marx line: "I like a cigar, but I take it out of my mouth now and again."

Delicately, I enquired: "And what is the situation regarding your cancer?"

"Oh it turned out I didn't have cancer. I was wrong, but you can't take chances like that can you?"

Just been to Lynch's Irish Bar to watch Arsenal beat Aston Villa. The weather has sort of improved. Very sunny today, but extremely windy and the beach was a sad place, deserted apart from the three English hacks seeing if the beach was deserted.

Tonight we are taking the media bus to the media centre to search for a decent restaurant. We have to stay within striking distance of the centre because it is virtually impossible to get a taxi home.

The media buses back to the Watford Gap Marriott only run until midnight. We have seen less of Jacksonville than just about any other Super Bowl city because of the transport problems.

SUNDAY FEBRUARY 6

Last night turned into a search for a decent place to eat that wasn't triple-booked. The worry became that we didn't really want to eat in any restaurant that could accommodate us, but we eventually struck reasonably lucky before taking the media bus back to base.

The Super Bowl game itself was close but not exciting with the New England Patriots beating the Philadelphia Eagles 24-21 to be crowned World Champions, as the American say, unaware or uncaring that American football is only played professionally in the States and Canada.

Israel v Republic of Ireland, Tel Aviv March 2005

WEDNESDAY MARCH 23

The predictions of security delays at Dublin airport turn out to be true. An hour is the average amount of time it takes to go through the system, which ultimately turned out to be due to little more than questioning. Rumours that everyone's suitcase and hand-baggage would be searched prove unfounded. Apart from the customary "Did you pack the bag yourself?" and "Are you carrying anything someone has given you?" it was security business as usual, just snail-slow.

I was asked if I knew anyone in Israel, if had I been to any Middle East countries previously and, inevitably, what were you doing in Iran, sir? Not drinking, that's for sure.

In days gone by journalists and players used to chat and socialise (they spoke and we paid). These days the media barely see the Ireland players who are invariably last on the plane. They sit at the front in a curtained-off area, are first off the plane and out of the airport before the press have made their way to the carousel where hopefully our suitcases will arrive. Soon we will be fined for looking at a player. A glance? Ten euro. A stare? Twenty.

The five-hour flight included a help-yourself service bar at the back of the Israeli charter plane, a facility that was fully taken advantage of by some of the passengers. One guy went for a pee and seemed totally oblivious to the 'map of Africa' on his light coloured tracksuit bottoms as he walked down the aisle. Even worse, he wore the same soiled tracksuit bottoms on the return journey, the map of Africa then including Madagascar and a few other islands.

The Israeli media are not best pleased with Ireland and rightly so. There were a few local reporters and a television camera crew at Tel Aviv airport, but neither manager Brian Kerr nor any Ireland player spoke to the home media. In fairness, though, they shouldn't take it personally. The modern Ireland are like that with everyone.

Ireland have no scheduled press conference tomorrow [Thursday] and as there are no newspapers in Israel on Saturday, the Sabbath, it means, in effect, their papers won't have a word from anyone in the Irish camp in the buildup to the match as the Friday press conference is no use as there are no Saturday papers.

This is an incredibly insensitive situation and one that could, and should, be avoided, though it underlines the 'them and us' attitude between those involved in football and those who write about it.

Tel Aviv airport is one of the most modern in the world. There is no sighting of any armed police or soldiers to the disappointment of news reporters who wanted to file a 'ring of steel' security story. Mind you, whether it will stop them filing such stories is another matter.

Arrived at the Tel Aviv Hilton five minutes before midnight, tired but had the energy to turn on the television in my room – on CNN I saw Michael Jackson arriving at court wearing his pyjamas. He's ill apparently. No word on his current condition, but we can rule out stable.

THURSDAY MARCH 24

With no Ireland press conference to attend, we all troop off to see Israel whose coach Avram Grant says Ireland are the model for Israel. One of his players informed us: "We're all confused. A few years ago we were told Turkey were the model, but they disappeared without sight.

"Then it was South Korea, the wonder of their professionalism and dedication. After South Korea it was Greece, but after winning Euro 2004 they've done nothing, so now it's Ireland. If we get a good result on Saturday it'll be someone else."

This, I think, proves the old adage coaches and players know what they're talking about because they have played the game and we don't because we haven't.

The Ireland players arrive at the stadium to train causing a hack-rush towards them.

"How does it feel to play for a Jewish club?" Tottenham's Robbie Keane was asked by local TV. Keane gives the sort of answer he would probably have given had he been asked when he last had a pee. Ask Robbie any question, you get the same answer.

Work done, a few of us walked along the beachfront and had a coffee in a café called Mike's Place. We didn't realise it was here that five people were killed last month by a suicide bomber.

While most places here have armed security guards they soon fade into the background and Tel Aviv is using the presence of almost 4,000 Irish supporters – the biggest group of visitors from any country to the city for more than 30 years – to promote tourism and show Israel is not paralysed by fear, terrorists strikes and politics. The local papers are fascinated by the Irish fans, noting that many visitors "wore shorts despite the cold weather" – it was 75 degrees.

Today is Purin, the Jewish holiday that is celebrated by wearing fancy dress costumes and drinking a lot. The Irish call it 'Any Weekend' back home. One Ireland fan named Hazel Broch showed pride at being both Jewish and Irish by wearing a green wig claiming to be a "LepraCohen." Nice one.

GOOD FRIDAY MARCH 25

At this point I must tell my favourite Jewish joke. A friend of mine is half-Jewish. He has a two-skin.

The Republic of Ireland press conference was notable for some unusual questions asked by the Israeli journalists. One asked Kenny Cunningham of Birmingham City: "We know all about security and such problems, but what is it like being an Irishman living and working in England?"

Cunningham made the sort of reply Robbie Keane gave to the guy who asked him about playing for a Jewish club. They have the gift of the gab, or should it be the gob, the Irish players.

I was a told a story about one Ireland player taken to dinner by Brian Kerr soon after he was appointed manager. The player was not used to choosing his own meal, so played safe by ordering what the boss ordered, in this case halibut steak.

When he was served, the player took a mouthful and said: "Boss, I think I should tell you … this steak tastes of fish."

Back to the hotel to write match previews and, for some, a trip to the capital Jerusalem, which is an hour away by bus (or to you, 90 minutes). Our guide took us to the Church of the Holy Sepulchre, the centre of Christian worship in Jerusalem – within the church are the last five stations of the cross and each stop is marked with a decorated altar. The Via Dolorosa represents the route that Jesus followed from condemnation to crucifixion, but the marvel at being at the centre of so much history was a little tainted by coming out of the church and seeing "the fastest internet connection in Israel" at the Holy Rock Café.

There was also a restaurant that served bacon (!) and eggs within two minutes walk from the wailing wall, where we were respectfully asked not to make calls on mobile phones or take photographs. Meanwhile, market shops selling t-shirts with slogans such as 'Shalom Y'All,' 'My Sister Went to Jerusalem and All I Got was This Lousy T-shirt', 'Member of the Israeli Secret

The 1968 European Cup semi-final second leg between Real Madrid and Manchester United. Sir Matt Busby's pre-match press conference before a couple of dozen reporters and two fans – one is smoking a cigarette. Not a TV lens or a radio microphone in sight. These days such a press conference would be attended by around 200 media members, televised live and certainly no fans or cigarettes present. Yes, I am there somewhere.

A Press XI (well, XV) that played Guinness on Queen's Park Rangers' Omniturf pitch during the Eighties. Back row, with newspapers worked for at the time: Martin Hardy (Daily Express), Jeff Powell (Daily Mail), Ian Gibb (Daily Mirror), Michael Calvin (Daily Telegraph), Colin Gibson (Daily Mail), Mick Dennis (Sun), David Millward (Daily Telegraph), Malcolm Folley (Daily Express). Front row: Peter Shreeves (ex-Tottenham assistant manager), Malcolm Macdonald (ex-Newcastle etc), Barry Flatman (Daily Express), Tony Stenson (Daily Mirror), Christopher Davies (Daily Star), Harry Harris (Daily Mirror). QPR "loaned" us a couple of trainees at half-time as we were losing heavily. Admiring one of the well-endowed players as we showered afterwards Martin Hardy memorably remarked: "F*** me. Do they also come in pink?"

Andy Cowie (of Colorsport, left) and Simon
Bruty (now Sports Illustrated) show me a yellow
card for wearing a suit at a media cocktail party
in Singapore in 1989. Or maybe it was for the
hanky?

This was not owned by Bon Jovi but you would certainly be drivin' on a prayer in it. The old (olde?) Triumph Herald was a Maltese taxi, 1989. I don't think the concept of MOT's had reached the island at the time.

The Colosseum in Rome. It was a 50,000-capacity all-seat amphitheatre. The press facilities left much to be desired.

Not exactly a super bowl. My Albanian shower and shower base, 1993. Be grateful I spared you the toilet.

I travelled with Frank Stapleton and an Irish TV crew to Kosovo when the Republic played Macedonia in 1999. The devastation from the Balkans war was horrifying.

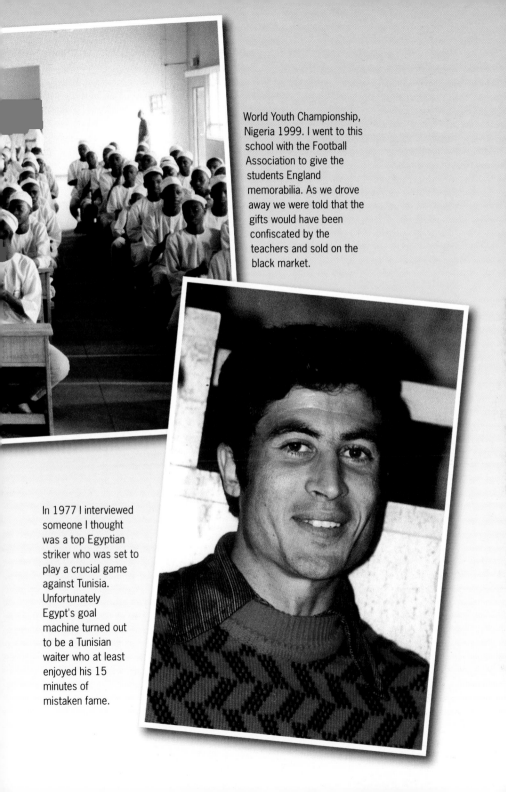

World Youth Championship, Nigeria 1999. I went to this school with the Football Association to give the students England memorabilia. As we drove away we were told that the gifts would have been confiscated by the teachers and sold on the black market.

In 1977 I interviewed someone I thought was a top Egyptian striker who was set to play a crucial game against Tunisia. Unfortunately Egypt's goal machine turned out to be a Tunisian waiter who at least enjoyed his 15 minutes of mistaken fame.

Super Bowl XXXVI in January 2002. The names of those killed at 9/11 were displayed during the game in New Orleans.

FIRST COAST SHAG CLUB – 2005 LESSON SCHEDULE
JACKSONVILLE MARRIOTT -- BIMINI LOUNGE
FREE LESSONS --- PARTNER NOT NECESSARY

Six Weeks Series of Lessons	INTERMEDIATE LESSONS Wed. 6:45 – 7:30 p.m.	BASIC LESSONS Wed. 7:30-8:15 p.m.	INTER/ADV WORKSHOP Sun. *** 6:00-6:45 p.m.	BASIC LESSONS Sun. *** 6:45-7:30 p.m.
1/19 – 2/27	Tim & Janis	Ted	Vickie	David & Diane
3/02 – 4/10	Vickie	David & Diane	Tim & Janis	Tim & Janis
4/13 – 5/22	David & Diane	Tim & Janis	Vickie	Vickie
05/25 – 06/03	Tim & Janis	Vickie	David & Diane	David & Diane
07/06 – 08/14	Vickie	David & Diane	Tim & Janis	Tim & Janis
08/17 – 09/25	David & Diane	Time & Janis	Vickie	Vickie
09/28 – 11/06	Tim & Janis	Vickie	David & Diane	David & Diane
11/09 – 12/18	Vickie	David & Diane	Time & Janis	Tim & Janis
12/21 – 01/29	David & Diane	Tim & Janis	Vickie	Vickie
02/01 – 03/12	Tim & Janis	Vickie	David & Diane	David & Diane

LINE DANCE LESSONS EVERY SUNDAY FROM ___ p.m. WITH VICKIE & FRIENDS

Just in case you thought I was making it up, yes there WAS a First Coast Shag Club in Jacksonville.

Super Bowl XXX in Tempe, Arizona. We fired live ammunition at a can in the desert. The kick-back from the shot was incredible. Nick Halling won the competition as he reminds me every time we meet.

Euro 2004, Braga. One side of the
stadium was carved in rock.
Amazing.

The street in Tehran known as Bobby Sands Street, which the Iranians renamed after the IRA hunger striker. The British Embassy had to move their entrance to avoid the address 'British Embassy, Bobby Sands Street.'

A chilling message outside the old American embassy in Tehran where 66 U.S. hostages were held for 444 days after Iranian students took over the building in 1979.

The Shah of Iran's summer residence (before his downfall). Designer: D. Trotter (Peckham).

During the 2002 World Cup, Japanese hotel rooms were so small unpacking proved difficult going on impossible.

Japanese children drew the Republic of Ireland players as part of a welcome party. Roy Keane's was taken off!

The Sad Bastard Bar in Munich. My second home at Germany 2006.

The Super Bowl/Rain Bowl, Miami 2007. It bucketed down throughout the game and everyone was issued with a poncho as the stadium was completely open to the elements.

My last European trip as a Daily Telegraph staff man in Sofia. From left to right: Jon Brodkin (Guardian), Matt Barlow (then Press Association, now Daily Mail), me, Tom Dart (Times), Jamie McPhilamy (Sun photographer), Martin Lipton (Mirror), Tony Banks (Express), Glenn Moore (Independent), Neil Ashton (Daily Mail) and Mark Irwin (Sun).

Police: My Job Is So Secret Even I Don't Know What It Is' and – heading the bad taste league – a top with a Superman 'S' symbol with 'Super Jew' printed on it. You could also buy a computer game called Terrorist Wars if you so wished, which none of us did. In terms of taste and profiteering it was, as one Irish journalist pointed out, more Wall Street than Wailing Wall.

SATURDAY MARCH 26

Shabbat. The Sabbath. No hot food available in the hotel for breakfast today, so it's a continental breakfast (though every breakfast I have abroad is continental, I guess).

Most of the press decided it should, indeed, be a day of rest before departing for the stadium where all 44,000 tickets have been sold for the first time in 16 years for this vital qualifying game.

Five minutes before kickoff I had a sudden rumbling in my stomach that told me whatever the time and place I had to spend a shekel. There could be no waiting until half-time. Needless to say I was at the wrong end of the row in the press box, so everyone had to stand up to allow me through. I walked very carefully towards the toilets only to discover that all the cubicles were in use. The toilet that was NOT occupied was the disabled loo and, though I normally respect such facilities, mother nature was telling me to forget such formalities right now.

I did what I had to do and as I opened the door there was a fan in a wheelchair waiting to go in. As if to justify invading his space I limped back to the press box, even grimacing with imaginary pain to underline my right to have used the disabled toilet.

Ireland took the lead after four minutes with a goal by Clinton Morrison from the narrowest of angles. Instead of pushing on and going for the second goal that would have put the outcome beyond reasonable dispute, Ireland sat back, were too negative and Abas Suan scored an equaliser in stoppage time. It felt like defeat for Ireland though they have only themselves to blame and overall it was a fair result. Group Four is the tightest of all the European qualifying groups where none of the top four have beaten each other.

Back to the hotel at midnight, pack, and up at 0530 for a far too early departure to the airport.

EASTER SUNDAY MARCH 27

Some members of the press pack seem to have over-celebrated Ireland's point with too many pints and their sore heads are a sight for sore eyes.

Security questions at the airport again – while we have nothing to hide, if someone did would he be likely to own up to receiving a package from someone? I was told they have to ask all these questions for insurance purposes.

Again, no sighting of the players who were the last to board the plane. It is no exaggeration to say they may not have been on the plane and we wouldn't have known. As the aircraft taxied down the runway Milo Corcoran, President of the FAI, who has had a heart problem, was taken ill – we had to turn back and he was rushed to hospital. We later heard his condition was improving, unlike the guy with the map of Africa tracksuit bottoms. A five and a half-hour flight home – tailwinds putting half an hour on the journey. Obviously the wrong sort of tailwinds.

Arrived back in Dublin about 3.45pm, a three-hour wait for my connecting flight to London and reached home at 10pm.

Knackered y'all.

Amsterdam Tournament, July 2005

FRIDAY JULY 29

Up at 6am, and spoke to the nation at 6.20am via talkSPORT about the Champions League draw.

Uneventful journey to Gatwick, thank goodness. We arrived at Schipol only to be told "it will be 10 minutes before we reach the terminal ... we've landed on an airstrip that is seven miles from the airport building." I thought that was called Rotterdam.

Caught the train from Schipol to Centraal station and felt it was appropriate to be given a Queen Room at the Renaissance hotel.

Wrote some football news during the afternoon before heading off for the game between Ajax and Arsenal. Upon arriving at the Amsterdam ArenA. I was told there was no pass available for me on Sunday when Arsenal play FC Porto. Welcome to the new season...

The ArenA is an indoor stadium and it was like a sauna, except no-one was wearing just a towel, though it was so hot we were all ready to throw one in. It was sweltering and thoughtfully the media were served piping hot expresso coffee throughout the match rather than cold drinks.

The guy next to me appeared to be trying (and as far as I was concerned, succeeded) for a place in the *Guinness Book of Records* for smoking the most cigarettes during a game, but the stink of his fags at least took my mind off the whiff from his armpits which didn't appear to have been on first name terms with soap or water for some time.

Arsenal won 1-0 against hosts Ajax with a late goal in an absolutely crap match. I returned to my Queen Room just before 1am. I watched CNN, which is what people do in hotel rooms abroad, finding out what's going on in countries they've never heard of and don't give a toss about, before going to sleep around two.

SATURDAY JULY 30

Awoke at 6am refreshed after four hours' sleep (he lied) to the sound of rain pelting against the window. Today is a free day, no work until the second game tomorrow evening. What am I going to do all day? There are four or five other English journos in Amsterdam. Looking through some tourist leaflets I noticed there is a 'romantic dinner cruise', though there is little romantic about English hacks abroad. Or at home for that matter.

I went for a stroll after breakfast and the window-ladies are on offer very early these days. Most of them have all the allure and attraction of David Mellor. Most are about 10 years older than him too. For research and reference purposes I visited some of the, er, adult shops ... some of the gadgets are just incredible ... eye-watering. There was one I could not imagine how a girl would use, so I asked (research and reference). "It's for the man, sir," I was told and immediately felt a surge of pain rushing through the third floor. I made my excuses and left without making a purchase.

The drugs scene here is incredible. You don't need to puff the waccy baccy, just breathe the air. I love the banners outside the Coffee Shops – 'Over 18s only'. Mind you, the same should apply to most of the new wave of legal American-style coffee shops, but only because you have to be 18 to afford the extortionate rip-off prices for piss-weak coffee that seems to become more expensive the longer the word is. Latte – £165. Cappuccino – £230. Cinnamon sir? That's an extra £100. And don't you love it when they offer an extra shot of coffee? That is to give it a minimum of flavour, otherwise it's basically frothy milk.

There's a great greasy spoon in Bromley and do you know what they call the coffee there? Coffee. It comes in a mug (usually chipped, of course) and is not 50 per cent froth, but 100 per cent coffee. No cinnamon. Just good old coffee. It costs just over a quid per chipped mugful. And get this, it actually tastes of coffee.

Anyway, in Amsterdam you don't really go to a Coffee Shop for coffee, oh no sir. You go there to sample the old waccy baccy. Dope – not on a rope, but in Rizla's.

I once went into a Coffee Shop here and actually asked for a coffee. My defence was that as someone who doesn't partake in either legal or illegal cigarettes I am naïve to such things. A girl came over with a tray of various rolled up delicacies, some rolled with paper so big it would have been like smoking a roll of lino – which being a non-smoker I would have preferred. Eat your heart out Bob Marley.

What did I do? Well, sweating like Michael Jackson reading the latest Harry Potter, I thought I'd give myself time, so I went to spend a euro, but the loo was locked. In fact it was like Fort Knox. Or Fort Locks. The manager opened it – "we have to keep it locked because people go in there and shoot up." I managed to sneak out without being spotted, not too difficult as by then you couldn't see halfway across the room.

On this occasion I strolled round the centre of Amsterdam, amazingly resisting the urge to buy any rubber masks or drugs. I did have one strange experience outside a sex shop (note OUTSIDE). I was looking in the window for possible Christmas presents when a voice said "hey big boy, wanna come in?" It was a lifesize model doll by the door 'dressed' in very little. A sensor must pick up someone close to 'her' and activate 'her' – I was that someone. However, rest assured in years to come I shall boast I was hit on by a model in Amsterdam wearing only a bra and panties. Starting now.

Next week is Gay Pride weekend (weak end, ha ha) so appropriately I had a spot of lunch before returning to my, er … Queen Room. Turned on

CNN and a talking head told me OJ Simpson had been fined $25,000 for stealing satellite television from a company called Direct TV, he was wired up to someone else's cable or something. They're finally getting tough on celebrities in the States then.

No doubt OJ maintains his innocence and will continue to look for the real pirate. I was shocked when I heard the news. OJ a thief! I just hope this one indiscretion doesn't ruin OJ's reputation.

I started to write a feature for next week, read the *Daily Mail*, which I'd paid £1.50p for and did a bit of surfing (the rain was that heavy). Met up with the other hacks at 7.45pm in a place called Susie's Saloon. Three of them had been playing pool and watching the Twenty20 cricket final on TV, as you do in Amsterdam. They had been on the Guinness, but others in the bar were on something, I was informed by one who knew, called skunk. Like the animal it stank. The whole bar stank of stale skunk, so I sat outside watching the boats go along the canal, supping a pint.

We moved on to an Argentine steak house, six of us by now. Amazing. The restaurant also stank of fags. They don't do air conditioning here, and while the food was excellent and the chat good, the environment sucked.

SUNDAY JULY 31
Woke up at 4.30am. Managed to get back to kip before getting up at 6.30am. God knows why I got up. I mean, there's nothing to see or do apart from smell da skunk, mun. The shirt I was wearing last night stank, but seemed very happy.

Half past six. It's not like I could stroll along a white sandy beach with the warm sea lapping at my tootsies. In fact, walking in Amsterdam is a minefield. It's the dog shit capital of the world. Honest. Maybe they can't get anyone to clean it up because they'd want time and a turd.

Do dogs ever tread in dog shit? Or are they cleverer than us? The deadliest sound in the world is the silent footstep. If you see any dog's pooh in the kerb over here it's because the mucky mutt couldn't hold himself until he reached the pavement, no doubt feeling a canine clot for not lasting those extra few seconds. You really have to concentrate when you walk otherwise your shoes will be covered in a shitzu's visiting card.

Anyway, having got up I pondered going back to bed and had an argument with myself about this, which somehow I managed to lose. I phoned reception and asked for another room to get away from myself. Breakfast didn't open till 0730, so I cheered myself up by doing some expenses.

The inevitable CNN was switched on and I watched a feature on Lance Armstrong, serial winner of the Tour de France. He now says he wants to sit around and watch TV and drink beer. What a lazy bastard he turned out to be.

Wrote half a Millwall feature for later in the week. Went for a thankfully shit-less stroll and bought some Dutch mouthwash. Jeez it was strong, almost taking not only the coating off my tongue but the entire tongue, too.

Just to make sure, because I was playing with dental fire, I asked the chambermaid to translate the directions on the packet. Bad breath is better than no breath, but it turned out I was incorrectly gargling with the stuff neat. I should have put just a few drops into a glass of water.

Arsenal beat FC Porto 2-1, but the main excitement came a few minutes before half-time when Diego Maradona appeared on the sidelines. The owner of the Hand of God is the new technical director of Boca Juniors, who are also in the competition. At half-time the players and even match officials were lining up to shake the hand of the man who robbed England of World Cup glory in 1986. The hand of God in the city of the dog.

Republic of Ireland v Italy, August 2005

MONDAY AUGUST 15

After an award-winning bacon sarnie, I made a few calls, did a bit of work, packed and drove to Gatwick to find the plane had been delayed. Wrote my Ireland piece at the airport where there was not a mayo/coleslawless sandwich to be had anywhere. Even on the plane it was whatever and mayo in every sandwich.

I refuse to believe I am the only person in the world who prefers his sandwiches without preservatives. They put mayo in the sandwiches so they can be on display longer. When I become Prime Minister that will be the first legislation I'll pass. The No Mayo party. Apologies to Simon of that ilk on BBC Radio 5Live, but sometimes there are casualties in war.

The stewardess took pity on me and gave me two voddie and oranges (or is it voddies and orange or perhaps even voddies and oranges?) instead of the regulation one. People marry for less.

Read the papers. It seems like there is a worrying shortage of teachers in England. At this rate by 2010 pupils will have to have sex with each other. And the hotel guy Russell Crowe hit with a mobile phone is to get £5 million in compensation. Crowe can't risk going to court as an ABH charge would probably preclude him from being able to film in the States again. So rather than do bird, Crowe is paying up. Bird? Crowe? Oh never mind.

Got to the Herbert Park hotel. I like it here. My room has a CD player, which makes me think "what a great room". Of course, I don't have any CDs with me, but it's a status symbol. I shall ask the other lads if they have a CD player in THEIR room and go "huh" if they haven't.

Went to bed. Turned on the news and there was something about a paparrazzi suing Pamela Anderson for allegedly 'abusing him verbally and physically'. Most guys have to pay for that. Read the Irish papers and woke up at 1.37am still in the reading position, so to speak.

TUESDAY AUGUST 16

There was a belter on talkSPORT from Alan Brazil speaking about who the greatest sportsman of all time was. Lance Armstrong, who recovered from testicular cancer to win the Tour de France seven times, got AB's vote. "Has to be him, he's battled back from dying." Eat your heart out Lazarus.

Had a good Irish breakfast (which, without wishing to damage Anglo-Irish relationships, is not really any different to a full English breakfast) before setting out on a mission of mercy. For whatever reason I packed only one pair of underpants and socks, so in fairness to the good people of Dublin, I owed it to them to buy some new underwear for tomorrow and Thursday.

Attended the Ireland press conference. It's always good to meet up with the Irish journos, a smashing bunch. Pretty routine quotes, but later I did pick up what I think is a belting story which should be used front page.

The English contingent in Dublin is a little low on numbers. One of the guys has brought his wife, while one or two of them are flying in tomorrow so tonight I'm having dinner with Jon Brodkin of the *Guardian* who is a vegan. Lentil medium rare sir? He's a good lad, who became a vegan after working in an abattoir during a school holiday. He probably took the job to earn the money because he couldn't make ends meat.

We had what Bill Clinton would no doubt call a threesome as Jason Burt from the *Independent* joined Jon and I for a splendid dinner. Mr Vegan had his usual salad. That's all he ever eats. Salad. For everyone else that's something on the side, like the blonde at number 38. But for Brodders a salad is as good as it gets. He should live in a hutch. I'm amazed he weighs more than three stone. I suppose at the weekend he gets tucked into a nice Sunday Salad.

Jon is one of my favourite journalists and people, but his [lack of] eating habits fascinate me.

WEDNESDAY AUGUST 17

Breakfast TV is a strange creature. Not sure which channel it is, but I discover a discussion on cervical cancer. Just the topic I want to hear before the little hand reaches seven.

On GMTV there is a rather fit girl interviewing a group I've never heard of. A very old episode of *Friends* is on another channel – so old that the series was called Just Met.

The breakfast room was full of Americans this morning, which meant butts that were either as large as the Grand Canyon (both sexes), petite (female) or ginormous (male). And why do those with the biggest butts insist on wearing shorts? American butts are something else. There are no half measures with them (no ifs or butts). They either work out every day or eat/drink nonstop (is beauty in the eye of the beer-holder?).

One woman's butt was so huge it could have had its own national anthem. And she was wearing the inevitable shorts, which should really have been called huges. XXXXXXL. It was almost as if she was saying "I've lost two pounds, you know", which would be like throwing a deck chair off the Queen Elizabeth.

What you often get with Americans is guys who are only about 5ft 4ins in their stockinged feet who obviously have a major hang-up about being short, so they pump iron to the extent they are almost as wide as they are tall.

Big butt Americans have mastered the art of getting the maximum on their plates. It's an art to get 38 sausages, half a pig, 18 tomatoes, 22 eggs, eight waffles and the obligatory slice of melon – "hey, gotta watch the figure you know" – on a plate.

Having said all that, I like Americans. They're usually friendly and chatty, if a little insular. Memorably I was once asked: "So is it the same sun in London as we get in Tampa?"

I treated myself to a digital voice recorder and also had a haircut – by an Indian! He didn't quite scalp me. He kept talking about his grandmother – or his 'naan' as he called her.

So to Ireland v Italy, which the Italians won 2-1. A swift after-match Guinness and to bed where I watched a commercial for a product that claimed to be "new and improved." How can anything be new and improved? If it's new, what was it improved on?

FRANCE V FAROE ISLANDS, LENS, SEPTEMBER 2005

SATURDAY SEPTEMBER 3

To Dover and then to Lens for France versus the Faroe Islands – France play the Republic of Ireland in a World Cup qualifying tie next Wednesday, hence my visit. Upon disembarking Le Shuttle at Calais I drove for almost 70 miles without (a) seeing any roadworks or (b) a traffic jam. Maybe there can be no roadworks in France or indeed anywhere else on the continent because the European cone mountain is camped along roads in England (appointments not always necessary).

Whatever, Calais to Lens and return was a roadworks and traffic jam-free journey. But two miles back on the M20 when I return you can bet the road signs will flash '40-mph speed limit ahead'. I would imagine the three Albanians in the boot will get out and say: "We're going back to France."

Why is the sign for roadworks a picture of a man digging when you never seem to see a man actually digging when there are roadworks?
Another thing while I'm on a roll. The signposts in France were so good we (Jon Brodkin of the *Guardian* allowed me to be his chauffeur) found the Hotel Artois without any problems.

It was a small hotel on the outskirts of Lens. The good news was that it was a 10-minute walk to the stadium. And back from it, for that matter. The bad news was a few years ago someone had a brilliant idea: "Let's build a hotel right slap bang alongside this road where lorries hurtle along 24 hours a day."

I was in room six and Jon in room eight, but as he's a vegan it was an organic huit (think about it). I sat in my car in the hotel car park with the air conditioning on and engine running listening to Wales v England on a crackly 5Live. What do you mean 'saddo?'

The game in Lens was predictably onesided with France winning 3-0. The French players, most of whom play in the Premiership, gave Jon and I a wide berth in the interview mixed zone. Notepads were rather empty, not a popular situation to report to the office, but salvation came in the form of Arsène Wenger, the Arsenal manager who was working for French television.

Arsène recognised us and came over to chat. "Do you have two minutes to talk about France?" we asked/begged. The most media friendly manager in English football was his usual obliging self and gave us a basis for our Monday morning reports. A true class act, merci Arsène.

Back to the hotel by about half past 12, stopping only for a cold litre of the liquid our hotel was named after. I wrote for 20 minutes or so before I decided I was tired enough to fall asleep despite the Motor Show inches from my window.

SUNDAY SEPTEMBER 4

Woke up at 5.30 – "I love the smell of diesel in the morning" – and finished my report. I had what can only be described as an 'interesting' shower, drying myself on a towel so thin it was really just a large hankie. Brekkie – two boiled eggs (well, I'll be bound) and, of course, soldiers and we hit the rue, Jacques.

Bit of shopping at Calais and home by midafternoon. Unpacked then packed for Dublin the following morning. Dull it isn't.

THE REPUBLIC OF IRELAND, AUTUMN 2005

MONDAY SEPTEMBER 5

Up at sparrow's fart (a phrase that is one of Australia's best exports) in order to claim a place in the inevitable M25 traffic chaos, which as usual did not disappoint.

After the road to hell, there was the equally unsurprising delay of a mere two hours at Gatwick. No probs, I'll have some coffee and toast. How naïve. Impossible to find. I could buy mayo-covered sandwiches, or steak and chips (just what you need at 8.30am), but not what amounted to a breakfast. Gatwick doesn't do breakfasts. The only jam I had that morning was on the M25.

There was a six-strong hen party complete with 'Sarah's hen night' T-shirts on the plane. One of them asked me what the Temple Bar area of Dublin is like. "Plenty of bars but no temples," I replied wittily waiting for the girls to collapse with uncontrollable laughter. Instead I received that look that told me my gag was in fact as funny as a broken leg.

Was upgraded at the Herbert Park hotel – again. A Polish girl was on the check-in desk and I've got to know her from previous visits, impressing her with the way I pronounce cities like Lodz and Katowice correctly (thanks to Nick Szczepanik).

I like this hotel. Every room is quiet (I bought a CD entitled 'Best of the M25' with the sounds of coaches, lorries and cars hurtling along to make me feel at home), I have a kingsized bed and the breakfast is the best. Wrote my piece in my nice room.

Most of the English hacks are over and the weather is good so my guess is that the evening's entertainment will involve thirst-quenching exercises.

It did. I consumed three pints of Guinness in an effort to boost the local economy before adjourning to a Chinese restaurant for a splendid meal. A hack pack from the *Daily Telegraph*, *Sun* and the *Daily Mail* put the world to rights, if you hadn't noticed.

TUESDAY SEPTEMBER 6

Closer examination of the bill from last night, which I thought at the time was a little excessive, underlined my suspicions. We each paid 70 euro – a total, obviously, of 210 euro. However the bill was 175.70 euro of which 76 euro was for wine. A 10 per cent service charge was added which obviously was not noticed making the total 193.30 euro.

So we ended up giving a tip of 34 euro, roughly 20 per cent of the bill, which is probably why the manager offered me his wife as we left. Good as the meal was it was not worth almost 50 quid (with or without the owner's missus) and at £25 a bottle the Sancerre could have been downgraded. C'est la vino as Del Boy would say.

The Ireland press conference was predictably bland. The Ireland players boycotted it after the Dublin evening paper ran a story that Ireland manager Brian Kerr and Roy Keane had a row when some players went to a nightclub last Friday. Kerr denied any row, claiming the players had permission to go out and there was no curfew. By boycotting the press conference – which meant every news organisation, Irish, English, and French 'suffered' for one paper's story – the players merely added fuel to the fire.

The Football Association of Ireland PR man handed out statements, which said it was not actually a boycott – "the players just want to focus on the game." I asked: "By that, does it mean they were not focused on every previous game when a player accompanied the manager to the pre-match press conference?" He replied he would come back with a new statement – the words horse, bolted, and stable-door spring to mind.

The French arrive this evening, confident they can win tomorrow. I usually think Ireland will lose, but they continue to punch above their weight. Obviously I want Ireland to win, but covering World Cup finals "without a country" means you can move around and see a number of teams, which is usually good fun.

If Ireland fail to qualify it means there will be no pre-World Cup training base on some Godforsaken Scandinavian island where the elk is the local delicacy. It would also mean we would not be billeted for a month or whatever in Germany with a bunch of millionaires who almost throw-up at the sight of a journalist. We would also not have Irish players pretending to talk on a mobile phone that is switched off whilst walking through the mixed zone, where the press, or crème de la scum as we are also known, beg for quotes, with their well-practised "sorry, I would like nothing more than to stop and chat with you but I'm on the phone" expression as they pass the hungry hack pack, whose pens are poised for the next banality.

"Swap you Duff for Kilbane?"

"You've got Keano? Brill. What did he say?"

"I haven't decided yet..."

At France 98, with no Ireland, Her Majesty's press would have a nice light breakfast before taking the on-time train to some sun-kissed French city where the ugliest girl looked like Miss World and then we filed 450 words on what the Brazil coach said about the game against Morocco. Our hard work completed, we would then ensure the French wine industry did not go bankrupt.

Of course, with the World Cup being in Germany the local wine cannot be consumed next summer with or without Ireland. No country that produces crap wine should be allowed to stage the World Cup – it should be one of the conditions. Germany should never have been given the World Cup. Four weeks of Blue Nun or Black Tower would send any self-respecting hack mad. Or rather, madder. Wine on a stick.

Oh Mr Pissporter whatever can we do … we wanted to drink some decent wine but we ended up with you.

Mind you, the 2008 European Championship is being jointly hosted by Austria and Switzerland, those two hugely exciting countries with a fine (cough) wine pedigree. All in all there is little to look forward to in the coming years. Can we fast-forward to the 2010 World Cup in South Africa? I'll probably be murdered in Joburg, but at least I will have had a decent glass of wine before my throat is cut. It's all about priorities.

WEDNESDAY SEPTEMBER 7

Had a serious, industrial strength curry last night. It had the 'wow' factor, I promise. I ordered chilli chicken masala to vindaloo strength, but was challenged/dared into upgrading it to a phal – "what are you, man or mouse?" the biryani brigade asked. So a phal it was. Normally when you ask for a meal to be upgraded they err on the side of caution – not the Chandni in Pembroke Road, Dublin. This was phal-plus.

As I took the first mouthful of hot coal I smiled and said "not bad" wondering if they would be the last words I would utter before my tongue melted. It was man against chilli, but I have to say it was splendid curry. As I was in charge of ordering after the previous night's financial suicide we managed to get away with 40 euro per head.

Jon Brodkin joined us for a lettuce leaf and caraway seed (to madras strength). As we left the restaurant Neil Custis noticed a piece of parsley on the top of Jon's naan. "Could you put that in a doggy bag for Mr Brodkin, please?" he asked the rather bemused manager, who, for some unaccountable reason, didn't know what the hell he was talking about.

It's now almost midnight and Ireland lost 1-0 with World Cup qualification now out of their hands. If they don't make it to the finals in Germany the manager, Brian Kerr, will probably be sacked, but I don't particularly like him anyway. Failure to qualify would mean a series of meaningless friendlies next spring, which no-one really gives a monkey's about. Depressing. Right, time to hit the scratcher. Got to be up at 6 for my 8.30am flight back to Blighty. Back here next month for more fun and games.

TUESDAY OCTOBER 4

Gatwick. French Air Traffic Controllers' strike. What a surprise. Delays. The French go on strike and I can't fly from London to Dublin. So here I am, doing what so many people do at Gatwick: Sitting in a chair and waiting for my delayed flight. I feel I should be paying council tax here. Packing was not easy. In Cyprus, where Ireland are playing on Saturday, it will be 80 degrees. In Dublin, where I will meet up with the travelling media, it won't be 80 degrees. So I have T-shirts and jumpers (not for goal-posts).

The flight to Dublin was uneventful – apart from a stewardess stripping, a mass fight and a crash landing.

The Dublin airport hotel has constant identity crises. We joke that every time we stay here it has a different name (last time it was Janet). Now it's the Clarion, a recent change because 'Holiday Inn' is still crossed out in the airport shuttle bus notice. It's been the Crowne Plaza and God knows what else, but whatever its name might be, it is still soulless. A couple of the other English hacks are here – we have to check in at 11am and it's a big risk flying out on the morning.

WEDNESDAY OCTOBER 5

Woke up at 7.40am. At 7.42am there was a knock at the door – the chamber-person wanting to know whether she could service the room. I can think of at least six journalists who would ensure said chamber-person would never forget the occasion if she knocked on THEIR door at 7.42am. Had a full Irish breakfast, wonderful. Especially the good old Irish Cumberland sausage. The flight over to Cyprus was 4 hours 50 minutes. The plane was full and we had to buy every drink and bit of food.

Some passengers (there were fans and media on the official flight) were not bothered by this and enjoyed a small reservoir of booze. One fan must have consumed 10 bottles of wine (the small size you get on board), three champagnes plus a voddie and something. When we landed he thought it would be a good idea to get out of his seat before the plane had stopped and when it did come to a halt the plane had a bit of a shudder. He went, excuse the pun, flying into another passenger who, selfish bastard, seemed very unhappy at having a pissed 16 stone guy fall on him. Some people...

By the time we arrived at the hotel and checked in it was gone 10pm, so I just had a couple of drinks sitting on the balcony (shirtsleeves ... very warm) before hitting the pit. There is a lot of negativity about Ireland manager Brian Kerr, who will almost certainly lose his job if they don't reach the World Cup finals. Ireland should have done better under him.

THURSDAY OCTOBER 6

A bad and far too early a start to the day. Woke up at 4am to the soothing sound of someone revving a motor scooter full throttle ... throttle being a word that not only came to my mind but to others who were also witness to the would-be suicide biker (at least if we ever got our hands on him).

Got back to kip before having breakfast on the veranda. The weather is wonderful ... at 9am it was sunny and in the mid-70s. I enjoyed a typical Cypriot breakfast of baked beans on toast before going to the stadium in Limassol for a farce of a press conference.

Once again manager Brian Kerr has decided not to speak to the media, putting up Andy O'Brien and Gary Doherty instead – neither of whom is likely to play. This has become a tradition with Ireland – whichever player is put up before the media we feel like saying "bad luck on not getting picked to play in the game." The PR within the Football Association of Ireland needs a serious upgrade.

Our cabbie waited for us outside the stadium – everyone here is called Stavros, needless to say (even the women). Back at the hotel I made a dash for the pool, which is the temporary media office. The sight of 15 hacks around a pool tapping away on their laptops was one to behold. The only movement came when mobiles rang which eventually meant a sprint inside so sports desks back home did not hear the sound of water in the background.

In the evening we did what we experienced travellers tend to do when away and that is to eat in the wrong place paying double the odds. It's been going on for as long as I can remember, so it's unlikely to change now. One of the boys said the excellent fish restaurant we went to three years ago was in a hotel guide, so he went to this room returning with its name. Stavros the cabbie drove us there but … yes, it wasn't the same restaurant.

However, it seemed lively and Stavros showed us to our seats before Stavros took our order. Stavros recommended the grouper so we took his advice and the fish duly arrived with boiled spuds and canned veg. I wondered if when that fish goes to an orgy whether it is grouper sex. The bill was a bargain, I don't think, £50 each. Only travelling journos could eat an average meal and pay Ramsayish prices.

Jon Brodkin, who's a vegan, wasn't with us. "He's a teetotaller," said Neil Custis of the *Sun*.

"No," I said. "I've seen Jon drink three or four pints…"

"Exactly. He's a teetotaller," said Neil in a manner that suggested there could be no further discussion.

FRIDAY OCTOBER 7
Brian Kerr speaks at last. A hostile 10 am press conference with Kerr not

helping his cause when asked why he had not held a press conference previously this week. After mumbling that according to his schedule he was not due to (which is bollocks) he said: "You must have the wrong schedule."

By 11am assorted hacks surround the pool and by noon (10am back home) most of us have finished, able to concentrate on topping up our tans. It's a hard life and all I can say is it won't be long before I will be freezing my nuts off in eastern Europe. It's not much of a defence, I agree, but it's the best I can do.

In the evening there was the traditional eircom night when the sponsors take over part of a restaurant – all food and drink for the media is free. There was a hen party from Vietnam ("is the capital Ho Chi Minge?" one of the, er, chicks was asked). There was also a party of Eskimos from Greenland – yes, someone did ask a girl if she was called Nell. But no nose-rubbing. Or anything else rubbing, honest.

The first three quarters of the 'entertainment' was excellent ... plates and glasses balanced on various heads ... dancing ... audience participation ... then later a girl came on and sang for an hour in Greek (we think). Greek singing eventually becomes like the sound one has when constipated. Also, just when you think she is finishing and you prepare for a huge sigh of relief, the song carries on. And on. We didn't so much get the 12-inch version as the 12-mile version.

Three journos contemplated suicide. Two discussed the possibility of asking the manager if there was any chance of a sponsored silence. One reporter went for a pee and never returned. The food was okay, but I am not sure whether Greek cuisine is one of the greats in the world. Still, it was a splendid gesture once again by eircom, probably the best sponsors in the world.

We left at 1am and some of the lads went into town for "a nightcap" – a bloody big cap by all accounts. They were the ones who emerged at 1pm the following afternoon looking like death barely warmed up. I returned to the hotel, and supped a voddie and orange (well, three) with some of the Irish lads before hitting the pit.

SATURDAY OCTOBER 8
My dad's birthday! He's 82 years young and is quite simply the nicest man in the history of the world. He is not just my father but also my hero. I have never heard my parents row. I told them recently this was not natural and if they were to be a proper married couple they MUST row. They said they would do their best. When we met again they said they had done their best, but ended up laughing. My dad did say that if they ever DID have a row he would have the last word – "sorry."

Had the same breakfast sitting in the same seat as the previous two mornings because this is what people do when abroad. See someone in your seat and you feel your space has been invaded. Served by the same waitress (Anita) ... the Groundhog Day breakfast. Spent three hours round the pool preparing for the game, which kicks off at 8pm local time, 6pm at home.

Checking out was the usual chaos. There's always someone who hasn't left his key, paid his extras or what have you. The coach, scheduled to leave at 4.15pm, left promptly at 4.50pm as per the obligatory delay. Then ... mayhem. Fifteen of us do not have our press passes for the game for reasons, trust me, far too boring to go into. They would be distributed at the stadium. The passless 15 had to hang around for an hour at the stadium by the main entrance for the Pass Man to arrive, in which time some lager-than-life joker above us thought it would be really funny to throw a glass of beer over us. Hilarious.

Ireland were awful, the worst I have seen in 19 years, lucky to get a 1-0 win. Afterwards an Irish fan about 17 (age and IQ) who had enjoyed a few wine gums and was bizarrely carrying a blow-up dolphin abused me as I waited for the players to come out. He swore at me and after a minute of this I said to him: "If your parents could hear you now they would be so proud." Which seemed to shut him up temporarily.

We took off at 2am local time, and it was about 7am when Neil Custis and I arrived at the Herbert Park hotel. His travel agent had not confirmed late check in and so they had let his room from the previous night. Neil was less than pleased at 7am on a Sunday morning, no sleep, knackered and having to find another hotel.

SUNDAY OCTOBER 9

A lost day. Had virtually no kip, maybe a couple of hours. Going to bed about 7.30am, a time when I am usually getting up for my 12-mile run followed by a thimbleful of carrot juice for breakfast, is not natural. Even if I could sleep for six hours it becomes more difficult with the Herbert Park hoover final in the corridor.

Wrote my match report, gave the players some stick and rightly so. Can't really remember what I did apart from write, lie down and read the papers. Telephoned the boy Custis and neither of us could be arsed to go out to dinner. Had room service, including four euro tray fee which is not tray bien.

The bad news was that at 1am I changed rooms. The hotel's air conditioning unit was outside my window and the night unit (don't ask) kicked in then. So after having almost zero zzz's the night before, at 1am I find myself changing rooms. Do you think I was in a good mood?

MONDAY OCTOBER 10

A heart attack on a plate breakfast revived me, ready for the Brian Kerr press conference. Oh no, he didn't do one. Left it to two players who won't play on Wednesday night against Switzerland, of course.

Had a Chinese meal that night with Neil Custis (*Sun*), Colin Young (*Mail*), Matt Scott (*Guardian*) and Russell Kempson (*Times*). Neil has a demanding job covering Manchester United for the *Sun*, not least because it is almost easier to get an audience with the Pope than speak to the players. He does it well and is also a great tourist, his sense of humour a huge bonus when we are away for days or weeks on end.

WEDNESDAY OCTOBER 12

(Phone and laptop problems took up a lot of time yesterday).

Breakfast with Scotty of the Guardian. What it is about the Guardian? Jon Brodkin is a vegan and eats only one apple and lettuce leaf a day so it seems. Scotty is tucking into a plate of prunes for breakfast. If I joined the Guardian would I be compelled to eat strange things?

What will probably be Brian Kerr's last ever press conference as manager of Ireland was less hostile than of late, but he's still a dead man(ager) walking.

Day of the game came and went. Ireland did what Ireland do, which is draw and they are out of the World Cup. This means I will be covering Ukraine, Togo and South Korea in Germany next summer. Three and a half weeks of Togo and crap wine.

Went straight back to my room after the game in case the office needed me. Booked alarm call for 6am, cab at 6.30.

THURSDAY OCTOBER 13

At Gatwick in the coach taking us to the terminal someone farted down one end, so to speak. It was without doubt among the most horrendous farts I have ever smelt – and I was halfway down the coach. Passengers were moving from the area and a little girl said to her mum: "Someone's done a smelly botty burp."

And how.

SUPER BOWL XL, DETROIT, JAN/FEB 2006

SUNDAY JANUARY 29

At the Radisson Hotel near Thiefrow (aka Heathrow). Staying here so I don't have to get up a disgusting hour in the morning to drive here. The hotel gives you 15 days free parking, so should allow the locals ample time to remove the wheels etc.

Can't remember when I have been less excited about a Super Bowl. Pittsburgh Steelers versus Seattle Seahawks is not the sexiest match-up ever. It's been tagged steel versus cappuccino (Seattle being the home of Starbucks). It's also being held in Detroit where the temperature is minus five degrees. Detroit is not the most appealing city in the USA, well not in January or February certainly.

Anyway, got to the Radisson and my room is so far from the lift it would probably have been quicker to drive here anyway. I think the room is nearer Gatwick.

MONDAY JANUARY 30

The day started with a double SNAFU. My 7.15am alarm call did not materialize, neither did my breakfast-in-room at 7.30am (the 'insurance' alarm call). Still, such complicated requests are a bit much for a big international airport hotel. The girl on reception apologised and said I could have a free breakfast which hardly benefited me, but of course I was delighted to save the DT a few quid.

Security at Heathrow were very interested in (a) my Iran visa and (b) that I lived in Bromley where the shoe bomber came from. The answer to the question "why I was in Iran?" – "to cover the 2002 World Cup playoff against Ireland" – brought blank looks. They were also, as usual, interested in my visas from Israel, Nigeria, Russia, Ukraine and Serbia – a terrorist's charter. I think I bemused them in the end.

At the check-in I noticed the girl had 'Espana' under her name so in my best Spanish (which is the same as my worst Spanish) asked her where she was from. "Colombia," she replied. "Oh, I have been there," I said in a rare outbreak of honesty which soon ended. "Bogota ... loved it, people were so friendly," I said, not telling her that a couple of hours after arriving I was pickpocketed.

"I am from Cali," she said. "Oh, my favourite team is America de Cali," I lied. "Really?" she said. "Oh yes," I replied with well practised economy of the truth when an upgrade is on the horizon, reeling off some America players, sad bastard that I am remembering them.

"Tell you what sir," she said, smiling. "I am going to upgrade you to business."

"Muchas gracias," I replied and headed towards the business class lounge. Those days at Morley College many years ago when I learned some Spanish (just enough to be upgraded) seemed worthwhile.

There were 100 spare seats on the plane and I had one next to me – upgraded and space. In space! The flight to Chicago was, not surprisingly, pretty uneventful. I read the papers, did my Tuesday for Wednesday piece, had a kip, drank a few glasses of California's finest and ... well, not much else really.

At Chicago I discovered a problem with the US cable for my laptop. One end fits in the electricity socket, no problem, but the other end is too small to fit in the laptop, so it's as useful as a chocolate teapot.

In the country where everybody hopes everyone else will "have a nice day" about eight times an hour, Detroit is going one step further to ensure the nights, too, are enjoyable. All police leave has been cancelled for the Super Bowl.

Every officer in Motor City USA will be on duty this week – plus troops from nearby counties – with police working 12-hour shifts seven days in a row. To keep their own house in order some hotels insist on male guests signing a no-party form upon checking in, which is another way of saying no ladies of the night will visit the room to help the occupant have a nice day (or night). Do I look like a Super Bowl Oliver Reed?

The precise pronunciation of the city that never heats is not Deetroit, "oh no sir," said a member of the host committee, pointing out the city's roots are French. "It is Dehtroit with the accent on the last syllable." This, from a country that pronounces buoy "booee".

In any language, what is undeniable is that Detroit has a serious claim to be the USA's smoking capital. While California, where smoking is banned in public places, is a breath of fresh air to non-puffers, lighting up is almost mandatory in Dehtroit. A non-smoking table even in a first-class restaurant means one surrounded by second-hand smoke.

TUESDAY JANUARY 31
Having stayed up until 11pm the previous night, fighting off jet-lag, I was pleasantly surprised to wake up at 5.30am.

I lay in my pit for a while before going down to the accreditation centre at 7.30am because that was the time it was opening. Correction, that was the time I and many other hacks were TOLD it was opening. It was very pleasant and enlightening to spend 30 minutes in line with a bunch of South Koreans.

At 8am, I trundled in and made my way to the International Media Section which was unmanned, or unpersoned as I should say in this PC age.

So I waited with dozens of American hacks to be accredited while the International Media Section remained closed.

The media gifts are almost non-existent these days. From having a useful computer bag each year with the Super Bowl logo, we were this time given a note-pad, but not even a pen. Made up for that by noshing on a freebie bagel and cup of coffee in the media centre. A girl memorably asked me: "Would you mind keeping an eye on my bagels while I get a paper, please?" Americans are wonderful.

Got in the media coach to go to the stadium for media day, a quiet intimate affair involving 3,000 hacks and every player from both sides who all have to do an obligatory one-hour interview session. These include searching questions such as the one to Ben Roethlisberger: "If you were a car, what car would you be?" The Pittsburgh quarterback has a hamburger named after him, surprise surprise, called a Roethlisburger (what else?).

There are no real characters in this Super Bowl. Usually there is some player who was shot while his hooker mother was selling drugs to an undercover cop or what have you. They're all good guys this year. Boring.

The hard work done, we adjourned for the media brunch, which comprises around 10,000 calories on a plate. You can almost feel the arteries clogging up with every mouthful.

Back to the Marriott hotel to write an article on Roethlisberger and told front desk again that despite turning off the heating the noise continued. They would fix it, I was assured, which meant I could put my mortgage on nothing happening.

Went to the media party at the Fox Theatre which was okay, but nothing to write home about, though I suppose in effect that is what I am doing. Arrived back about midnight, pleased I had not succumbed to jet lag. I was less pleased the noise was still there, my mortgage safe. I phoned the front desk and they sent up a guy who took my heating unit to bits, great fun at 0030. He said he could do nothing about the noise. It was made by the dry riser (as if I didn't know) of the hotel. So front desk found me another room which … are you sitting down … had the same problem. I was then moved to the 47th floor – from the 28th – by now it was close on 2am and I was knackered. The new room was inferior to the original room and it, too, had the dry riser noise, but I was beyond caring. So I was messed around for two hours and given an inferior room with the same noise.

I spoke to the front desk night manager and said I would be seeing the duty manager to make an offer how much I should pay for my stay. The rate is $190 per night and I offered $10. He said that would be unacceptable. "Well it should be a lively little chat with the duty manager then, shouldn't it?" I said before putting a pillow over my head to sleep.

WEDNESDAY FEBRUARY 1

Good start to the day. My 500-word piece asked for yesterday did not go in. Space problems. Or rather, lack of it.

Went to see the duty manager about my faulty dry riser (as you do) and he was very apologetic. "Your rate is $190 a night," he said. "I will dock half of that from last night."

"How about I have a meal in the restaurant to the value of $95?"

"Okay."

So now I have to decide (a) whether to have a $95 meal alone in the rather splendid restaurant or (b) dine with another hack. Not an easy decision.

My early impressions of Detroit are positive. Even the weather is warmer than expected … about 40 degrees. The city has made a really big effort to clean up its act – literally – and the people have a friendly attitude towards you.

"Hi … my name is Peter and I am your mugger today. Excuse me sir … if you would, please, just give me all your money then I will be on my way. Thank you sir. Have a nice day."

In between the slave-like schedule for a working hack that is the Super Bowl I managed to find time to visit the Motown museum, which was wonderful. It is the former house of legendary producer Berry Gordy, and where they used to make all the great recordings. Totally fascinating, amazing memorabilia including Michael Jackson's glove. I visited the recording studio where they had the original sheet music from a Temptations hit. Sadly, but perhaps inevitably, I was invited to become part of the 'New Temptations' with the guide teaching us how to do the Temptations dance. As the only white guy of the group I stood out in more ways than one.

Opposite the hotel there is a jewellers with a sign outside "Come inside and have your ring cleaned." Have they never heard of double entendres here?

Went into Greektown for dinner last night with Nick Szczepanik from the *Times* and Simon Veness from the *Sun* and his American wife. Simon is in a wheelchair after tearing his cruciate ligaments playing football last Saturday and I was chosen to be the pusher because I have a lot of practice doing it – mainly due to my luck. Found a restaurant called Hellas and had a rather splendid chicken hellas washed down with American rather than Greek or Cypriot wine. No disrespect to Greek or Cypriot wine, but it's crap.

THURSDAY FEBRUARY 2:
Usual place in the breakfast restaurant, served by the same waitress who asked me the same questions – "orange juice and coffee sir?" I then went to the buffet and asked the guy for a scrambled egg because I can't bring myself to say "sunny side up." The bill comes to exactly the same and I leave exactly the same tip. Another Groundhog Day breakfast.

The highlight of the trip so far was undoubtedly the Rolling Stones' press conference. The Stones are playing the half-time show – three numbers in 12 and a half minutes. The set is a closely guarded secret, but I reckon they will do *Start Me Up* plus *Dancing in the Street* (in honour of Motown).

Mick Jagger was a star. He was asked about Janet Jackson's wardrobe malfunction when her boob popped out at the previous year's Super Bowl. "Network television," said Sir Mick. "They're always worried about how many times you are going to say f*** on air..." Just hope those broadcasting it live had a time-delay.

Jagger was terrific, great energy ... took the mick (sorry) out of everyone. "America has changed over the last 40 years like us, but we both retain our core values," he said managing to keep a straight face. The Stones are being paid $3.5 million dollars for their 12 and a half minutes, no doubt to their huge satisfaction. Paul McCartney did the half-time show last year and it is reckoned sales of his records went up by 250 per cent the week before and after the Super Bowl.

Had lunch with Keith Webster, editor of *First Down*. We used my $95 freebie lunch, but couldn't make it up to 95 bucks so I will have a couple of freebie breakfasts too.

Wrote the preview in the afternoon and then went to an international media party bash in Windsor, just over the Canadian border. It was a mile and a half away, but it took an hour at both borders to get through and we were the only coach. We were there for 90 minutes so it took longer to get there and back. The food was crap – crab cakes and other crabby things. Had three voddie and oranges and some brie and left. A wasted evening. Could not bring myself to have a photo taken with a mountie, or ask him if he always got his man. Or if he had a brother who was a lumberjack and was he okay.

But overall Detroit is okay. The city's made a big effort to ensure people feel good, downtown has been cleaned up, weather has been warmer than expected. So far so good.

FRIDAY FEBRUARY 3
The hotel is crazy. I think the entire population of Detroit is here now.

Residents must wear a fetching lime green wristband as ID (aka the no hooker wristband). The lifts take an eternity to arrive and when they do you find the first two are so crowded you need to be an ant to get in.

Preview filed, work has now finished until my report on the game on Sunday. Problem is there is little or nothing in the vicinity of the hotel. The nearest shopping mall is apparently 25 minutes away by taxi which means the plastic will remain intact, a Super Bowl first.

Spent a lot of the day reading Ed McBain's last book, a novel way of passing the time. Went to the hotel shop to buy a Gatorade and snack, returned to my room to find the top of the Gatorade had apparently been superglued on. Back I went to ask the girl if I could change it for one that opened, she took the Gatorade and ... yes, you guessed it. "You must have loosened it sir," she said smiling that you-didn't-really-loosen-it smile.

Because I am a professional I decided to attend the Super Bowl XL Cheerleading Spirit Clinic even though it would not make any copy for the paper. I watched and admired the girls' athleticism and movement as they went through their routines.

In the evening Nick and Ken Elliott of the *Evening Standard* along with yours truly took the shuttle bus to Birmingham and enjoyed a splendid Italian meal. Ken has triplets, three boys, who will be 13 soon. A trio of Kevins – for what he is about to receive...

The NFL guide who was on the shuttle bus was interested to hear about the Motown museum where she had never been. "They have an incredible collection of records on the walls," I said, adding rather distastefully: "Including Marvin Gaye's last recording – *I Heard It Through The Carbine*..."

"Oh really," she said and I suspected had I said his last record was called *I Once Had A Pet Elephant Called Tiny* she would still have said "Oh really."

Returned to the hotel and decided to have a nightcap, ordering a screwdriver for myself and Ken. What I did NOT order was a nonalcoholic screwdriver, though that is what was dished up. There may be just a few things in the world that I am an expert on, but knowing whether I've been served a screwdriver or simply an orange juice is most definitely high up the list.

This was a job for the manager, not the bar steward who served me simply OJ. Trying to lighten the situation I said: "I can always murder a screwdriver but could never murder an OJ." After I said it I wondered why I bothered.

There followed a tasting session involving four different people (using straws) before it was decided that yes, sorry sir, we did give you a nonalcoholic screwdriver. Problem was, there'd been so many people tasting the OJ was half gone, so when the voddie was poured in it amounted to a voddie and a dash. However, I need not have worried about it being too strong as the voddie had been watered down.

SATURDAY FEBRUARY 4

The weather, as the locals predicted, has changed. It is snowing. Photographer supreme Dave Shopland, whose surname is entirely appropriate, told me the shopping mall is a $40 cab ride away, which of course was no deterrent to him. Master shopper Dave probably bought the cab, too. Even sharing, the prospect of paying $40 for effectively the right to shop did not appeal to me. This is going to be the No Shopping Bowl.

Collected my game credentials and was given some earmuffs, gloves and a hand warmer. Wonder if I should tell the tax man? Most importantly I acquired two VIP tickets for the Motown Legends concert at the Detroit Masonic Temple, an unlikely venue. Artistes appearing include the Four Tops, The Miracles, Freda Payne, Brenda Holloway (I may tell her she has a jail named after her), Martha Reeves and the Vandellas plus The Former Ladies Of The Supremes (or FLOTS I suppose). Really looking forward to this with the Rolling Stones to follow tomorrow.

Did a piece for Pittsburgh radio station and told their listeners how popular the Steelers were in Britain (hey – even got a wheel named after them, I quipped wittily) and that most of the folks back home would be rooting for them, oh yes sir, we love our Steelers back in Blighty. As ever, give them what they want to hear.

"Saw" the Premiership games on my laptop in my room on the BBC web site (okay ... the score-flashes) while watching the snow fall before attending my Get A Life class. Had the world's biggest omelette on room service as did not think the Detroit Masonic Temple would provide grub AND music.

In fact never got to find out what the Detroit Masonic Temple had to offer. In hindsight and after 17 Super Bowls I should have realised that the one thing you can't do is to go anywhere on the eve of the SB unless you (a) walk or (b) have transport laid on to take you to AND from your destination.

The hotel was so crowded it took 20 (!) minutes to get to the taxi rank outside the main lobby and after waiting for 45 minutes, in which time six taxis came along ... we called time on Tamla.

Initially there were 22 people in front of us in the queue, sorry line. After the sixth cab had been and gone the people-count was 24, which may, just may, have had something to do with the Russian bellhop with the bulging pockets who was organising the queue/line.

There was also the worry of getting back to the hotel after the concert. The nearest metro was about a mile and a half away, acceptable on a warm night in Miami or San Diego, but not when the snow is coming down in a mini-blizzard.

So the night before the Super Bowl, Nick, Ken, and myself sat in a sort of makeshift bar in the lobby of the Marriott drinking cocktails which cost $7 each. As we had all eaten before leaving for the taxi queue/line we didn't really want to eat again so after three rounds of $7 cocktails we called it a day (why do we wait until night to call it a day?), returning to our rooms at 9.30pm because there was no Plan B. Sad beyond belief but that's Super Bowl eve for you.

SUNDAY FEBRUARY 5

One of the truly unforgettable conversations of my life, which took place at the stadium, ensured Super Bowl XL would remain in my memory even if the game was probably the worst of all 18 I have seen. Before the match I went to buy the now obligatory barrel of popcorn and two draft Buds – only one for me – and the girl refused to serve me the Buds as I did not have any ID. I showed her my credentials (as they say) but she said no, sorry sir, I need to see your driver's licence.

"I don't have it with me. I am from London. I do not drive here," I replied with just the slightest whiff of sarcasm.

"Sorry sir, no ID, no beer."

I told her I had never been so flattered in my life. "You need proof I am 21?" I asked, though was less impressed by the amused Seattle fan behind me who said: "He's so old he could be a Rolling Stone." My incredibly funny response – "hey, you, get off of my case," went over his head. Fortunately the guy at the next Bud counter was happy that, yes, I was 21 (or over) and served me with a couple of drafts.

The day had started with the discovery that the Irish bar whose website claimed it would be showing Chelsea versus Liverpool (11am kick-off here) did NOT in fact have the match on a live satellite link. So we went to the pre-game brunch and topped up our arteries before heading off to Ford Field, a fabulous stadium it must be said. There, I said it.

The pre-game show included the Four Tops (managed to see them eventually) and Stevie Wonder, though I wondered if it was the best of taste for the male support dancers to have white walking sticks. Even less PC was the record the NFL chose to play after each score – *Rock 'n' Roll* by Gary Glitter whose image has lost much of its shine.

The Stones did the half-time show with, as predicted, *Start Me Up* their opener. Their second choice was staggering – *Rough Justice* which just happened to be the title track off their latest album and a song which few knew. The better known *Satisfaction* finished the set with old rubber lips proving to be a true star.

Back to the hotel for the post-match dinner – a sort of protected species goulash – washed down with a glass of vino and a coffee. And yes, when the waitress inquired if I wanted sugar I did ask for brown sugar.

Pittsburgh 21, Seattle 10. Not the best of Super Bowls, but Detroit tried its best to put on a show and make visitors welcome.

2006 World Cup, Germany, June 2006

WEDNESDAY JUNE 7

In a cab en route to Heathrow airport and the driver is from Nigeria. I have had him before, if you'll excuse the phrase, and he's a good lad because he laughs a lot. Even when I say something like "I hope my plane isn't delayed" he laughs.

Today will be spent (apart from flying to Munich) being accredited and settling in the Hotel Exquisit, which would be a fabulous Scrabble word. I was tempted to look the hotel up on the internet but decided against it in case it's NOT exquisit. It's hardly likely to say that of course. I mean, "non-exquisit hotel, traffic noise 24 hours a day and especially night, dirty rooms, dreadful food and aggressive staff" is unlikely to feature on the hotel web site. More likely is "a wonderful hotel where there is complimentary champagne all day and you will have no problem with your internet connection." We'll see.

I have tended not to do too well with hotels at major finals. Two years ago in Oporto the hotel advertised as being three kilometres from the city centre was indeed that – as long as you could walk across water. If on the other hand you could not it was a 25-minutes bus or taxi ride around the bay. In 2002 in the Far East the rooms in Japan were tiny – unlike the prices because buying a coffee would make even Bill Gates ask for time to pay.

At Euro 2000 the Hotel President had probably never been visited by any president. France 98 was okay. For Euro 96 I was based in Newcastle where even in June and July the weather was not exactly Auf Wiedersehen sweat. I am due a decent hotel in Germany. Well, I think I am.

Mr Happy the driver has started to talk to me about Iran making a nuclear bomb. Just the sort of lighthearted conversation I need at 6.30am. I put forward the theory I heard on some TV show that the war between Iran and Iraq was caused by the two countries sounding so similar they kept getting each other's post and were pissed off so went to war to sort it out. He didn't know what I was going on about which is fair enough, but he still laughed his wonderful laugh.

At Heathrow airport, a good start as I was happily upgraded from goat curry class to business for reasons unexplained. Chatted with ITV commentator Peter Drury who said he still owed me £120 for two Footballer of the Year dinner tickets – I told Peter not to leave the country. I swear I heard a Nigerian cab driver laugh in the distance.

Take-off was delayed for 30 minutes because the vehicle to "tow" the plane in position got lost. How? David Baddiel and Frank Skinner were on the plane – they are doing something for a pod-cast link during the finals. A sign of the times or rather a sign of the *Times* as that's who they are working for.

Had an enjoyable business class breakfast, even managing to open my carton of milk for the coffee without it squirting all over the place. They can be man's inhumanity to man those mini cartons. Many a shirt and/or tie has been ruined by them. I spent the rest of the flight congratulating myself on this momentous achievement.

Munich's Hotel Exquisit lives up to its name. It is fabulous. Correction. My room is fabulous. Correction ... my suite is fabulous. From the outside the hotel looks pretty average. From the inside initial suspicions are confirmed. But my suite is magnificent. It contains a hallway with a table and trouser press. Separate loo (with paper on the left AND the right of the throne, not really sure why) and bathroom. Then there is a lounge with a TV, a three-seat sofa, an armchair, table and desk. Next is the bedroom with a double bed and ample wardrobe space.

The guy on reception gave me my key and a blue thing "which you need to access the pay movies," his smile giving me the impression he was confident of a two-week vacation in the West Indies on the profits of said pay movies in room 109. Unless there is a catch this will be terrific for the next three weeks. There is even a place I can sunbathe if (a) the sun appears and (b) I have any spare time.

I've no idea where the other lads are staying but this seems fairly central. Most importantly, I have been in Germany for two and a half hours and haven't mentioned the war. Or the 1966 World Cup Final.

Germany 2006 going well. Accreditation is next.

Ah, the glitches have started. The computer system at the accreditation centre was down which meant around 100 journalists with better things to do than hang around while the system was repaired were not happy – I heard "what the **** is going on?" in 12 different languages.

The media centre at the stadium was empty. Two days before the World Cup kicks-off and not a list of players, no stats, nothing. Even the media shuttle bus went AWOL. Still, a minor hiccup and a bonus is that the stadium is only about 15 minutes on the Metro from the hotel.

My *Telegraph* colleague John Ley sent me a text saying he can't get his laptop to work, his hotel is 30 minutes from the courtesy bus station and he missed the shuttle because he took the wrong train attempting to get there. Still, thankfully it was after only 20 minutes that he realised this.

All in all I've had a result, it seems. Decent accommodation, well, very decent really, my laptop works, I'm near a Metro and only a quarter of an hour from the stadium. It's all too good to be true. No doubt I'll be mugged tonight or get food poisoning. Maybe both.

Dinner with Mick Dennis (*Express*) and Jeff Powell (*Mail*) in a Bavarian restaurant not too far from here. Mick is the best all-round journalist I have ever worked with and it's a shame he was sports editor of the *Evening Standard* only for a brief spell.

Initially Mick was an excellent agency and then *Sun* reporter before moving indoors – in my early *Telegraph* days Mick was on the backbench, part of the sports desk's decision-making process. He was inspirational in terms of keeping the spirits of everyone high and now as football correspondent of the *Express* he writes a spikey Wednesday column.

Jeff has probably done more to raise the standard of tabloid football writing than anyone. In my early days on the circuit he helped me a lot, including the occasional and deserved rollicking. He is someone I still look up to because he has maintained an incredibly high standard of writing for what must be going on 40 years.

A good first day at the 2006 World Cup.

THURSDAY JUNE 8

Last night's dinner in the Haxenbaur was memorable for the size of Jeff's knuckle of pork. If that was a knuckle then the fist would be enough to feed a third world country for a month. Everything seems to be knuckles over here; it's the land of the knuckle. I had knuckle of muesli for breakfast.

I chose my table – when you are in hotel you always select a table on the first day that becomes 'yours'. It's like an animal marking its territory, though the waitress didn't seem too impressed when I peed on the table-leg.

The World Cup seems to be the best kept secret in Munich. Two nights before the kick-off and there were hardly any flags, signs or what have you about the World Cup. Maybe Germans are still uneasy about displays of nationalistic fervour.

More and more of the British hacks are arriving here hourly, all wondering how they will file copy from the stadium tomorrow. FIFA have effectively put up a signal ban, forcing the media to pay arms and legs (and knuckles) for special wi-fi cards available only from them, which will enable us to log on. It's almost censorship, restraint of trade. I have Bluetooth access from a mobile, a 3G card, a wireless connection, landline connection facilities and an ISDN computer cable which probably means I will fail to file in five different ways.

Went for a lunch time stroll and noticed a sign that said "kuntkost", but perhaps the less said about that the better.

My suite is still fantastic. I keep waiting for workmen to start drilling outside but it's quiet, big and comfortable. I ordered my first class train tickets to Nuremberg (for Mexico v Iran on Sunday, the big one) and to Stuttgart for France v Switzerland on Tuesday. Journos here have free first class rail travel with a special Bahn Card which is a truly magnificent perk.

FRIDAY JUNE 9

The hunt for a decent German white wine continues. I was chatting to the hotel manager about this vitally important matter and he said: "My colleague is a bit of a wine expert, he may be able to help." Ah, progress. The wine expert came over and I said to the manager: "Ask him for the name or names of some good German wines." Question was duly translated. Reply? "Reisling." Not exactly what I was hoping for.

One of the best German wine stories comes courtesy of Jack Steggles, who worked for the *Daily Mirror* for much of his career, and you need only the most basic knowledge of German to understand it. Jack said: "I was in a bar in Germany and when the barmaid asked me what I wanted. I told her 'dry white wine, please' and she gave me three glasses." Wonderful.

The hunt also continues for a Togo (our adopted country here, don't ask why, they just are) T-shirt. Went to a couple of stores with a huge World Cup merchandise section, no Togo gear. One girl said: "Are they in the World Cup?"

"Yes."

"Oh, but how about a nice Germany T-shirt?"

My first row of the World Cup arrived and surprisingly it was about boiled eggs. Having claimed my territory yesterday I returned to 'my' breakfast table for my Groundhog Day start to the day. Once again I kicked off with knuckle of muesli and fresh fruit salad and asked the waitress for two boiled eggs, three minutes please.

Yesterday the knuckle of boiled eggs was fine, though my request for knuckle of toast (ie soldiers) was refused. Germans don't do toast in the morning (and let's raise a glass to that). Anyway, today's eggs arrived and they were runny, very runny … could have gargled with them had I the desire which I didn't.

I called over the waitress and said: "These eggs are not three minutes." She replied: "Yes they are." The confusion, not that there should be any, is that yesterday's egg boiler cooked them in what I consider the proper way. Put eggs in saucepan with water and when it comes to the boil, boil the eggs for three minutes. Easy peasy. That, mein fraulein, is a three-minute boiled egg. Today's egg boiler put the eggs into the already boiling water and boiled them for three minutes. Big difference. "So you should have asked for five-minute eggs," said the frowning fraulein. "Well, no … had I asked for five-minute eggs yesterday I would in fact have had five-minute eggs which would have been too hard. It is subjective what constitutes five minutes when boiling an egg. In future I shall specify that I would like either a five-minute egg (or eggs), the five-minute period taking in pre-boiling time or a three-minute egg (or eggs) which does not include pre-boiling time."

For some reason the forlorn fraulein, bemused of Bavaria, didn't seem to know what the heck I was going on about. I ended up having knuckle of croissant with strawberry jam.

Spent the morning on my terrace lounge reading the *Daily Telegraph* and updating my World Cup stats – the sun has belatedly arrived in Munich.

Security getting into the stadium was a pain in the Arsenal. Had to wait for about 35 minutes along with all the Hillmans (Hillman hunters ... punters) before being bodily searched by a male body searcher who seemed to enjoy his job a little too much for my liking.

The good news is that the scare stories about not being able to file from the stadium unless you buy a special wi-fi card from T-mobile proved to be untrue. I have managed to log on using my 3G card – so the place it was not expected to work is virtually the only place it HAS worked. The World Cup is going far too well.

The stadium is fabulous. The grass looks almost as good as my lawn. Almost. A better than usual opening match with Germany not over-impressive in beating Costa Rica 4-2.

SATURDAY JUNE 10

A familiar face at breakfast. Tim Collings of Reuters, who greeted me with: "Can't stop, got to get to some training ground somewhere." So it was breakfast for one again. I'm not working today (a Saturday, no paper tomorrow) and to the best of my knowledge no-one else from the Brit pack is in town. So not only is it breakfast alone for solitary old me, but also lunch, afternoon tea, dinner, supper ... you name it, I'm solo.

After yesterday's boiled egg saga I decided on a change – fried eggs with chillies, confident my Odol mouthwash would ensure no-one realised I'd eaten half of Mexico for breakfast. So, two pieces of toast with chilli fried eggs, plus two cups of strong (not that there is any other variety here) German coffee, which is always reliable. Mother Nature didn't know what had hit her.

I am delighted to report that after only four days here I have cracked German. Drucken on a door handle means push, the other word beginning with Z means pull. This is important for strasse cred. Knowing 'drucken' and 'ein grosse bier bitte' should see me through my time here. That's the lingo taken care of then.

Result. I managed to buy a Togo T-shirt. A real replica (as the guy who sold it to me said, laughing, everyone's a comedian these days) which set me back eight euro. One wash and it'll fit a Barbie doll no doubt. Unsurprisingly, the shop where I bought the T-shirt was owned by Turks. I reckon there are as many Turks as Germans, maybe more, in the vicinity. I doner know why that is.

It's now 2pm, an hour before England v Paraguay, and I have done little apart from buy a Togo T-shirt, eat some chilli eggs, and write the diary. Oh, and watched the first episode of *Life on Mars* on DVD.

Watched England v Paraguay in a bar drinking Becks – how patriotic can you be? It was a scrappy game in which England started well but fell away badly. A 1-0 win, although I expect knives are being sharpened for England head coach Sven-Göran Eriksson. Trinidad and Tobago held the Swedes.

Now I am going, alone of course, to see Serbia & Montenegro against Holland at what looks a different, but decent bar across the strasse from my hotel where I have my suite.

SUNDAY JUNE 11

God knows why (I blame the chilli eggs), but I had a dream about Chris Coleman, the Fulham manager, last night. What a waste. Could have dreamt about anyone ... but no, I get Chris Coleman.

Having been awakened by the dream I decided to have a 3.37am leak, as you do, a decision I regretted when, walking through my suite to the loo with my eyes pretty well closed ... I trod on a plug. I probably woke up the entire population of Munich with my one-word expletive which then spread to Stuttgart when I then fell over and hurt my arm on the table. A double whammy in the true sense.

Breakfast was surreal. As I sat down at 'my' table Me, *You And A Dog Named Boo* was being played, an unlikely accompanying record to my knuckle of muesli and fresh fruit salad followed by knuckle of two chilli fried eggs on toast. I was the only person in the breakfast lounge. It gets no sadder. Well it probably will later on. The staff, who are very friendly, all know my name.

Of course it isn't surprising they remember my name as I'm the only guest here it seems. I feel like Norm out of *Cheers* when I come down to reception. Instead of "Hey Mr Pedersen, how you doing?" from Woody with Norm replying: "Well Woody, man meets beer, falls in love with beer, drinks it and has another…" I get "Hello Christopher, how are you today?" I wish I was Norm. Even normal.

I am now on a train to Nuremberg with Dion Dublin, Alistair Bruce-Ball and David Oates who are covering Mexico v Iran for 5Live. They are trying to get their tongues round the Iran players – well, how to pronounce their names, that is. At yesterday's press conference the Iran coach was asked what he thought of the Holocaust, with the game in Nuremberg and all that. Unsurprisingly he did not comment on a rather delicate subject and it will be some achievement if there is a less tasteful question at Germany 2006. By the way, the best chant so far is, remarkably, from the Germans, not always known for their sense of humour. "Three World Cups and one World Pope."

The (free) first class travel is excellent. Airconditioned, plenty of space, comfortable seat – and that's just the loo. Very pleasant. Even better, the BBC boys have a car meeting them at Nuremberg station to take them to the stadium and said I can join them. The World Cup is going far too well. By now I am normally issuing fatwahs on the organisers, hotel manager and anyone else who dared to cross my path. This time it's all going smoothly. I am worried.

Security was heavy at the Nuremberg stadium. The heavies were going to confiscate my hotel key "as you could use it as a weapon." I replied: "Then how the hell would I get back into my hotel room, sorry suite, you dumb-ass if I have thrown it at someone? You may as well take my laptop too as that is far heavier and therefore more dangerous." Well, I didn't actually SAY that because I am basically a coward, but I certainly THOUGHT it.

In 2002 at the World Cup in Japan the security staff confiscated a woman's breast pump because, they said, it could be used as a missile. Anyway, I have a decent view in the press box for a game that no-one outside Mexico and Iran gives a toss about. I must also be one of the few people to have visited both countries (boring World Cup fact number 957).

Mexico 3 Iran 1 was a better game than I had predicted. Incredible atmosphere, the Mexicans are barmy, but nice barmy. In the middle of the Iranian section was a red and white flag "Millwall on Tour." Incredible. Best T-shirt so far is Never Mind the Ballacks, though unsure whether Germany captain Michael Ballack will wear one.

Tom Humphries of the *Irish Times* told me a great story about a train journey. All the announcements were made in German and English until one was made only in German. He saw some Germans shake their heads and mutter something so Tom asked what was happening.

"Ze train is being diverted," one German said. Tom asked why which seemed fair enough but soon wished he hadn't. The way the German replied came out as "they have found a bome in Ohm."

A bomb, or bome, had been discovered near the railway line. "It's your fault," said one German smiling at Tom. "Well, maybe my granddad's," Tom replied, returning the smile.

Tom then added: "I hear Ohm is lovely, quite unlike anywhere else. In fact there's no place like Ohm." He didn't really say that, but he might have done had he thought of it. Maybe not then.

MONDAY JUNE 12

My diet here is crap. Yesterday I ate a knuckle of chilli fried eggs on toast and fresh fruit salad for breakfast. At the stadium we can only buy cold snacks, so lunch was a cheese and tomato roll with orange juice. After the game, at the station, every hot food seemed to end in 'wurst' which in my mind speaks for itself. I could not bring myself to eat anything ending in 'wurst' and could not be arsed to queue for what seemed three days to buy a croissant.

When I arrived back at my hotel after midnight there was no room (or even suite) service, but I found a small box of three After Eights and a little complimentary bag of jelly beans which they leave on your pillow so you can ruin your teeth before going to sleep. Three After Eights and some jelly beans washed down with a Coke – I bet no other person on the planet had that for dinner.

No match for me today, no other members of the Hack Pack in Munich, so once again it's three games on my own in a pub. Sad? Moi?

I have to preview the France v Switzerland game being played tomorrow, which I wrote on the train coming back from Nuremberg on Saturday so today's work is out of the way, leaving me even more time to … er, do nothing.

Once again the only person at breakfast. Is everyone avoiding me? An empty breakfast room save for the lonely, sad English hack. Not only that, the waitress fraulein – MY waitress fraulein – just brought my knuckle of chilli fried eggs on toast without even asking me what I wanted – like, how boring and predictable am I (or did you know I was going to say that?).

It's 11am – only another 12 or 13 hours before I can go back to bed. At least Italy are playing tonight.

It's 4.30pm and I am watching Japan v Australia and my room, excuse me, my suite has not yet been serviced. I need a good moan, I've been here five days and it's not natural to go that long without a whinge. I'm a football journalist abroad for heaven's sake. However, this isn't really a good enough reason.

Probably my best row came in Cagliari at Italia 90. The television in my room did not work and I had to cover Egypt v Holland from the box, which is difficult when there is no picture. I asked … and asked … and asked … but nothing was done.

An hour before kick-off I took positive action. An Irish journalist said last Friday recalling the incident: "I shall never forget the sight of you walking across the hotel foyer carrying a television, putting it down on the front desk and saying: 'This TV does not work, can somebody please get me one that works as soon as possible.'" And they did.

Ah, those were the days. In Germany everything works, runs on time and things people say will be done are done. It's no fun.

7.45pm, room still not serviced, but my first row of Germany 2006 has got to be better than an unmade bed and towels on the bathroom floor, which if I am honest makes me feel at home. Can't think of anything to row about. Tough times.

8pm, I decided to go downstairs to the courtyard to have a coffee and read some magazines. Guess what? no-one else there. Is this a wind-up? Breakfast? Happy hour? I'm doing solitary. Next stop Death Row. Or better, Heathrow.

Got an hour before Italy v Ghana and I'm Ghana watch it in 'my' bar opposite, where I shall sit in the same seat as I did on Saturday for Argentina v Ivory Coast and have knuckle of penne arrabiata as it's the only thing on the menu I can understand. The bar is called Mozart (not originally because they were Chopin and changing the name), but it is now officially the Sad Bastard Bar.

TUESDAY JUNE 13
Things are looking up. Three people in the breakfast room – three American women who were unaware "this cute little World Cup" was on when they planned their trip. The German word for breakfast is fruhstucken. If one morning the service is poor, would I be able to get away with asking: "I suppose a fruhstucken's out the question?" Ok, probably not.

Anyway, enjoyed my usual fruhstucken and then off to Stuttgart where I bumped into Alan Green and Graham Taylor on the train. Had a good chat with them and then a load of hacks from El Salvador boarded and sat near us. Always keen to practise my Spanish, I said to them that in 1981 I had interviewed Pipo Rodriguez, their former national team coach who, as a player, scored a goal against Honduras that sparked a 7-day war between the two countries. I wrote the piece for the Observer and it's not every day you get to interview someone who's started a war. The El Salvador hacks were so impressed by this they did an interview with me about my interview with Pipo (great name for a peeping tom). I'm big in El Salvador.

Yess! I've had a row, thank goodness. In fact, two rows – like buses, they come in pairs (like twins). First row came when, upon arriving at the stadium in Stuttgart at 2.30pm to see Togo against South Korea on TV before France v Switzerland and security wouldn't let anyone, not even the media, through the gates until 3pm. As many of the media, notably radio guys, had work to do, programmes to be on, there was just a teeny weeny bit of dissent. In fact, there was almost a full-scale riot. By the time they opened the gates at 3.10pm there was a huge crowd (many with bad breath) irate, to say the least.

Upon eventually being allowed in, security confiscated a bottle of water from me. "Nein," said Herr Security.

"But it is exactly the same plastic bottle of water that I can buy there [pointing to a stall five metres the other side of security]."

"Yes but you cannot bring it through here."

"Who says so?"

"Me." (it's getting good now).

"You?"

"Yes. You cannot bring it through."

"I want to see in the security regulations where it says I can't bring through exactly the same type of bottle of water that I can buy five metres away."

"You are not bringing it through here."

"If someone bought a bottle of water there [pointing] and brought it out, gave it to me, would I be allowed to bring it through?"

"No."

Germany 1, England 0.

Into the stadium and I asked the Help Desk (yeah, right) why the gates weren't opened till 3.10pm.

"I'm sorry I can't help," said the Help Desk guy with no sense of irony. "Maybe ask security."

So to security. "I am sorry but I don't know," said Mr Security.

"But you are security, you MUST know."

"Maybe someone else can tell you, try the Help Desk." Towel taken off back of deck chair and thrown in.

To complete the memorable pre-match scenario a bit of a filling came out of a tooth (where else, I guess?) while I was eating a knuckle of ham and cheese sandwich. Oh, and for the first time my Orange 3G card doesn't work. I am only able to log on by my Bluetooth (which doesn't have any fillings missing).

The day just got worse and wurst. The France/Switzerland game was crap, 0-0. I am now on a train back to Munich. It's allegedly a 2 hour 20-minute journey, so it'll be midnight by the time we arrive. No hot food – again, breakfast apart.

Today's intake has been the usual knuckle of chilli fried eggs etc, a knuckle of cheese and ham sandwich at the stadium where the only hot food was something ending in "wurst," no thank you ma'am, a piece of cake and a knuckle of brie in a roll for what will be dinner on the now moving train.

Match days in another city make it difficult going on impossible to have anything hot to eat. I keep suggesting to the organisers they should have 'international' food like pizzas, lasagne or cheese and Marmite on toast available in media centres. They say "what a good idea, Christopher," and then dish up rolls. My influence is waning (which pre-supposes it was ever at a level to wane). Some of the other troops might be in town tomorrow for the 'derby' between Saudi Arabia and Tunisia, so could be a decent nosh-up afterwards rather than the Sad Bastard Bar.

WEDNESDAY JUNE 14

Today I celebrate a week in Munich and what better way than with a knuckle of chilli fried eggs on toast? This is a strange World Cup for me, the first major tournament I can remember when I have been 'alone'. No running mates around. There has never been a finals of any type when I've been the only journalist in an official media hotel.

Being based in one city has its advantages and disadvantages. Those who are on a two-days-here, one-day-there move-about schedule are knackered (if not knuckled) and frustrated about the constant packing and un-packing. I don't have that problem, just long hours by myself.

I have seen little of Munich because I can't really be bothered to go into the centre, find a restaurant and go through the 'table for one please, yes, I know, sad bastard,' routine. Hopefully some of the other boys will be in town to watch Germany v Poland which is the late game tonight after covering the earlier Saudi Arabia v Tunisia.

I can't tell you how much I am looking forward to this game – mainly because I am not looking forward to it at all. Plenty of scope for puns here though ... just deserts ... sands of time ... the Saudi's were sheikhen ... just three that won't see the light of day in my report.

Wrote a follow-up to the France v Switzerland game. Now it's 2.30pm and I am on the media coach (which in turn is one Metro stop away from the hotel where I have a suite) going to the stadium.

The coach is full of Arabs, not surprisingly as it is Saudi Arabia v Tunisia. Bar takings at the stadium won't be too good today. At least neither team can complain about playing in the heat.

By the way, I loved this agency report:

'Sex workers in Berlin have gone into extra-time at the World Cup and are doing double shifts to cash in, a German newspaper said Wednesday. "Berlin's hookers are groaning – all brothels are creaking at the seams," mass daily *Bild* reported.

"In some establishments the girls already have to put in double shifts owing to the World Cup," the paper added. German police said last week there were no signs of forced prostitution being on the rise. Be that as it may, with around a million fans having come over for the month-long football showpiece and with prostitution legal in Germany, supply is clearly meeting demand.

Bild quote Josephine Conte of Berlin's upmarket Bel Ami establishment, one of 400 "joy houses" in the city, as saying demand has gone through the roof and that her employees were having to put in "special shifts."

She explained: "We have VIP reservations right through to the end of the tournament. Sometimes we don't know where to put all the men!"

As payoff lines go that's up with the best.

THURSDAY JUNE 15

Today is going to be a long one. Long Thursday, a public holiday. I am the only Englischer Mann in Munich, no game and the matches on TV are, with the exception of England v Trinidad and Tobago, vin ordinaire.

Ecuador v Costa Rica is at 3pm which could be fun, but hardly raises the pulse (can't see the Sad Bastard Bar heaving at the seams for THAT game), then England v T&T, followed by Sweden v Paraguay at 9pm, if I haven't died of being terminally lonely by then.

I have a couple of previews to do, notably Holland v the Ivory Coast, sorry, Cote D'Ivoire as they prefer to be called (not where I come from chaps).

It is now 5.20pm and it suddenly occurred to me that apart from speaking to the desk and my mother, the only other word I have uttered to a human being today is "danke" to the fraulein waitress as she brought me my knuckle of chilli fried eggs which I didn't even need to ask for.

Just seen Ecuador beat Cost Rica 3-0. A feature of Germany 2006, well the tournament I am experiencing, is the TV coverage. Too many of the presenters/pundits have dodgy teeth. Honestly, the quality of dentistry is very poor. Watch any American TV show and everyone has piano key teeth, white, even and expensive, probably cost more than your house. Not a poor tooth anywhere to be seen. Even some guy buying a drink in a bar has teeth most of us would kill for. A passer by in the street, some unknown extra in a movie scene, grins and shows his $10,000 smile. Americans make fun of everyone else's teeth and they have a point.

On English TV they tend to make sure the talking heads have reasonable teeth, but over here too many smiles are like looking at a row of condemned houses. Having said that, no one's teeth will EVER be worse than the Queen Mother's, sorry ma'am. Like, how bad were HER teeth? You prayed she never smiled because all you ever saw was a row of black stumps, tombstone teeth. One would have thought the Buck House dentist could have done something to nanny's nashers.

Anyway, I digress. It's a bit off-putting when some German Alan Hansen is pontificating about Costa Rica and his teeth are in a worse condition than their back-four. And with as many gaps. One station has Steffen Freund, famous for never scoring a goal throughout his career with Tottenham, as a pundit. His teeth are as good as his finishing. I shall remain on Germany 2006 tooth-watch throughout the tournament to inform you of updates.

When the Germans have a public holiday they mean it. Like, everywhere is closed. Couldn't even get a knuckle-of-anything roll. The hotel's room service could only offer me "some cheese".

So apart from the knuckle of chilli fried eggs as Groundhog Day breakfast, I have had a [sad bastard] bar of plain chocolate, which I had put in the fridge for an emergency (it's arrived) and a Powerade. I hope the Sad Bastard bar can serve me my penne arrabiata later.

Watching England v T&T in the Sad Bastard Bar with laptop for company. How garbage are we? Sven will get stick but the players deserve an absolute panning too. Two goals … three points … and lucky England.

The Sad Bastard Bar is far emptier than last night, unsurprisingly. There are only about a dozen people in my local, one is smoking, think he's an Arab, and my guess is he is smoking camel dung. The smell, and he is about 15 feet away, is disgustingly pungent.

How anyone can get pleasure from inhaling dried camel pooh is beyond me. But then he probably wouldn't like cheese and Marmite on toast or a knuckle of chilli fried eggs. Through the smog Sweden v Paraguay seems a decent match.

FRIDAY JUNE 16
Usual breakfast, if you don't know the score by now you have not been paying attention.

Earlyish start for Stuttgart where the Holland v Ivory Coast game should be a cracker. On the way to the Metro two guys came up to me and asked me for directions to Marianplatz. Having almost a taxi driver's knowledge of Munich by now ("you'll never guess who asked me the way to Marianplatz today…") I was able to tell them they needed to take the U8 to Forettmaning – in fact, I am going that way, follow me guys.

It turned out they were from Colorado Springs and were on vacation (aka holiday, but you can't tell 260 million Americans the word is in fact 'holiday'). They are Denver Broncos fans needless to say and we were soon chatting about the motorbike accident Pittsburgh quarterback Ben Roethlisberger had been involved in. They did not seem to find it at all strange that some English bloke should know anything about Ben's bike accident or even knew who he was.

I remember being in Florence once (nice girl) where a group of Americans on the next table were wondering how the San Francisco 49ers had got on the previous night. I was able to tell them the result, who scored the touchdowns, etc. Again they seemed to think it was perfectly natural that some limey in Florence should know chapter and verse about the NFL's Monday night game.

Train journey to Stuttgart was uneventful. I wrote my previews to Australia v Brazil and Iran v Portugal, and was told I shan't be covering Paraguay v Trinidad & Tobago, the last game in England's group which will be played simultaneously with our boys inevitably failing to beat Sweden, in Kaiserslautern next Tuesday (not worth the time and money, would have to stay the night) which means another free day – well, a nogame day.

The security at the stadium was once again a pain. They will not let anyone bring in a drink that is not one of the official sponsors', sorry, corporate partners'. So if you have, say, a Pepsi you have to scrape off the label (if it's a plastic bottle) or throw it in the trash can. Or drink it on the spot. This has lead to one mass protest where several hundred people arrived at a ground wearing branded clothes of a non-corporate partner, causing mayhem as the security cordon demanded they removed every last stitch!

The security measures are ridiculous. They search your bag, but are not qualified to do so. The basic technique involves opening the bag and peering inside. They asked me to open my sunglasses case, but didn't bother with my camera case while two parts of the bag simply weren't looked in. We have to go through this process twice before getting into the media stand, each time taking about 15 minutes including queue time. And it is a pain in the arse. No sympathy please.

The game was, as anticipated, excellent, Ivory Coast just lacking the ruthlessness to punish Holland, who won 2-1. Afterwards I took the media shuttle back to the station, the coach packed full of international hacks. A

Chinese snapper (female) had breath that could be smelt at probably 10 paces. The shuttle was due to leave at 45 minutes past the hour, but by half past it was chocca. However, even though a fly would have struggled to get into the packed bus the driver insisted on keeping us waiting for 15 minutes in searing heat and strange smells.

Splendid night out in Stuttgart with my son Kerry plus his mates Mark, Charlie and Pete who are over here for a week, living in a mobile home type vehicle. Eventually we found a tasty pasta place where food and liquid was taken on board. For me it was unusual, but welcome to speak to people while eating. Or just to speak to people really. Or just not eat alone.

We witnessed the memorable sight of a Dutch fan, the worse for wear, falling down about a dozen concrete steps, getting up and walking – ok, staggering – on totally unharmed. Just watching him tumbling was painful, but alcohol can have a great numbing effect. Not the following morning though.

Got to my scratcher at about one, another wonderful hotel where I had another suite. And I am back to the same hotel next Wednesday for Australia v Croatia.

SATURDAY JUNE 17
Went for breakfast and bumped into Australian midfielder Tim Cahill's parents, who I met at a barbecue last summer. In fact, the breakfast bar was full of Aussies – the parents, wives etc of the Australia team were all staying in the hotel.

To Frankfurt for Portugal versus Iran, second time I've seen Iran in a week. They'll be calling me the Ayatollah soon. Did a piece with talkSPORT at 2pm, the Paul Hawksbee and Andy Jacobs show, one of the best football programmes on the radio. Among the topics we spoke about was the French player who had a haemorrhoid operation last week but was back in action after six days. "Obviously has piles of talent," was my starter for 10

2006 WORLD CUP

bad puns. H&J have maintained an incredibly high standard over the years to make it one of the funniest, most entertaining of sports programmes.

Portugal 2 Iran 0 was neither funny nor particularly entertaining. Average springs to mind and that's being kind. I've had a mixed bag of games, but the Ghana 2 Czech Republic 0 match I watched on the rattler returning to my Munich headquarters, was breathtaking. Ghana should have won 6-0.

So ends the second week of Germany 2006. The football has been generally good with five or six belting games. Argentina (modesty does not prevent me from reminding you they were my pre-World Cup tip) look the best team so far and pulverised Serbia & Montenegro 6-0.

Arrived back to the Hotel Exquisit and some dry cleaning, which I had left earlier in the day, had been delivered. Alarmingly, also included in the package were three pairs of knickers, two bras and a blouse. I know it's the weekend but ... As they aren't my size I shall return them to reception in the morning.

Saw an enthralling Italy 1 USA 1 in the Sad Bastard Bar. American defender Eddie Pope was sent-off. Does that mean Pope gets a one-mass ban plus VAT? Maybe he'll star in a new movie – *Benedict Like Beckham*.

You know the Americans who asked me for directions? They came into the bar. Spotted me. So I had dinner with two blokes. Hey, it's been almost two weeks away.

SUNDAY JUNE 18
Breakfast was crowded by recent standards and among the guests was Steffen Effenberg, a terrific midfield player for Bayern Munich and Germany in the Nineties. All blond hair and blue eyes, too. Mysteriously, he was wearing a tracksuit with "Cassius Clay The Greatest" on the back.

Today is Brazil versus Australia, so the atmosphere in Munich later tonight will be superb. Samba versus Sydney, football versus Foster's. I have been allocated a ticket for the match, but there are some journos less fortunate. They were christened 'the Waitlisters' by Dion Fanning of the *Sunday Independent* in Ireland.

At Holland versus the Ivory Coast, Dion told me there had been 286 Waitlisters, the international hack pack beggars at the gate, hoping to claim one of the returns/cancelled tickets/no shows. The Waitlisters look at we Ticketers with a combination of envy and anger.

"Why has HE got a pass and not me?" Their inferiority complex is obvious as the media class system kicks in. The Ticketers have a certain arrogance and spring in their step. Us and them. We have considerably more tickets than yaoooouuuuw.

Match tickets must be collected by the Ticketers (if they want to stay Ticketers) 90 minutes before the game and the Waitlisters (who hope to become Ticketers by hook or by crook) start hovering then, edging closer to the front as the clock ticks down. An hour and a half before the game begins, the list closes. If you have a ticket and arrive at this point you will not get it, even if the reason for your delay has been the interminable body and laptop bag searches necessary before you enter the stadium, kidnapping or a holdup.

To date there has only been one exception which came after what Dion called "a media uprising" when the shuttle delayed a contingent of hacks who had left plenty of time to pick up their tickets. Faced with the indignation of a busload of Ticketer hacks determined not to become Waitlisters, FIFA begrudgingly relented.

There are many different approaches to wait-listing. Some like to get to the stadium early, have a chat with the girls at the desk and let it be known that they are immensely agreeable, nothing they can do will upset them and will happily accept any decision they make, especially if in involves a ticket at the end of it. That necessitates charm, charisma, nice teeth and good breath.

More commonly, the hapless Waitlisters arrive just as the waiting list is being opened, shout loudly, then swear, shout even louder and then swear louder in whatever language they can before demanding the immediate appearance of the head of press or even FIFA President Sepp Blatter, who one of the Waitlisters always knows "very well – so be it on your head..." It is wait-listing bullshit, the Waitlister knows it and worse, the people in charge of the ticketing desk know it too.

It was fascinating as proud-to-be-Ticketers watched the Waitlisters waiting for the moment when the names of those who were lucky enough to be upgraded from Waitlister to Ticketer had their names read out like Rowan Atkinson in the *Secret Policeman's Ball*. It is almost cruel that it isn't even done in alphabetical order, so the tension goes all the way.

Dion said Waitlisters' hearts sank when a man in a FIFA pinstripe suit appeared from behind the stage, consulted with two other men and began the process without any consultation with the women who had been handling the situation and who some of the Waitlisters had been working on big time. Maybe even dinner.

Life is not easy for Waitlisters.

Watching Brazil at the World Cup is just about as good as it gets. Their history, reputation, fans, the colour, atmosphere make for a wonderful spectacle. All those nights at Selhurst Park in the cold seem worthwhile. They were a shade lucky against Australia and 2-0 certainly flattered them. You know it isn't your day when a Brazilian substitute called Fred scores against you in the 89th minute.

I hope Oz can beat Croatia and qualify for the second phase, though. I'll be there in Stuttgart to watch them later in the week (which is a way of saying I am not sure whether it's Wednesday or Thursday).

Tom Humphries of the *Irish Times*, one of the best sportswriters in the world, is in the Exquisit till Tuesday and is allegedly joining me in the Sad Bastard Bar later. Tom has had offers to join English newspapers but has stayed with the *Irish Times*, which is their gain. His Locker Room columns on Mondays are essential reads. It is difficult for a sports journalist to be genuinely funny while writing about football or boxing, but Tom manages this better than anybody.

MONDAY JUNE 19

A moment of hilarity in the press box after Brazil v Australia yesterday. The France v South Korea game was on TV and a Korean player called Hu was booked. A hack from China and one from Brazil had the following conversation and you have to think how it sounded as they spoke:

China: "Who was booked?"

Brazil: "Yes."

China: "No, who was booked?"

Brazil: "Yes he was."

China: "Who was?"

Brazil: "Yes."

China: "No, not yes ... who was booked? Which player?"

Brazil: "Hu."

China: "No, I am asking you..."

Brazil: "I told you. Hu?"

China (to me by now): "Who was it who was booked?"

England: "Hu."

Brazil: "I told him..."

China: "What number player...?"

At this moment the fun and games ended. Shame.

I was joined at the Sad Bastard Bar by Tom and Liam Mackey (*Cork Examiner*) where we cheered Hu and the gang. Sadly, Hu did not score because we were desperate to start a "who scored?" routine. Liam had to catch the 12.30am train to somewhere, getting in at 5.30am. We said that we would assume he had arrived safely, so don't ring us Liam, not necessary.

Tom and Liam were hugely impressed that Juliet, the Vietnamese waitress, was so attentive of our party. I didn't like to say that it might have something to do with the fact that previous time I was there, the bill came to 26 euro and instead of giving her 30 euro, taking into account the usual 10% tip, I had inadvertently given her 40, thus trebling her expectations.

Should be a relatively easy day today. A 600-word follow-up on Brazil's Ronaldo and that's it. No game for me.

Breathwatch: the standard of breath at Germany 2006 is poor. Very low. I have noticed different aromas from different countries (is that breathology?) – hard to describe so far, but the Chinese female snapper is by far the worst. However, there was a guy from Brazil sitting next to me in the press box yesterday and I could smell his breath even when he wasn't talking to me, a serious achievement, especially outdoors.

Teethwatch: they don't have any dentists in Croatia. They can't have. The Croats in the hack pack have by far (collectively) the worst teeth. No two teeth seem the same colour or size. I dread any of them smiling, when they do it looks like a motor accident.

More on these important subjects later.

So much for the easy day. I ended up writing 1,400 words today, a Ronaldo followup, a piece on Harry Kewell and a preview to Paraguay v Trinidad & Tobago. Decided to go for a walk to get some roll-on underarm deodorant to take to Stuttgart, security not allowing spray-on stuff at stadiums.

Back at the hotel I put on my Togo T-shirt (okay … I know … I know) to watch them lose 2-0 to Switzerland on TV. Next up is Ukraine versus Saudi Arabia, Spain v Tunisia is the 9pm game, but if Tom's around and fancies a nosebag in town that match may be sacrificed.

TUESDAY JUNE 20
Did not watch Spain v Tunisia last night, first game I have not seen. Had a splendid dinner with Tom Humphries in a Rathaus at Marianplatz. And,

honestly, the Bavarian red wine was excellent even if it sounds a contradiction of terms.

Tom was the journo who conducted the controversial interview with Roy Keane just before the 2002 World Cup that effectively caused Keano to be sent home by Republic of Ireland manager Mick McCarthy after the mother of all rows. Tom was recently at a school near Dublin doing a Q&A session, first question came from a 13-year-old boy.

"Are you the journalist who did the Keano interview in Saipan four years ago...?"

"Er ... yes..."

The boy was seen whispering something to his pal.

"What are you saying...?"

"I'm just telling me mate that me dad said you were the * * * * who * * * * * * up our World Cup in 2002..."

Tom has now left the Exquisit, so once again I am Home Alone. It'll be the Sad Bastard Bar for me tonight to watch England v Sweden. Working conditions uncomfortable – it was bloody hot as I wrote my Serbia & Montenegro v Ivory Coast preview on the sun terrace.

Been watching CNN and the Saddam Hussein trial is still going on and on. Have you seen him? I must say he looks terrific. Trim, smart beard, nice suit – being locked up is obviously doing him good. Like being in a health farm.

What puzzles me is that he has quite a lot of grey in his beard but his hair is jet black. Not a sign of a grey hair anywhere. How can a guy nearer 70 than 60 have a grey beard and totally black hair? Is his hair going prematurely black?

Right, off to the Sad Bastard Bar to watch Sven's adopted country hopefully beat the country where he was born. I am pessimistic. And rightly so, it turned out. We cannot beat the Swedes. A 2-2 draw also gives us a serious injury to Michael Owen and a great goal from Joe Cole, but Sweden deserved to win. So it's England v Ecuador on Sunday in Stuttgart, which means I will almost certainly cover Germany v Sweden on Saturday.

WEDNESDAY JUNE 21

Last night was the usual Groundhog Bar routine. Dinner at the Sad Bastard Bar with Juliet not even bothering to ask me what I wanted to drink or eat. One night she'll even know what time I will arrive and it'll all be there on the table.

The heavens opened for the first time during the finals. I was preparing for a lazy if wet day before going to the Ivory Coast v Serbia & Montenegro in Munich tonight when the desk rang – could I get to Bad Kissingen for a press conference? I made the train to Nuremberg by the skin of my better than average teeth. And didn't I just love saying to a taxi driver when I arrived in Nuremberg: "Bad Kissingen." What a dateline – "By Christopher Davies, Bad Kissingen." Got back about 9.30pm to see most of a drab game between Holland and Argentina, both of whom have already qualified. Tomorrow I'm off to Stuttgart and Australia v Croatia, which could be lively.

As expected, I have Germany v Sweden in Munich on the first day of the knockout phase games followed by Portugal v Holland in Nuremberg on Sunday, 9pm kick-off so staying over.

THURSDAY JUNE 22 and FRIDAY JUNE 23

Why no diary Thursday? Because at the end of one of the most frustrating days/nights of my career at 2.30am I was in the back of a taxi being driven from Stuttgart to Munich, the journey costing 350 euro.

And why was I taking my most expensive taxi ride ever? I had covered Croatia v Australia and to cut an incredibly boring story short (be grateful) I turned up at the Maritim Hotel, checked in and was given the key to room 754, opened it to find an Australian guy already in the room.

"G'day mate, seems to have been a bit of a cock-up," he said, posting an immediate candidate for Understatement of the Year. Indeed. Despite checking me in and being given a key (albeit to a room already occupied by Bruce) the Maritim Hotel in fact had no booking for me, even though I had a booking confirmation.

Nicky, our diamond of a sports desk secretary, sorted my life out as I stood like a Waitlister outside the Maritim. I was finally told I had a hotel a mere seven miles outside the city confirmed for the night.

Or not.

A nightmare chain of events had begun with English referee Graham Poll making the biggest error of his career in failing to sendoff Croatian defender Josip Simunic despite showing him two yellow cards, which will sadly give a lot of people a lot of pleasure. Will he ever live this down?

At 1am, relieved that I now had a bed for the night, I went to the FIFA Help Desk or as it turned out, the No Help Desk, to ask whether this new hotel was nearer the stadium or city centre. Nearer the stadium a local yokel told me. The No Help Desk said they would phone for a taxi "that will be here in four to 10 minutes." I should have smelt a knuckle of rat – "four to 10 minutes?"

Naively I allowed the 1.15am media shuttle to leave. By 1.30am there was no sign of a cab. The No Help Desk re-phoned (if there is such a word, to be honest, don't care). "Five minutes Mr Davies."

I said: "Phone them back and say if it isn't here in five minutes I get a free trip." He did and they were unappreciative of my request. To the extent they put the phone down on him. Bad tactical error. So it was now gone 1.30am, the shuttle bus had left, next one was at 2.15am and the cab company was now flatly refusing to come to the stadium. Apart from that life was great.

Another cab company was phoned and a cab turned up at 2am by which time I had taken grumpiness to new heights, or depths. "You say * * * * a lot," observed the boy from the No * * * * * * * Help Desk.

A 30-minute ride to God knows where and I finally arrived at the new hotel about 2.30am. It was full – "and we were this afternoon," was my greeting. I am tired, hungry, miserable, foul-mouthed, short-tempered and willing to not only mention the war but start another one – my usual self then.

The thankfully friendly fraulein spoke to the Travel Company's 24-hour help line who said that "there must have been a glitch with our computer to not show it was full." That's OK then.

The Travel Company person working the graveyard shift phoned around, but unsurprisingly there were no hotels available. The next Stuttgart-Munich train, a slowie, was 4.20am. I could hang around the station till then (risking my laptop and other such stuff, so not really advisable) catch it, get home heaven knows what time or, as I did, took a cab. Cost? A mere 350 euro. The office will love that. God bless the Travel Company.

It was in the back of loads-a-euro cab that the nightmare continued. A kip was impossible as the driver, far too cheerful for my liking at that hour, had satnav, so every few minutes I heard a voice telling him where he should be going.

Got back at the Exquisit at 4.30am confident that no-one in the world, probably in the history of the world, had ever been in a worse mood than me.

Today (Friday) has been a downer. After all the positives of the World Cup I feel deflated. The double hotel cock-up wee-wee'd me off mightily while three hours' kip is never the best preparation for the day. I am also still coming to terms with Graham Poll's three-card trick during Australia v Croatia. Bottom line is, what Graham did (or didn't do – i.e. send-off a player having shown him two yellow cards) is unforgivable and probably inexplicable. Had it not happened, the World Cup final could have been his – one mistake, albeit a humdinger, and he's out of the tournament. And people say referees aren't accountable.

I like Graham. Having collaborated with him on a book I got to know him well and he gave me the sort of insight into refereeing few journalists have been afforded. I am surprised more football writers don't make a bigger effort to include referees among their contacts. We write about the referee in almost every match report yet too many journalists (and commentators) have a less than basic knowledge of the laws, getting away with this because supporters are not clued up either.

I believe football hacks probably have less awareness of the laws of the sport they cover than most sports journalists. Mind you, managers and players are the same. They will often bang on about how you have to have played the game to know what it's like, but never having refereed (or taken the trouble to learn the laws even to a better than average degree) doesn't stop them from telling the referee, who HAS learnt the laws fully, that he was wrong.

For me, one of the saddest developments in football in recent years is that Premiership match officials are now driven to and from stadiums in safe cars. This came about after too many referees were verbally insulted or even physically attacked in the car park. One ref had to drive through a red light at West Ham as fans started to bang on his car and attempted to open the doors after a game.

This is a knock-on effect from the constant criticism (aka passing the buck) by the losing manager who blames the referee for his team's defeat, seeking to divert attention away from his own failings. Supporters have been brainwashed by serial moaning managers and assume that when their side is beaten the ref must be to blame.

I know of many cases where managers have slated the ref at a press conference yet have given him good marks in his official report to the FA. "Sorry mate, you know how it is," one manager said to the referee by way of justifying such hypocrisy and double-standards.

In fact, the referee is the most honest person on the pitch. Yes, he will make mistakes, but they are honest mistakes. When a player makes an honest mistake like missing an open goal or allowing the ball to slip through his hands it is … well, a human error. Refs aren't allowed to make them though.

Referees become back page news because managers use them as convenient scapegoats for defeat. Most refereeing decisions are subjective … the referee's opinion … made in an instant at real speed without slow-motion replays from different angles. How much easier it is to spot an error then?

Christopher Davies steps down from his soapbox and makes the familiar journey to the Sad Bastard Bar where the words sorrow and drown immediately sprang to mind.

SATURDAY JUNE 24

It occurred to me while I was at said bar last night, being served by Juliet, that I may not return. Just in case, I asked Juliet for chilli con carne so I could hear her say it with her Vietnamese twang. But then … read on.

Didn't wake up till 10.50am this morning, which is nature's way of telling me that I was officially knackered. Meant I missed my chilli fried eggs. But a man needs a breakfast, so where did I go? Yes, the Sad Bastard Brekkie Bar for knuckle of croissants, strawberry jam, freshly squeezed OJ and a cup of German coffee.

I had an unexpected visitor while wearing only my underpants this morning. I was on the phone when a guy just let himself in my room, said "pardon me, sir," checked the mini-bar, walked out saying "just checking mini-bar…" (which I had managed to pick up on) as I stood there in my Marks and Spencer specials.

Chatted to Paul Hayward to see how his World Cup was going. I worked with Paul on the *Daily Telegraph* for more than 10 years before his move to the *Daily Mail* and rarely have I met a journalist so ego-free (or even chilli fried ego-free). He may just be the most popular writer in what I still call Fleet Street. His columns are wonderfully crafted and hit the spot, with Paul's own brand of humour a welcome bonus.

And so to Germany v Sweden, Germany winning 2-0 without breaking sweat. Had arranged to meet Tom Humphries and a couple of the other Irish journos in town to watch Argentina v Mexico. Received a text from Tom, who's staying in the Exquisit: "Rather than go into town which will be packed, we are in Mozart's." So breakfast AND dinner in the Sad Bastard Bar, where the previous night I thought I was making my last visit. Wrong.

You can take the man out of the Sad Bastard Bar but...

SUNDAY JUNE 25

Surely it was my last night (again) in the SBB? Argentina 2 Mexico 1 was a stunning game with a winning goal in extra-time by Maxi Rodriguez worthy of such a fabulous match.

I am now in Nuremberg for Portugal v Holland. Met Jon Brodkin of the *Guardian* on the train, hardly a word was exchanged, not because we don't like each other but we were both writing our Germany v Sweden match reports.

There is a clear hierarchy at media centres/stadiums. Those with Access All Areas accreditation are the big knobs. There are nine categories of access – as a humble hack I have three, a 3, 6 and 7 which is public area, media stand and media centre. That probably makes me a little knob, which, on top of being an honorary member (no pun intended) of the Sad Bastard Bar, is not good.

We little knobs look at the big knobs with a combination of awe and jealousy. The first thing we LK's do is peek at the name on the BK's accreditation to see who he is. Mostly they are FIFA guys with names you have never heard of, many you can't pronounce ... some from countries you've never heard of. Doesn't matter. He's a BK, you aren't. Respect.

As BK's they deserve it. You allow them out of the lift first because as an LK you know your position. BK's first, MK's and especially LK's, the smallest of the small ... pond life second. You wonder in your dreams ... even for a day ... you might be an Access All Areas Big Knob. How wonderful to walk past the shit of a security guy who has delighted in his "sorry, you can't go there" attitude … looking him right in the eye, proudly wearing your AAA (BK) identification.

You know he's desperate to stop you, but the sudden realisation that you are, even if he has no idea why, a big knob … an Untouchable … Access All Areas … got that sunshine … ALL areas … and you smile the surly smile of a BK as you walk past … his arm, desperate to be stuck out blocking your path, has to stay by his side … ALL areas … read my lips baby. ALL areas … make my day.

Back in the real world (cup) David Beckham has just done what he does best, scoring from a superb free-kick even if he was helped by the Ecuadorian wall breaking up. A less than convincing England win ensued, which will keep the hack pack with them for another match rather than allowing them to spread their wings and covering other countries.

Nice quiet game between Portugal and Holland – just the 16 yellow and four red cards, a World Cup record. The referee lost the plot and control in a game that left me bemused. How can professionals be so unprofessional? It means England will play Portugal in the quarter-finals, who will have Deco and Costinha suspended, while Cristiano Ronaldo might be injured after the Dutch kicked him off the park. Sven's appetite for the opposite sex has got him in trouble quite often but he won't mind having Lady Luck with him that night.

I am now on the 1.10am train from Nuremberg back to Munich, having decided against staying. The train gets in to Munich at 2.25am, so it won't be mega late by the time I get back in my hotel suite, complete with 3seat sofa, armchair, table and desk etc.

The World Cup is taking shape now – Germany v Argentina (the big one) and Portugal v England (the medium one) are two tasty-looking quarter-finals. I'll see what the desk wants me to do for the rest of the week tomorrow. I am booked to stay in my hotel suite until Tuesday.

MONDAY JUNE 26

Got back to my suite at the Exquisit at about 3am and managed around five hours' sleep. Last night's was a demanding game to cover, never have I seen a match where the referee showed 16 yellow and four red cards. Few people have.

It is very, very hot out here and even hotter in the media shuttle buses. They are very popular with the media because (a) they are free and (b) because they bypass the outer-perimeter security search, which is time-consuming and ineffective. I had a body search yesterday and the guy didn't notice the mobile phone in my shirt pocket. Just the 40-minute wait for that. Ridiculous.

So because of (a) – particularly (a) – and (b) the media shuttles have become the must-take way from the station to the stadium. However, they have become a victim of their own popularity. Yesterday in Nuremberg the shuttle was full beyond imagination. Sardines? Dream of being a sardine. That would be an idyllic existence. By the time the shuttle bus moved off it was so crammed that synchronised breathing was necessary.

It is 9pm and my name is Christopher Davies and I am a Sad Bastard (applause from other SBs). Hey Christopher…yeh!!! I get sad hugs in turn from all the other outed SBs. I don't have to tell you where I am watching Ukraine v Switzerland. The place is a magnet. I promised myself I wouldn't go there…no…no…no…but I have all the willpower of Posh Spice and a shopping spree. The SBB is like a magnet. This MUST be the last visit surely but I said that yesterday and the day before.

TUESDAY JUNE 27

My last full day in Munich. Tomorrow I shall be off to Hamburg – six hours on the train – for the much anticipated (not) Italy v Ukraine game on Friday night. After that, down to Frankfurt for Brazil v Spain or France then home for a couple of days of R and R before probably returning to Dortmund on

Tuesday for a semi-final. I have packed most of my stuff – or rather stuffed most of my packing in the case. I just have to put the rest in and jump on it.

Italy are all style and sexy. Ukraine are all ugly, crap names and lousy clothes. Italy have Luca Toni (OK, he sounds like a sports drink, but a sexy one), Alessandro del Piero and Francesco Totti. Ukraine have Volodimir Yezerski and Vladislav Vashchuk – no comparison with even the worst Italian names. While the Italians play for Roma, Juventus or Palermo, Ukraine players play for Kryvbas Kyvvyi Rih, Krylya Sovetov Samare and Dnipro Dnipropetrovsk. No wonder they put in for a transfer. They want to play for a team they can pronounce.

Well, I did it. At 8.37pm tonight I did it. I left the Exquisit and walked past the Sad Bastard Bar. When Juliet waved, my conscience (even if I had to look up the word) was pricked. I watched the France v Spain game in town, the French winning 3-1. But the biggest result of the night was Sad Bastard Bar 0, Sad Bastard 1.

WEDNESDAY JUNE 28

Incredibly the staff did not form a guard of honour, or even dishonour as I said auf wiedersehen to the Exquisit to head for Hamburg. A last knuckle of chilli fried eggs on toast served by a fraulein whose name I never did find out. The very nice guy at reception said he hoped I had enjoyed my stay as he handed me a bill that Bill Gates would have had his chief accountant haggle over. I gave one last tearful look at the Sad Bastard Bar and it was goodbye from me. And so to Hamburg.

No Sad Bastard Bar in Hamburg, but the sad bastard remains. No other troops in town until tomorrow, but again I have a fabulous hotel with – yes, a suite. All open plan and very swish. I went out for a walk around the block, but no restaurants or eateries, so came back and ate in the hotel's restaurant. Table for one please. As usual. I think the Germans have a new slang word – a Davies. It means a table for one.

THURSDAY JUNE 29

It took me 15 minutes to work out how to turn off the air conditioning and all the lights plus drawing the curtains before I went to sleep last night. All done by a remote control that wasn't remote or control enough for me. Best of all is that the floor by the wash basin and in the toilet is heated. I can do what a man has to do with warm feet. Marvellous.

Breakfast was different class. Among the freshly squeezed juices were cucumber and carrot, plus something pink which I couldn't understand the label of. Real men don't drink pink, though. Eight different types of yogurt, four different melons – the chilli fried eggs are history. Lovely fresh fruit salad with freshly squeezed orange juice, some French toast and bacon to follow. For dessert, two croissants with bilberry jam, whatever a bilberry is, but it was tasty.

Did a preview to the Italy v Ukraine tie which has obviously captivated the universe. Then tonight … not sure … not heard from anyone so maybe the other troops are coming tomorrow from wherever just for the mouth-watering match.

Went for a stroll about 8pm and I saw an Eastern Market. Worth checking out, VERY worthwhile it turned out. There was a stall that was cooking Indian food … I went in search of paradise and found heaven. Chicken jalfrezi, pilau rice and vegetable curry … 11 euro.

Washed down with a glass of white wine that was … well, chilled. It was not the best ruby I have ever had, but I struggle to recall one that was more welcome.

I sat down on a sort of communal bench by a table that seated six (there were about 20 such benches to accommodate the customers of all the stalls) and enjoyed the ruby so much I almost forgave the guy sitting next to me who lit up when he had finished some dish from Syria, probably knuckle of sand. A coughing bout from yours truly did not seem to have any effect on him. Anyway he left and then there were two … me at one end and some guy wearing a tracksuit top and trousers, very smart mate – at the other.

My plate licked clean, I got up to leave, which had uncomfortable consequences for Mr Smart Track Suit. The bench went up my end and down his like a seesaw and he fell off, probably not expecting the bench he was sitting on to suddenly fly ceilingwards as it did. He didn't appear to find being on his ass particularly funny, but he was in a minority of one, the three kids on the next table finding it apparently one of the funniest things they had ever seen.

I wandered away from the unlikely cabaret to see what other stalls may take my eye. There was one that sold Chilean wine and to rewash down my gift from above I had a glass of chardonnay. As I was supping aforementioned liquid a girl working on the stall asked me if I had 30 minutes to spare (I could have said I'd just had 30 days to spare) as she was organising a wine-tasting competition.

Eight of us sat down at a table with a proper bench and were poured six different types of wine, all from Chile. We were even given a bowl to spit out the wine if we so desired. The three women spat and the five guys swallowed. Make of that what you wish.

The eight tasters set about their arduous task. We had to write down marks out of 10 for each wine with the winner a sauvignon blanc. There was quite a big crowd watching and the session was completed when the spitters and swallowers were given a bottle of the winning wine.

I returned to my suite and watched the third episode of *Life on Mars*, an excellent series that I missed when it was on TV. I can see there is an element of sadness about watching a DVD on your laptop in a hotel room/suite, but the comforting effects of the jalfrezi and sauvignon blanc overcame this.

FRIDAY JUNE 30
Ukraine versus Italy tonight, two teams who have almost limped to the

quarter-finals, but one now has a chance to be one game from the final. As 'small' countries tend not to get within touching distance of the big one, World Cup logic says Italy will beat Ukraine.

Some of the troops will be in town tonight, but as the game kicks-off at 8pm local time no chance of dinner afterwards, especially if there is extra-time and penalties. I shall leave for the stadium at about 3 o'clock to ensure I get a decent seat in the media centre for Germany v Argentina, slightly more appetising than my match.

I am now at the Hamburg media centre eating a Greek salad. An eventful journey here. One stop on the train and I boarded with an elderly guy who went to the special section at the end of each carriage for pensioners. Sitting in the area were three people – a mum, dad and son who each had a bike – either side of the carriage with the bikes in between them.

The old guy really let rip, both barrels AND the hand gun. He was obviously telling them that they had no right to sit in 'his' area and they were defending their stance (if sitting down can be a stance). Now you probably think he was bang to rights and the Bike Family were defending the indefensible. The weakness in his rant was that the carriage was empty apart from the Bike Family, Mr Rant and Sad Bastard.

They had sat there because had they sat somewhere else their bikes could possibly have caused an obstruction. And like me, Mr Rant was only going one stop, but it didn't stop him having a one-stop rant. I wondered if there was a German equivalent of "on your bike."

The media shuttle to Hamburg stadium was the usual collection of bad breath and bad smells. Some guys are unaware that after three weeks away doing your laundry is a fine investment. Surely they must be able to smell themselves – or do they constantly think it's the guy NEXT to them? I'm all for a bit of self-denial but…

At the stadium I watched Germany beat Argentina on penalties. It is what Germany do. Win shootouts and reach World Cup finals.

SATURDAY JULY 1

I shall know later today my plans for next week. If England beat Portugal I shall be in Dortmund next Tuesday for Germany v Italy. If England lose it's auf wiedersehen Germany. No more knuckles.

Reading on the wires about Germany and penalty shootouts and came across the homework and background they do for such eventualities. As the Germans prepared for the penalty series, a member of their coaching staff slipped a piece of paper into goalkeeper Jens Lehmann's gloved hand. On it were the names of Argentina's penalty takers and the direction in which they usually shoot.

Lehmann stopped shots from Roberto Ayala and Esteban Cambiasso, correctly guessing both times, and nearly saved the other two shots as well.

The Arsenal 'keeper discretely consulted the list between the penalties, keeping it in his right sock. "We didn't know the order they would shoot in, so he had to look," said Germany team manager Oliver Bierhoff. "We have a very detailed scouting program. Our goalkeeper got very detailed information. He was told who usually takes penalties on the Argentina team, he was shown videos of all the penalties they had shot in the past two years, who shot them, whether they shot left or right."

Might explain why Germany are serial shootout winners.

And so to Frankfurt for Brazil v France, a France 98 final rematch. There could also be a Germany v Brazil final for the second successive World Cup, which would not necessarily be good for the game. Not exactly an indication of how the sport has moved on.

England are out of the World Cup after doing what they usually do. Reach the quarter-finals and lose a penalty shootout, this time to Portugal, then look for someone else to blame. For the fifth time since 1990 we lost a penalty shootout in a major tournament. We lack the mental strength and inner confidence to win these things.

If there is a silver lining it is that I will be flying home tomorrow. My World Cup is over at pretty well the point I thought it would be. I shall have been away for 26 days and my garden and fish need me.

Germany 2006 has been more enjoyable than I anticipated. Having good accommodation helped. The free first class travel was an enormous perk. It is impossible to say how much this cost the organisers because I can't remember an occasion when journos took the seats of what would have been paying customers, the trains were generally far from full.

The organisation was terrific. A hole can always be picked but FIFA/Germany have done an absolutely first-class job of organising the most difficult, demanding and moaning profession in the world. The people have been incredibly friendly and helpful (the odd security guy apart). My computer has worked regularly. The weather in Munich was almost too hot, hardly a major problem. There was a glitch with the Stuttgart hotel but I'd give the trip 8.5 out of 10 and that is a good mark, I promise you.

The chilli fried eggs, the Sad Bastard Bar, yes it's been fun. On July 12th I go into hospital for a total knee replacement operation, the result of a mugging – or rather attempted mugging – in Marseille some years ago...

From Hock to the Doc.

Germany v Republic of Ireland, Stuttgart, Aug/Sept 2006

TUESDAY AUGUST 29

Seven weeks, one total knee replacement operation and other statistics best not made public since returning from the World Cup in Germany, and I am preparing for my first competitive international of 2006/07 in ... Germany. However, I am travelling to Stuttgart via the scenic route – Dublin.

We fly to Stuttgart on Thursday afternoon for the Euro 2008 qualifying tie, but new Republic of Ireland manager Steve Staunton and the players are holding their Thursday press conference on Wednesday (this is Ireland) at 10.30am, straight after the scheduled Wednesday press conference, hence my early departure for Dublin.

The day started at the dump. Took some garden refuse (at first it didn't want to go) and an old hi-fi down to the council dump. I thought it would be a case of pulling the hi-fi unit from the boot and putting it on to the rubbish pile. Oh no, not any more. Each type of rubbish now has its own skip and woe betide anyone who puts the wrong type of rubbish in the wrong tip.

The recycle Nazis are watching. The skip was about six feet high, so I had to ask a burly lorry driver to help me lift my old Pioneer system up and over into the correct skip. Life used to be easier than this.

The desk wanted four pieces from me before I left for Gatwick Airport. Three news pieces and a bit on Ireland who have a new player in the squad with the magnificent name Sean St Ledger, who sadly does not play for Derby. St Ledger (Derby) would be a player/club combo hard to beat (even by a short head). Whatever, St Ledger (Preston) is not bad either.

Security at Gatwick was tighter than Joan Collins' face, though I thought being asked if I had any hair gel was a tad over the top (my bald pate being one of my more charming attributes). "Sorry sir ... we have to ask." Thankfully there was a party of six noisy, screaming kids on the plane. What better than the sound of happy kids playing and shouting? Rather than read a book, a paper or just relax, we had The Bash Street Kids giving it large.

I shall be staying at the Herbert Park hotel (as usual) and I hope my groundwork on Rosa, a receptionist from Bilbao, during my last trip pays dividends with an upgrade. Needless to say I practised my O-level (o = ordinary) Spanish on her and even more needless to say I told her I was an Athletic Bilbao fan. "My second club," I said with all the sincerity of of Ashley Cole telling Cheryl why he was late home.

The media conference scheduled for 10.30am tomorrow has been put back to 1.30pm because most of the Irish journalists are in England, covering the Roy Keane press conference at Sunderland where he has been appointed manager. I could have had an extra night at home. Well, I couldn't as the ticket was booked but...

WEDNESDAY AUGUST 30

Gracias to Rosa I have an upgraded room complete with CD player and one complimentary CD – Tony Bennett's greatest hits, which is unlikely to get an airing, it has to be said.

Turned on *Sky News* as you do when you are in a hotel (assuming the hotel has *Sky News* that is) and there was a piece on pint-sized pop star

Prince, who is getting divorced. There was a clip of him collecting his belongings from the house formerly known as his.

Michel Platini, who hopes to be the next UEFA president, is staying at the Ireland team hotel, over here for a 10-day crash course in English. He wanted to be sure of his subjunctives. Platini was one of the truly great players of his generation. I remember being in Portugal for a pre-Euro 2004 cocktail party thrown by the [failed] Morocco 2010 World Cup bid. I was chatting to a few English hacks, eating, drinking and enjoying the hosts' hospitality when Platini entered the room. There was that collective turning-of-heads that happens when someone famous comes in, with murmurs and whispers. Platini and his entourage made their way across the room, by coincidence towards us. As he approached our little group Platini left his entourage, came over to me and shook my hand. "Hello, how are you?" he asked me. "Fine, yes," I replied as he continued his walk. To say the other lads were well impressed would be an understatement. The captain who led France to Euro 84 glory and probably next UEFA president going out of his way to shake my hand.

I did not tell them that I had never met the guy before because sometimes you just take what life gives you.

Six players were put up at the Ireland press conference and only one was of any interest to me, Reading striker Kevin Doyle who will play against Germany. About 18 months ago, when he was a right winger for Cork, his dad had a 100 euro bet at 150-1 that his son would play for Ireland within two years. Nice bet.

At the press conference I found myself talking knees with Cathal Dervan who used to work for the *Star* in London. Cathal told me about his recent cartilage operation. As he was being examined the nurse looked at his foot and asked: "What's that?"

"A birthmark," replied Cathal.

"Oh ... how long have you had that...?"

THURSDAY AUGUST 31

I am sitting in the Aviator restaurant in Dublin airport. Opposite me are two girls, about 40 I would say. Fish and chips and beef madras with pilau rice is the order of the day. And the other girl was eating...

One girl has both dishes on her plate, which I swear I can hear groaning under the weight of the calories. I like fish and chips and even more I like beef madras but collectively? I don't think so.

Needless to say the waistline of the girl eating Jaws and half of India is a little on the large side. Extra large. XXXXL. The chair must be made of industrial strength wood. So must the table. She is confidently moving through her meal(s) and I must stay to see whether she can finish what must surely have been half the kitchen's fish and meal allowance for the day.

I had checked out of the hotel at noon, saying adios to Rosa. "When will we see you again Crees?" she asked.

"In October, Rosa."

"Oh, have you made a reservation?" (you know what's coming).

"Not yet, no."

"Well, let's do it now ... I will upgrade you again Crees ... we Athletic Bilbao hinchas [fans] stick together."

So when I come back for the Czech Republic game in October, I'll be reunited with Tony Bennett.

She's done it. Not a chip left on her plate. Remarkable. Now for a nice light dessert, probably sticky toffee pudding and banana split with extra double cream. I may have seen history made.

I enjoyed a late breakfast, the healthy option would you believe (nothing else left after Miss Food-fest had finished). Read the papers and wrote my piece.

Today's *Daily Telegraph* has a piece on Britain's most embarrassing surnames. Top is Cock, with a recent survey showing there were 826 Cocks in Britain. Other embarrassing names include Handcock (199 left), Glasscock

(238), and Willy (185). Also listed were Smellie, Daft, Slow, Poor and Bottom. Inter-marriage would be interesting. Smellie-Cock, Smellie-Bottom or Slow-Willy appeal to my puerile sense of humour, but top must be Cock-Daft.

"Madam, you are...?"

"Cock-Daft."

"No madam, your name, not your hobby."

Arriving at Stuttgart was a million miles from my last visit to Germany. The well-oiled World Cup organising machine was nowhere to be seen. We were shepherded out of a back door where our luggage was brought to us on trolleys. The Maritim hotel that was a hub of activity in June was, as Arthur Daley once said, as silent as a nun's fart, hardly anyone around, no cabs, very different to last time.

FRIDAY SEPTEMBER 1

After breakfast I went for a walk, a limp-free walk after my op. Weather was superb. Back for Steve Staunton's press conference, which was as exciting as constipation. And produced as much.

I cannot see Ireland doing anything under him apart from failing, though he isn't helped by having the worst squad of players in the 20 years I've been covering them. Steve sees every question as a hand-grenade and as soon as things start to go wrong, which will be tomorrow night against Germany, the knives will be out. He was speaking about a four-year plan at his press conference (translation – don't slag me off yet)

Tony O'Donaghue of *RTE* went into the centre of the city to do an atmosphere' piece and as he was speaking live to the nation a fan poured a pint over his head. Apparently Tony never even blinked, carried on with his piece and was rightly given a well deserved a round of applause at the end. And a beer...

I am fully prepared for tonight's eircom bash. On every trip abroad the Ireland sponsors take the press out to a restaurant, a magnificent gesture.

A few journos have to stand up to 'do a turn' ... tell jokes, sing a song or whatever. I have been working on some anagrams of the guys here. Christopher Davies is 'this sharp divorcee' – like, how accurate do you want? You get the idea...

It was in a place called El Greco's and was, as usual, most enjoyable. Tony O'Donaghue stood up to tell a joke and one of his TV crew poured a glass of beer over him. This could not turn into a tradition.

SATURDAY SEPTEMBER 2

It appears El Greco left some journos needing time in the intensive care unit this morning, sorry, mourning. One Irish hack wore sunglasses at breakfast. "If I took them off my eyes would come out too." He claimed his eyes were like two fried eggs – not chilli fried eggs – in a bucket of blood, a true wordsmith.

A lazy Saturday. Weather was again superb, so I walked into the centre of town, which was a sea of green and white. The Irish fans were drinking pitchers of German beer – each. God knows what condition they will be in by kick-off.

During the World Cup we took the media shuttle to and from stadiums, which had priority over traffic/security checks etc. This time our coach took an eternity to get to the stadium and find the correct parking spot. It remains a constant source of amazement that every media coach always seems to be directed to the wrong place, so a mini-tour of car parks or stadiums is experienced.

There was no media hospitality room as such in the stadium and water could only be bought in glass bottles (banned from the tribunes) or in plastic glasses, which had to be carried up four flights of stairs. This act made me so thirsty I needed a bottle of water to quench my thirst.

Ireland did better than most expected, but lost 1-0. It was the right result achieved in a fortunate way, a German shot deflected past Shay Given by Robbie Keane. Steve Staunton was sent-off for kicking a water bottle in frustration (sadly not towards me in the press box) and was very flippant about it. "Everyone does it."

Do they? He'll get a one-match ban.

The game ended at 10.30pm local time and it was 1am before our coach could leave, having to wait for the Irish hacks and snappers to finish their work. The traffic was still of M25 car park-like proportions and it was almost 2am before we arrived back at the hotel.

Win or lose the Irish celebrate and the Maritim hotel was in full swing. I made my excuses and left for my room where I packed and hit the sack about 2.45am ready for the dreaded 6.45am alarm call.

SUNDAY SEPTEMBER 3

Swore at the alarm when it went off what seemed like a few minutes after I had fallen asleep. Had breakfast and a row with the hotel desk because of the slow internet connection. The hi-speed (er...no) internet connection was done via T-mobile. Most hotels, you put the cable in the back of your lap top, log on, agree to the terms and 15 euro per day is on your hotel bill. Not with T-mobile. You have to pay by credit card and once connected you get low-speed connection "because others in the hotel are using the service too," I was told. "So as long as no-one else uses the service it's fine...?" I asked. No reply.

Going down to breakfast about 7.15am, there were still Irish punters drinking from the night before. It's very intoxicating when the lift doors open and the smell of beer greets you.

The coach was scheduled to leave sharp at 8am and left sharp at 0830 mainly because one hack was still asleep at 8am. He was given merciless stick when he belatedly arrived on the coach where some members of the press corps (corpse?) qualified for the penultimate rites if not the last variety To the airport and the sort of chaos that makes you never want to fly again.

Checking in took ages, not least because every suitcase had to go through an X-ray machine which broke down.

Bought a coffee and sat down at a table to start writing my match report. A woman sat next to me and lit up. Why me? I logged off and as I was putting my laptop away she said: "I am f****** entitled to smoke you know."

I replied: "You certainly are madam. That's why I said nothing, but it is within my human rights to move."

"Whad-daya mean, f***** human rights ... ya taking da f***** piss?"

"Madam," I said. "Can I ask you one question?"

"Yeah."

"Which finishing school did you go to?"

"Whad-daya mean finishing school?"

No further questions, madam.

On the plane I found myself next to an elderly Irish fan who seemed to have some kind of Coughing Tourettes. It was not quite "cough ... wanker", but he made some very strange sounds when he did cough. Only for an hour and 40 minutes thankfully.

Arrived back in Dublin at 12.30pm, so six hours and 10 minutes before my flight for Gatwick departs. Colin Young's flight to Newcastle leaves at 9pm, but he's managed to get a ticket for the all-Ireland hurling final at Croke Park this afternoon.

So here I am where it all began, the Aviator Bar, Dublin's equivalent of the Sad Bastard Bar. Is there no escape?

If all goes well and I don't die of terminal boredom (there's a bad joke there somewhere) I should be home between 9 and 9.30pm. Off tomorrow, but got a lot to do, Tamasha, the best Indian restaurant in Kent, in the evening then Tuesday morning off to France v Italy in Paris on Eurostar.

It is now 4pm and a Spanish girl on the BA desk allowed me to check-in early, taking pity on me presumably. Another round of body searches after my new knee, which has a steel pin in it, set off an alarm.

FRANCE V ITALY, PARIS, SEPTEMBER 2006

TUESDAY SEPTEMBER 6

On the Eurostar to Paris to report on the rematch of the World Cup final, at the start of qualifying for Euro 2008, after just a day at home.

The journey from the hotel in Stuttgart to my home on Sunday took 13 and a half hours. The 6hr 40min stopover in Dublin was increased by an hour because of a delay to the oncoming flight (that old chestnut), the airport so crowded there wasn't a seat to be had in a bar, restaurant or at any departure gate (and probably in a loo, too, but thankfully no proof of that). There was then another 30 minutes on the runway while, well, I don't know. At Gatwick, there was a 30-minute delay for our suitcases, which seemed consistent given what had gone on before.

The trip to Paris for France v Italy started with the realisation the Travel Company had booked me to check out of my hotel on the day of the game. Thankfully they managed to get a second night in the Mercure hotel, which surprised me given that Italy are in town.

However, upon arriving at the hotel it ceased to be a surprise that they could accommodate me for the night of the game. The Travel Company had said the Mercure was a city hotel (140 euro per night), but in fact it was only just in Paris, on the southern perimeter of the city and a 30-minute drive from the city centre. The Stade de France is in the north of Paris, so I'll be leaving about 10am for the game tomorrow night.

Apart from being in the Parisian equivalent of Dartford, the Mercure is slap bang opposite a Metro station with a main road outside the front of the hotel. The therapeutic sounds of trains and automobiles if not planes did not appeal to me, so I asked for a quiet room. I said I WANT A QUIET ROOM.

It is quite a quiet room. Well 'room' might be debatable as there is no window. No noise, but also no window. They are charging a hundred quid a night for me to stay in a cave. Should be called the Flintstone Suite. "Wilma ... send me up a brontosaurus sandwich."

To add to the fun and games there is a restaurant called the HIV just along from the hotel and yes, I am positive of that.

The only English language programme (apart from the porn channels, but that is technically mainly English grunting) is BBC World, unquestionably the most mind-numbingly boring channel in the universe. No human being can possibly be so bored as to watch that. It makes the test card seem riveting.

Wrote two pieces of 400 and 500 words on Italy defender Marco Materazzi, villain of the piece in the Zidane head-butting incident in the World Cup final, plus a preview to le match. There is no in-room worldwide web access. That facility is available only in the bar (honest) where a three-hour wi-fi card costs 15 euro (just over a tenner with no extra charge for passive cancer from French cigarettes).

Not sure if any other English hacks are here in Paris, but I can safely assume they are nowhere near the Mercure hotel (caves from 140 euro per night, reservations never necessary). I suppose it still beats working for a living but it's a photo-finish this time.

Ventured out about 8pm and my first impression was that I must immediately declare which of the gangs I should pledge myself to. The choice seemed wide. The Hoodies. The Tattoos and many more. Decided the only option was to eat in.

Easier said than done. Room service included a 'blink of chicken' (that was the intriguing translation) which the guy on the front desk and I agreed was probably some Mexican dish. There was also a lamb and pork Mexican dish. "Look, I'll waive the Mexican," I said expecting the guy on reception to almost die laughing yet incredibly his expression did not change. "Can you do me a nice cheese platter with some French bread?"

"Sorry sir, no bread."

No bread. What a pain.

Defeated, I went to the restaurant 20 yards next door to the 'hotel', confident with my new knee I could now outsprint the Hoodies and Tattoos. Sat down, waited to be served … and waited … and 10 minutes later I left. I'm not sure there was even any awareness of my arrival, let alone my departure.

I hot-footed – okay, warm-footed – it to a restaurant called, what else, Le Restaurant, 100 yards away which had air conditioning of chapel hat peg proportions.

So here I am, the Sad Bastard in the Sad Restaurant tapping at a laptop trying to look as if Drew Barrymore will be joining me at any moment. Or even Michael. Still, a steak is on its way. Very pleasant it was, too. Drew would have enjoyed it, I'm sure. Don't care so much about Michael.

So this is my job. Paris for a fabulous match staying in a cave in an area that makes South Central in Los Angeles seem like St George's Hill, Weybridge, unable to eat room service and alone again, naturally.

Travelling. Bloody hell.

WEDNESDAY SEPTEMBER 6

I made it through the night without the Boyz From Da Hood breaking into my cave. There are notices in the hotel about how pickpockets target the place, while at breakfast on each table is a warning to be careful with your handbag.

Nice place.

Chantal is the girl on reception and in an act of naïve optimism I asked where I could buy *L'Equipe*, the French daily sports bible.

Keen to ensure she gave me the right answer she thought long and hard.

"Mmm ... the nearest paper shop is 15 minutes away." Not the answer I wanted.

"You cannot be serious? Fifteen minutes? Can't people round here read?"

I'll never know because she didn't answer me.

I then had breakfast, which was crap. Scrambled eggs that were so unscrambled you had to drink them through a straw.

Coffee was brown water, bereft of caffeine and any taste or flavour. I've had stronger water.

Still, at least I didn't get my handbag nicked.

It is now 9am and I shall be in my cave for 8 or 9 hours before leaving for the game. The day was spent writing, escaping only for a sandwich at lunch time.

The journey to the Stade de France took almost an hour. A splendid spread was put on for the press at the stadium. Cured ham (what did it really have?), smoked salmon, fromage – excellent.

The game was better than anyone dared hope. France were breathtaking, playing some truly wonderful football. Thierry Henry ran the world champions ragged, a stunning individual performance as his team won 3-1.

An eventful journey back to Le Cave. On the Metro, about six sinister, unsmiling gendarmes came through the carriage searching dodgy-looking kids, arresting four for possessing drugs.

Not a classic trip despite an utterly memorable match. Right, pit time, alarm set for 7am, but I'll be awake long before that. Eurostar at 10.09am and then back to Blighty for a few days.

Hamburg v Arsenal,
September 2006

TUESDAY SEPTEMBER 12

The drive to Luton Airport was as interesting as a drive to Luton Airport can possibly be. I enjoy travelling with Arsenal. Amanda and Dan, who head the media PR team, are just about the best in the business, while I think it is impossible for Arsène Wenger to do a boring press conference. Wenger is a journalist's dream. He will answer any question and I am convinced that whichever business he had followed he would have risen to the top. His English is as perfect as can be for a foreigner, yet Amanda told me he asked her to make a note of any mistakes he may make and tell him.

On the 75-minute flight to Hamburg Jim van Wijk of the Press Association let it slip that his brother used to be Wolf in Gladiators, but now lives in New Zealand changing nappies. Jim has a photo of himself with Mr Nappy, but unsurprisingly refused to show us.

Arrived at Hamburg airport and went straight to the hotel where the official UEFA press conference was held. Arsenal's German goalkeeper Jens Lehmann said how good it was to be back in Hamburg after his recent World Cup exploits with Germany, ignoring the fact Germany did not actually play in Hamburg in the 2006 finals.

The Royal Meridian where the press are staying is wonderful. I have a view overlooking the lake. The rooms are sensational, mega-modern with a 42-inch plasma TV, which I'll struggle to get in my bag.

BEHIND THE BACK PAGE

I went for dinner with Jonathan Legard, the BBC Radio 5Live football correspondent and five-star good guy. Jonathan is not only the most professional of broadcasters who calls things how he sees them, he is engaging company with a great sense of humour. We enjoyed a splendid pasta washed down with a less splendid German wine and watched Bayern Munich 4 Spartak Moscow 0.

Got back to the hotel and went to bed at 1am turning on CNN to see what was happening in the world. A survey by American (where else?) doctors has revealed it is not good to give chocolate to girls with PMS as it only worsens the situation. Personally I would have thought it would be more dangerous to take chocolate FROM a girl with PMS, but I'm not an American doctor so what do I know?

There was also a piece on the Air Guitar World Championship going on in – yes, of course, Finland. No doubt the winner gets an imaginary cheque.

WEDNESDAY SEPTEMBER 13
Match day was one of those lazy days abroad … did some work bringing my stats and records up to date before having a stroll in the sunshine, noticing there was an Indian restaurant called Gobinda. Upon checking out, most of the boys were distraught to discover the mini-bar in our rooms had been free (a fact I had, through my network of contacts, discovered early doors). One journo went back to his room claiming he had forgotten something, returning with guilty-looking bulging pockets. But don't worry John Cross of the *Mirror*, your secret is safe.

The game went well for Arsenal, who won 2-1. Hamburg airport was closed after the game so we had a 90-minute drive to another airport with our arrival at Luton 2.30am. Forty-five minutes later I checked into a Days Inn for what amounted to 20 rather than 40 winks and was on the road by 8am, my journey to Bromley taking two and a half hours, roughly double what it SHOULD take, though it never actually does.

Levski Sofia v Chelsea, September 2006

MONDAY SEPTEMBER 25

My last European trip as a *Daily Telegraph* staff man. Voluntary redundancy beckons. The charter taking us to Bulgaria is an all-first class plane with two [large] seats instead of three cramped ones per row. It looks like some sort of 'leaving' drink will be had tonight.

Flight over was bumpy and the meal was tandoori chicken – thankfully I hadn't had a curry for 24 hours. Sofia airport was a throwback to the old Soviet days, still stuck in a time-warp. The duty free shop was a kiosk and the only after shave it sold was called Pour Homme. Having smelt it 'Poor Homme' is more appropriate.

One hack phoned his missus while we were waiting for our luggage and she asked what time he would be home. "I'm in Bulgaria," we heard him say. Apparently his wife was unaware and his dinner was in the oven.

The 30-minute journey to the hotel was memorable mainly for the guide's speech about the history of Bulgaria. "There are 27 mountains…" it began, and by the end we were looking for one to throw ourselves off.

Lovely Hilton hotel, very swish even if a design fault meant that the coach could not get up the drive to the entrance. As a football writer perhaps I am not qualified to comment on the building and design of a hotel, but to have a drive that coaches cannot use does seem a rather basic error.

Because of the two-hour time difference we didn't check in until 9pm. By 9.30pm we were heading to a nearby restaurant. It was excellent, with Bulgarian folk music and dancing which needless to say was fun for 10 minutes, but then became as entertaining as toothache. Or Greek singing. The menu was in English, including a piece on the roast lamb – "if this isn't enough we'll cook the whole lamb for you, but sorry, we need 24 hours notice."

One mouthful of the white wine was all the encouragement we needed to move on to the Shiraz, which was okay in a way a vintage French burgundy compares to battery acid. A selection of starters was followed by barbecued chicken breasts, spuds and unknown veg, but it was good overall.

Back to the hotel at 2am and straight to the pit. Not before receiving an offer from a guy on the door of the Erotica Club for us all to come in and part with our money. The 'no syringes' sign on the door did not give the impression of a classy joint. Like the casino in Donetsk where punters were asked to 'deposit their handguns before entry'.

TUESDAY SEPTEMBER 26

The two-hour time difference meant I woke up at either 6.30am or 4.30am. The power shower revived me, in fact almost knocked me out it was so powerful. None of the other hacks made breakfast. It was one of the better breakfasts with yours truly having a red pepper omelette.

I received a superb email from my *Daily Telegraph* colleague John Ley called Living Life Backwards.

Wouldn't it be great to live your life backwards?
You start out dead and get that out of the way.
Then you wake up in an old age home feeling better
every day.

Then you get kicked out for being too healthy.
Enjoy your retirement and collect your pension.
Then when you start work, you get a gold watch on your
first day.
You work 40 years until you're too young to work.
You get ready for High School: Drink alcohol, party,
and you're generally promiscuous.
Then you go to primary school, you become a kid, you
play and you have no responsibilities.
Then you become a baby and then...
You spend your last nine months floating peacefully in
luxury, in spa-like conditions – central heating, room
service on tap, and then...
You finish off as an orgasm.

Living my life the more traditional way, I took a stroll in the sunshine later in the morning. While many cities in Poland and certainly Budapest and Prague are almost totally westernized now, Sofia still has much of the old iron curtain about it. A coffee in a splendid café was accompanied by Barry White singing through a speaker of, it seemed, maximum five watts. The Sky Plaza was full of throwback clothes ... leather jackets so stiff you could not bend your arms. Nothing to buy, but fascinating.

Press conference at 4pm was a bun-fight – and the buns won. Simon Greenberg, the Chelsea PR guy who, rather staidly, prefers to be called Director of Communications ... anyway, PR guy Simon sat next to Jose Mourinho whilst wearing a Chelsea tracksuit. Someone even asked Jose if Greenberg was available for selection.

Dinner was ultimately enjoyable. We eventually ended up at a place called Spaghetti Company – you can't beat the local cuisine – which was a swish, modern restaurant and the food was very good. When it came to pay there were problems. The restaurant's credit card machine was faulty and would only take American Express which, as none of us had American Express, would NOT do nicely. They even refused sterling – a stark contrast from my last visit in 1987. Luckily there was a cash machine nearby, but it was a pain in the penne. Back to the hotel about 1am, swift nightcap and to bed.

American TV specialises in surveys that I believe are carried out by a race bred on a special island somewhere off the California coast. CNN say "a survey" (they didn't say by who) reveals sleeping pills can cause "sleep driving". Yes, you can, the survey says, take a sleeping pill or maybe two, go to bed, get up, drive somewhere and have no recollection of it. I can imagine Chris Tarrant saying: "Told you..." God bless American surveys.

WEDNESDAY SEPTEMBER 27

Breakfast was a chilli omelette, a sort of fried eggs with attitude. Went into the centre of Sofia with Jon Brodkin (*Guardian*) and Mark Irwin (*Sun*) to see some sights. The main Orthodox church was stunning, though goodness knows how many workers must have died while it was built. In those days cranes were just large birds. Bought some postcards and a T-shirt, but nothing else to buy really.

Arriving at the stadium I discovered there was no landline for me, even though one was ordered. As, unsurprisingly, I can get no Orange signal with my 3G card (no change there then) it looks like I will be putting 1,500 words plus teams over on copy via the company mobile phone. Going out in style.

Because of the two-hour time-difference the game kicked-off at 2145 locally, the latest start to a game I have ever experienced. The weather, having been superb over the previous two days – in the 70s during the day and still warm enough for shirtsleeves at night – has taken a sharp turn for the worse.

The Bulgaria T-shirt I bought is being worn under my shirt and the entire English press corps has been caught out by the cold and rain.

Good story from the game with Didier Drogba scoring a hat-trick as Chelsea beat Levski Sofia comfortably. No major hassles at the airport, but sat on the plane for 25 minutes while everything was loaded.

Arrived back at Gatwick at 3am. Incredibly it took 50 minutes to clear customs and reach the long term car park. On the road by ten to four and home by 4.30am.

I wonder what the Health and Safety people would say about such schedules? I have driven home many times from airports in the early hours when, truth be told, I should not have been behind the wheel. Eyes stinging and head thumping with tiredness. It is not natural for a "day shift" worker to drive for maybe two hours in the middle of the night, especially after a two- or three-hour flight when they have possibly nodded off. I believe all journos should be able to take taxis to and from airports under such circumstances, to be driven home by a specialized night driver. Sadly it will probably take a bad accident for any change.

THURSDAY SEPTEMBER 28

My last day after almost 20 years with the *Daily Telegraph*. Freelance life awaits me. I am now becoming, as someone tactfully put it, a prostitute with a pen.

Super Bowl XLI, Miami, Jan/Feb 2007

TUESDAY JANUARY 30

My first assignment as a hooker.

Why do we always wake up an hour before the alarm is due to go off when it is set early? Mine was due to go off at 5.45am, but yes, I woke at 4.47am – don't we just love the age of the digital – and cursing the fact.

The decision then is whether to attempt to go back to sleep until the alarm goes off (why do we say the alarm 'goes off' when it is really 'going on'?) or get up, give yourself plenty of time rather than the absolute minimum, nice cooked breakfast, and not have to rush. By the time I'd made my decision the alarm went on/off.

The house is like an igloo. I have never stayed in an igloo, but I am prepared to put my head on the block (of ice) and make the comparison. It's so cold if OJ Simpson was there he would wear gloves just to keep his hands warm. The reason for the cold is that on Saturday the central heating went on the blink. The house became progressively colder and by the following day I was wearing a leather jacket indoors.

Gas board guy came and said he could not turn the gas back on until I had a terminal fitted. I asked why this had never been picked up before.

"Sorry, can't comment on that," he replied when I told him, sounding just like a Premier League football manager when asked a direct question.

"So how much does it cost to have fitted?" I asked bracing myself for the answer.

He replied: "If we do it, about £1,500. Regulations mean we have to erect scaffolding around the side of the house to install it. We can't use ladders you see."

Now in the brace position what I did see was 1,500 big ones disappearing from my bank account. The terminal costs £30 – with £1,470 fitting costs. Only in England.

Mr Gas Board left Casa Igloo and the incumbent Eskimo phoned a local gas fitters. They put me in touch with a chimney sweep who fits terminals. I phoned him and he's coming round to do the job the day I return from Miami. The cost? Seventy quid. But like, how cold is the house going to be after 10 days without heating?

The other bad domestic news is that three fish died a few days ago, so it was no Wanda (sorry) I phoned the fish man. He came round, looked at the dead fish and said: "They've got herpes."

I've been accused of many things but...

The disease is actually called koi pox – you really couldn't make that up, well I couldn't and didn't. He reckoned it was probably caused by a bird having a wash in the waterfall part of the pond and enjoying a number one's or two's or whatever birds do. The other koi are poxless thank goodness.

And so to Heathrow for my first business trip of 2007 (the visit to Dundalk for the Irish Soccer Writers' Association's dinner was purely pleasure, I promise) – Super Bowl XLI between the Indianapolis Colts (who I think will win comfortably) and the Chicago Bears.

The cab driver was called Colin, one of those names that seems to have gone completely out of fashion. You don't hear of any babies named Colin (especially girls) these days. Trevor, Graham, Stanley and Brian are also total non-names in 2007. Anyone who is called Colin/Trevor/Graham/Brian/Stanley/Whatever is the last of a dying breed in the name stakes.

Colin was interesting... "I'm a plane spotter. I go to Biggin Hill a lot."
I prayed for a traffic jam-free ride.

Heathrow was manic without the street preachers. Flight over was uneventful and upon arriving at Miami I had to fill in the usual customs and immigration forms.

"Anything to declare?"

"Herpes and pox," I didn't say.

Have a nice day, sir.

The Deauville Hotel, Miami Beach sounds nice, but it would not even be in the top 100 hotels I have stayed in. It is soulless, the corridors lacking any warmth (so I feel at home). It is also a 30-minute drive from the media center, which is out at the Miami convention center, with shuttle buses to and from every half hour. The media usually stay in the hotel where the media center is based or at least close by. Half an hour in a shuttle bus will produce some magnificent media moans as the week progresses.

I went to the media center for accreditation, came back to the Deauville, but could not be arsed to go to the media party which would have meant getting the shuttle bus back to the media center and then taking another bus to wherever the party was. I was also jet-lagged, so I went to a Brazilian restaurant over the road and had a splendid dinner of spicy chicken, rice and black bean sauce.

To my Brad (pit) at 11pm (or 4am).

WEDNESDAY JANUARY 31

Awake at 5.30am, not too bad for a first nighter. Turned on the TV and there was a feature on a caffeinated doughnut. So now we can be overweight AND restless. Caught up with some of the English papers. I loved the photograph of ex-Rolling Stone Mick Taylor shopping in a supermarket. Apparently he was buying some white wine and bread in the store. It's only hock and rolls, but he liked it.

Miami (or North Cuba as it probably should be known) is warm today, about 73 degrees and sunny. Ends gloating.

Had a walk round the hotel area, not too much to offer apart from a wonderful beach and beautiful warm sea (I lied about the "ends gloating" bit). There is a Boca Juniors shop, which is almost a shrine to Diego Maradona, former star of the Argentine club. I had a look around, saw a T-shirt with the 'The Hand Of God' goal photo on it. The owner asked me if I would like one. No gracias.

There is no Super Bowl fever in the Miami Beach area. Not a sign, a placard, nothing. Amazing to put the international media in American football's equivalent of Yarmouth. I may as well be here on holiday. Don't say it.

Wrote a piece on the first two black – or African-American as they are called here – head coaches to go head-to-head in the Super Bowl. The race issue is a big deal in the build-up. In a sport where 75 per cent of the players are black there are only six black head coaches, around 20 per cent of the total. For some reason the white guy always seems to get the job. The Chicago Bears' head coach is called Lovie Smith and you have to wonder what his parents were doing when they registered his name. It's worse than Trevor.

The Deauville Hotel used to be one of the most famous hotels in Miami Beach. The Beatles once played here in the Napoleon Suite, while the Rat Pack apparently used the place to quench their thirst after … yes … a hard day's night.

Dean Martin, whose thirst was legendary, would have needed his own barman. This is the man who said: "I once shook hands with a teetotaller and the whole right side of my body sobered up."

Tonight was the Broward County Media Party at Gulfstream Park, an hour's journey from the Deauville and the question has to be asked – why? The venue was a race track just outside Fort Lauderdale and apart from a dozen parachutists landing on the track (and what were the odds against that?) nothing else happened.

We ate some nice food and drank some nice drink, but why the hell they transported goodness knows how many people so far for so little is puzzling. There must surely have been somewhere closer?

Home soon after midnight, and turned on TV to see what was going on in the world and discovered a news item about 'renowned socialite' Paris Hilton who has filed a lawsuit against a website where people pay to see her naked.

This is truly remarkable. There are still people who haven't seen Paris Hilton naked?

THURSDAY FEBRUARY 1

After doing some work I had breakfast in a Cuban café. I went to the media center and asked two Super Bowl information girls where I could find updates from the morning's press conferences. Not an unreasonable question. Neither knew. I then asked what time the shuttle bus left for the Deauville hotel. "I'll ask transport," one said. Minute later: "Sorry sir, they don't know."

I asked, jokingly (or not as it turned out) if she could perhaps try catering to see if they know – she said that was unlikely but she would try. Minute later. "Catering suggested I tried transport … sorry sir…"

The hotel's wi-fi service is very hit and miss, more miss than hit. Journalists on some floors have no wi-fi connection and have to work from the hotel lobby. However, the good news is that a free chocolate fountain has been set up in the lobby with a pile of melon, pineapple and strawberries. Average weight gain expected to be around eight pounds per hack.

Still no evidence that the Super Bowl is in town, apart from watching TV. American sports programmes are slick, professional and brilliantly presented. The trouble is, every commentator and analyst sounds the same. They may be the same two guys using different names. Even the way one looks across at the other for the 'handover' is the same. They really are Talking Heads.

British commentators are so much better, putting far more personality into their work. They give their own take and touch on what they are describing in whichever sport they are engaged in. You would never get a Sid Waddell, Henry Blofeld, Peter Alliss, Bill McLaren or Dan Maskell on American TV. In the States they all have to speak, commentate or whatever in exactly the same manner. I swear they ever wear the same suit, shirt and tie.

Tonight is the international media party sponsored by the South Florida Super Bowl XLI committee at Vizcaya. I shall attend.

I am glad I did as it was possibly the best NFL function I have been to (and I have been to a few). A breathtaking scenario of an olde Hispanic-style house overlooking the sea was helped by the warmest of nights (ok, I know … I know). The food was magnificent and a Santana-style band added to the occasion.

Wi-fi problems temporarily forgotten.

Hillary Clinton getting much coverage here. I wonder if she will become president. That's just what the White House interns need – Bill Clinton back with more time on his hands. I guess they're called interns because that's how he had them.

FRIDAY FEBRUARY 2

Further discussion about last night's international media party and I was reminded of an earlier occasion when the Super Bowl was held in Miami. They shut off half of South Beach and made all the restaurants free to media and guests for four hours. It's a tough job, but someone's got to do it.

That was when Richard 'Slinger' Matthews had the Brit journos' kitty (collected a day or so earlier) and spent the lot in 30 minutes on two local girls. He'd managed to find the only bar on the beach that wasn't free. Not only that, he also befriended apparently the only two girls who wouldn't melt on hearing the English accent and being informed of the status (i.e. a member of Her Majesty's press).

Slinger lost the kitty and the pussy at the same time, if you'll pardon the expression.

Moving on. I was chatting to Simon Mann of 5Live at the party and mentioned that in the recent Sports Journalists' Association poll for the best television/radio sports programme I voted for *Fighting Talk*, a Saturday morning show on 5Live which is great fun and makes sitting in an M25 traffic jam almost enjoyable.

"I'm really glad you said that," said Simon.

"Oh, why?"

"I write and produce it."

I genuinely did not know. Am expecting invitation to *Fighting Talk* real soon.

After another breakfast at my Cuban greasy spoon, I went to a press conference where it was confirmed the Miami Dolphins would play the New York Giants at Wembley on October 28 this year in the first NFL regular season game outside of North America.

Skysports.com have a guy here covering the Super Bowl called Alex Ferguson. Yes, that really is his name. Journos are required to say their name and their media outlet, so when Alex asked a question: "Alex Ferguson, Skysports.com but not THE Alex Ferguson," he said, clearing up any possible misunderstanding in case the guy from the *Wyoming Bugle* or the *Utah Gazette* thought the manager of Manchester United had suddenly appeared at the international press conference.

The wi-fi problems continue. The media center has free wi-fi access, but after spending 45 minutes working on my laptop three guys on the NFL's technical help desk were beaten. "Sorry, we can't get your laptop connected. We've no idea why. It won't work at the stadium either." Thank goodness he didn't tell me to have a nice day.

I am not alone in being wi-fi-less. A number of journalists in Miami covering the Super Bowl can't use their computers at the media center or the stadium while getting a signal at the media hotel is intermittent. This does present certain difficulties workwise.

The Super Bowl is not just about a game of football. There are stories and news releases and parties for football players building houses, football players donating money to youth centers, football players bowling at the Dolphin Mall. The week's activities are outlined in a book of 35 pages in which the game rates just one paragraph. On Thursday, the news release touting the pre-game show was 10 pages. The official reports on the teams' practices were one page each.

Billy Joel did a press conference as he is singing the national anthem. Well, he did THREE press conferences dressed in a leather jacket and a baseball cap. Old Piano Man didn't appear to know who was playing in the game. "I always root for New York," he said. He is no fan of the national anthem. "It's a tough song, not the greatest song ever written," he said. "*America the Beautiful* is actually a better song. Nobody remembers the lyrics, and they don't know what they mean. It's kind of a slog, really."

Nice one Billy. We love you just the way you are.

Dinner tonight was with Nick Szczepanik (*The Times*), a smashing guy who loves American sport and used to work in Miami. We took the media shuttle bus to the media center and found a splendid restaurant in Collins Avenue. I ordered a bottle of Gavi di Gavi, one of my favourite Italian wines, and when it was poured it was clearly (or to be precise, cloudily) corked. I told the waitress that it was corked and she appeared with another bottle, but claiming the manager said the original bottle was ok. She poured (re-poured?) the wine and it was probably three shades lighter than the original and tasted like Gavi di Gavi should. The defence rested.

It was (for the record) 76 degrees at 10pm as we ate outside. The Atlantic salmon did not die in vain.

SATURDAY FEBRUARY 3

Spent 90 minutes swearing at the laptop this morning, not an unusual occurrence for a travelling hack, before I finally managed to get a connection. The Super Bowl is back here in three years and even if I am not in Miami in 2010, I hope whoever is has better luck with their laptops.

Punxsutawney Phil, the weather-predicting groundhog (as in *Groundhog Day*, of which I've had a few), was in the news today. Apparently we can expect an early spring instead of six weeks more of winter. Do you remember the name of the town where this ritual took place? The photos in the Miami Herald had the name half hidden, but it was Gobblers Knob. Honest. And I thought Pratts Bottom and Badgers Mount were bad.

When we were in Atlanta for the Super Bowl, driving to a shopping mall we noticed a sign for a town called Cuming. Needless to say we all had our photo taken close to it, so we could say we were five seconds from Cuming. Little things. Of course, there is also the sign in London's East End – British Waterways Bow Locks.

A non-working day today, but going with Nick to Bay Harbor shopping mall in an effort to spend some good dollars-per-pound money. I failed apart from buying a book of Ed McBain short stories and the *Daily Mail*. Bay Harbor is so upmarket that most shops do not have prices on the clothes, which is God's way of telling you to walk on by … and not walk and buy.

Still not an ounce of Super Bowl fever. Amazing. If you didn't know the Super Bowl was on you wouldn't know it was on (you may need to read that eight times). Maybe this is because in North Cuba (aka Miami) it is mainly Hispanic or retirees in the city nicknamed God's Waiting Room. I don't think I have ever been to a major sporting event with so little local awareness of what is being staged.

Back to the hotel and I sat by the pool having an egg and bacon bagel washed down with a smoothie. Had 30 seconds to spare so read all the interesting bits in the *Miami Herald*. Florida is apparently suffering from severe drought, which has gone on for almost two years. It's so bad Cubans are walking here.

Back to the room and American TV – Arnold Schwarzenegger was doing some campaign speech about building a new infrastructure in California where he's governor. The speech lasted 45 minutes – that's how long it took him to say "infrastructure". There was an item about how the campaign manager for the mayor of San Francisco resigned when he found the mayor had been having an affair with his wife. I suppose when a guy has an affair with a girl in San Fran it is big news.

Went into the trendy area of Miami Beach with Nick (we are becoming the Odd Couple) and had an overpriced, not very good Italian meal. The main course was chicken in herbs with vegetables. I asked for a side order of potatoes. Dish came … no spuds. Explained to Ortiz what I wanted … si senor … came back with spuds … veg had been taken off the plate … it was third time lucky.

It was wonderful to sit outside and eat – or in my case, wait for my meal to arrive as ordered. But still not a drop of Super Bowl fever or atmosphere. This is the Non Bowl. The Quiet Bowl. The Secret Bowl.

SUPER SUNDAY FEBRUARY 4
It's raining. Don't worry though, it's warm rain. So now it's the Wet Bowl. The international media are not under cover in Dolphin stadium and the NFL have promised us ponchos, so we won't get rained upon. The Poncho Bowl, too.

An early start to Super Sunday by Super Bowl standards, well by my Super Bowl standards. I caught the 8.30am media shuttle from the Deauville hotel to the media center and then the 9am shuttle to the Radisson where there was a pre-game media brunch, though starting on the artery-clogging half a pig etc at half past nine isn't strictly speaking a brunch. But what the hell.

The best eater among the Brits who cover American football, and this subject is not even open to debate, is Alan McKinlay of the *Daily Mirror*, sadly absent this year, though the NFL's food bill will have been halved by Macca's no-show. He created a new Super Bowl record for the most food on a plate which, it turned out, was only his hors d'euvres. For Macca it is always the Food Bowl.

I had a salsa and peppers omelette with hash browns, bacon and sausages. Oh, and French toast. Within Her Majesty's working press it is known as a Small Macca.

Back at the hotel the wi-fi problems persist. The signal quality is "excellent" – or so the bubble on my PC tells me – but after an hour this allegedly excellent signal is not excellent enough for me to even log on. Very, very boring.

The Super Bowl is not the fun week it used to be. Because of budgets fewer papers are sending reporters so the coverage back home has been downsized. From having journos representing five or six English national newspapers, this time it's just Nick and myself. Simon Veness, who used to work for the *Sun* before moving to the States to write excellent and value for money (he said) travel books, is also here.

It helps to get David Beckham, or one of the six sports names who guarantee big coverage even if they only sneeze, in the Super Bowl story. Newspapers are living in a superstar era. Unless they can get Becks, Wayne Rooney, Cristiano Ronaldo, Freddie Flintoff, Jonny Wilkinson or whoever in the story – and ideally the intro – the Super Bowl will be marginalised in despatches. It's a shame because there are some terrific human-interest stories here and it IS one of the most-watched sporting events around the world. The Super Bowl can provide a different, alternative read to Ronaldo, Mourinho and England losing to the Cook Islands at hopscotch. But no Becks, no real coverage.

When leaving for the game, the hotel lobby is usually a hive of activity with security on hand to keep nonresidents out. Not today. There were three people in the Deauville lobby – there are more in my house most nights (when the central heating works that is).

The seven-mile journey to the stadium from our hotel ended up taking an incredible two hours. We had to take the hotel-media center shuttle, which is like going two miles the wrong way, and then with no bus priority lanes it was an M25-type snail speed journey to Dolphin stadium.

Pre-match entertainment was Cirque du Soleil with Billy Joel singing the national anthem, badly it must be said. Some say there is no such thing as a bad BJ, but Billy was not at his best. However, the way the NFL stage the entertainment show remains unsurpassed – breathtaking and with precision timing.

MONDAY FEBRUARY 5

It was the Rain Bowl, the Wet Bowl, the Brolly Bowl, the Sodden Bowl ... the first ever outdoor Super Bowl played in the rain. And how it rained. I watched most of the game wearing a poncho like most others in a stadium designed for sunshine. It wee wee'd down from start to finish and the fact it was warm rain was little consolation to those who had to use laptops during the Colts' relatively easy win.

During the second half when the rain turned into stair-rods there were a significant number of empty seats. Supporters fed up with sitting in the wet opted to watch the remainder of the game from the dry (if that is an appropriate word) of the bar. The rain affected the game too, with the ball dropped or fumbled an unusually high number of times. It was a close, intriguing, error-strewn game which the Colts should have won more comfortably. Not the worst Super Bowl I have seen, but certainly not the best, though definitely the wettest.

Went back to the Radisson for the post-game dinner, which was an ordinary buffet, at best. I started with a nice slice of turkey, plus slice of roast beef – a Mini Macca – but there were no spuds or veggies. To accompany the meat I had more meat. Hasn't America heard of meat, two veg and roasties?

Flight home doesn't leave until 8.30pm, which means a lot of time at Miami airport. The odd couple had their final breakfast in the Deauville. The *Miami Herald's* headline "Colts Reign" was spot on. The noon shuttle turned up promptly at 1.25pm and because we didn't have the necessary documentation, which we were unaware of – "Yellow form? No yellow form, sorry sir" – we had to pay 21 bucks.

Checked in at Miami airport where my new knee beeped as I was going through security.

"Do you have an implant sir?" I was asked.

"Yes, my knee is 36EE," I replied, waiting for high-fives all round at yet another example of my wit.

"Step into this room please sir," I was asked/told. A guy gave me the once over and even asked to see my knee. As he was built like a brick outhouse I decided against saying: "That's a lousy chat-up line" and rolled up my trouser leg to reveal a magnificent 10-inch scar. The Frenchman in Marseille who attempted to mug me, but ended up just kicking me in the knee has a lot to answer for.

I am now sitting in Pizza Hut having bleeped my way through security, eating a cheese pizza – a Micro Macca. It is three o'clock, so only five and a half hours until take off. I have just had a text from one of the journalists flying from Dublin to Rimini for the San Marino v Republic of Ireland game. The plane had to turn back because the wheels were jammed and wouldn't come down.

Have found some wi-fi at the airport. Maybe I should have stayed here for the week.

Barcelona, September 2007

MONDAY SEPTEMBER 3

Back on the continental trail after a seven-month timeout. I did not have the ideal preparation for the trip.

What happens when I am in bed is normally a subject I rarely speak about in public (be very grateful), but last night's events were unusual, to say the least. There I was, Sunday night, fast asleep when, at almost half past two, I woke up startled, frightened and for a moment believing someone was in the room attacking me. The lampshade and bulb socket in the light over the bed had suddenly decided to drop ONTO the bed, missing my head by about 18 inches. I shat myself. It's funny, but it isn't. It would have been funny if it was anyone else's bed, but the lamp god decided it was MY bed that should be the recipient of aforementioned shade, bulb etc. That made it decidedly unfunny in my view.

I've no idea what caused it, old age maybe. They say lamp fittings start to take after their owners (honest they do). But it was the mother of all unexpected and unwanted alarm calls. OK, you can stop laughing now.

I am off to Barcelona to interview their coach Frank Rijkaard. But first came the difficult bit – the M11, M25 and M1 en route to Luton Airport. There are three certainties in life – tax, death (which strictly speaking must surely come after life) and, completing the hat-trick, traffic jams on any road in England beginning with M. The M11, M25 and M1 did not disappoint in that respect.

Decided to have a romantic evening for one in the Travel Lodge rather than risk being delayed tomorrow, so I was delayed tonight instead. I take each delay as it comes. Just the three hours to do 75 miles. Why can't people go to the north of Scotland to have accidents rather than the roads I am driving on? Or rather, attempting to drive on.

The Travelodge was buzzing – not. They are great value for money, though, and there is no extra charge for the 2am Who Can Say "Goodnight" The Loudest In The Corridor competition or the 5am Door Slamming tournament.

TUESDAY SEPTEMBER 4

Beans on toast for breakfast – the sausages were celebrating their third birthday, hours that is. Nice easy drive to the airport, checked in no problems when ... the fire alarm sounded. The terminal had to be evacuated. Why me?

Well it wasn't just me. Chaos outside as everyone spilled onto the pavements and into the car parks, including a sheepish-looking stag party on their way to 'Shagaluf'.

I was fortunate, having managed to check in. Pity the poor people who had queued for 20 minutes and were just about to check in when ... everybody out. Of course, those passengers who had checked in had to go through security again along with those who were waiting to go through going through the procedure again – an interesting start to the trip.

The Hilton hotel in Barcelona is superb and does not have the outside lifts or other aspects that makes we vertigo suffers break out in a cold sweat. It may be difficult to appreciate what heights do to those with vertigo unless you are a sufferer. We would rather be in the Mile Low Club. In one Barcelona hotel I stayed in a while ago two wings were linked by a walkway which had glass windows AND a glass floor. It was like a glass cage and I didn't have the bottle ... it made my stomach churn. I was on the 15th floor and crossing the five metres of total glass, which I had to in order to reach my room, was a silent torture.

I used to wait until no-one was around, close my eyes and do the quick-step across the glass floor. That worked until one morning I closed my eyes, braced myself, started to walk briskly across and was unaware of someone from room service carrying a tray of breakfast coming the other way. I walked straight into her, and orange juice, coffee, croissants and goodness knows what else ended up clattering down onto the glass floor.

To make matters worse I carried on with my 'blind' walk and couldn't help her clean up the world's most frightening floor. My explanations fell on the deafest of ears.

Anyway, back on the safety of the Hilton's ground floor, a previous visit had underlined that the bar is not the place to drink unless you are a lottery rollover winner. I adjourned to a watering hole (why do they call it that when no-one drinks water there?) named Si Senor across the road and asked the bartender for a vodka and orange juice. I have never, ever seen anyone pour such a generous measure of vodka. People have married for less.

The glass was about seven inches tall (don't ask how I measured it) and he filled it with Absolut to within one inch of the top. Six inches of vodka. It was not so much a vodka and orange as vodka and a dash. Any less orange and it would have been put in with an Optrex dispenser. It may just have been the largest vodka ever poured.

The first mouthful was an experience of head-shaking proportions. Next time I have an operation I'll opt for a Si Senor voddie and a dash rather than an anaesthetic. I drank a second memorable mouthful and asked the bartender if I could have some more orange juice. "You mean more vodka?" he smiled. Wittily I said: "No senor." (the bar being called Si Senor). The alleged joke disappeared into thin air, but thankfully he topped the glass up with OJ. Even thus diluted it remained the strongest vodka I have ever drunk.

Three women from the US of A were on the next table and heard my accent. "Where you from?" asked Pam of Utah.

For reasons which may have had something to do with the small reservoir of Absolut I was poured, I thought I would tell them the answer – London – using the charades method. So ... two syllables ... first syllable ... sounds like ... I stood up and made as if I was running. "Toronto?" asked Betty of Cleveland which confirmed a lot about what I head heard about Cleveland. And Betty was drinking tea.

Dinner was taken in the Olympic Village dockside area, which provides the most pleasant of views and ambience or as Del Boy would say, ambulance. I asked for an orange juice, but still had enough vodka in my system that it immediately became a screwdriver.

WEDNESDAY SEPTEMBER 5

Breakfast was taken outside in the sunshine, the Hilton earning a bonus point for having baked beans available. Frank Rijkaard was friendly and well practised in the art of saying a lot, but giving little away.

After the Rijkaard interview I took a tourist bus trip round this magnificent city and saw far more in two hours than in what must be 15 previous visits. Barcelona is a classy place, the Gaudi architecture must be seen to be properly appreciated. Everywhere is spotlessly clean, the people obviously taking great pride in the capital of Catalunya. If you have never been there make every effort to visit what is for me the best city in Europe.

Back at the hotel I wrote the Rijkaard piece before adjourning to a restaurant where I ate a magnificent steak while watching the world go by.

THURSDAY SEPTEMBER 6

Returning to Luton was depressing. Walking out of the terminal I was almost ankle deep in dog-ends with the predictable collection of fast-food wrappers and other rubbish.

Barcelona had been spotless. Smokers – and in Spain smoking is almost obligatory – put their butts in rubbish bins (so to speak). In fact, all garbage is placed in such containers. The welcome home was sad but inevitable.

Milan,
January 2008

MONDAY JANUARY 21

The nation's gritters have appeared. The streets of Bromley, well my street, has been gritted and I could walk along the pavements without worrying about slipping over. The frustration is that I climbed straight in my car and drove to Gatwick Airport, so didn't need to walk anywhere but the pavements looked incredibly safe.

I am on my way to interview Kaka who, apart from having a name that sounds like the word we use to babies for dub-dubs (which in turn...) is the best footballer in the world, official. Kaka is the current European and World Player of the Year and plays for AC Milan, the current European and Club World Cup Champions. He is 25 and it is said he is also the nicest footballer on the planet.

Essential road works on the A21. I love that bit about essential. What sort of road works did they do previously? Unnecessary? Frivolous? OK lads – there is nothing at all wrong with the A21, so let's dig a frivolous hole, temporary traffic lights ... better still stop-go signs. That should be a good for at least a 20-minute delay.

Showing the foresight that comes with experiencing frivolous or essential road works on the A21 I had allowed an extra 30 minutes to the extra 30 minutes that always seem to be needed even if you just pop down the road.

The long-term car park at Gatwick Airport was its usual soulless self. What a business that is, airport car parks. The ultimate captive audience in many ways, you can charge what you like because what's the alternative if you drive to the airport? I tried to work out how much the car park must make per day, but gave up. Upkeep is minimal, not sure who pays for the airport shuttle buses, but they are a pinprick on the profits. In my next life I want to come back as the owner of an airport car park.

I am now at Gatwick having left home at 6am. The flight leaves at 9am, which gives me a chance to spend a lot of money on a croissant and a cup of coffee. Like, almost a fiver for a flaky French thing and a cup of froth.

I hope all goes well with Kaka. Everything has been arranged, but when you are meeting the best player in the world who doesn't speak enough English for an interview – a translator has, please God, been promised – at a club where media demands are huge then the worry beads come out.

I am comforted by the fact that those who know Kaka say he doesn't have a bad bone in his body, let alone any skeletons in his cupboard. He is an evangelical Christian, who was proud to announce he was a virgin when he was married in 2006. Kaka said life as an evangelical pastor appealed to him after football. At the World Cup finals in Germany that year he disagreed with the Brazil coach who allowed visits from players' wives and girlfriends (maybe both in one or two cases) for nookie nights. Kaka did not believe sex should be part of the World Cup.

Let's hope opposites attract.

When Kaka scores he raises both arms and lifts his head towards the sky – aka headquarters – thanking God for the gifts He has given him.

Whatever your thoughts on sport and religion in this respect, it has to be better than the current trend of pre-rehearsed baby-rocking, rap dancing, some act involving a corner flag or an obscure sign with hands and fingers celebration.

At the start of 2008 Carlos Tevez thought it would be a good idea to celebrate his winning goal for Manchester United against Birmingham by putting a dummy in his mouth. Why? Talk about dummier and dumber.

It was, he explained, to pay homage to his wife and daughter, Florencia, aged two-and-a-half and pretty well past the dummy stage I would have thought, who were watching the game back home in Argentina. Tevez placed the dummy in his shorts and when he scored took it out and placed it in his mouth.

Unsurprisingly it looked ridiculous as grown men tend to when they put dummies in their mouths for whatever reason. It was further evidence of how goal-scoring is becoming individual glory rather than something to celebrate with your teammates, even though players always tell you it doesn't matter if they score as long as the team wins ... then go to extreme lengths to plan and practise individual celebrations. When the ball goes in the net, many don't bother to share the joy of scoring with their teammates. Oh no. Instead they start a dance that seems more designed to get them on *Soccer AM*, or make some obscure sign with their hands and fingers – perhaps even stick a dummy in their mouth.

There is also the incredibly boring cupping of an ear by a visiting goal-scorer gesturing to home fans that he cannot hear anything – oh how original after 10 zillions ear-cuppings – or the finger over the mouth to silence the home supporters – see ear-cuppings. Both should earn an immediate yellow card produced for unsporting behaviour if only for the boredom factor.

When Alan Shearer scored, which he did regularly, he simply raised his right arm and ran to his teammates. He didn't engage in some weird ritual involving a corner flag. No wonder he's called boring.

Such over-egged celebrations tend not to occur in other sports. I never saw Australia wicketkeeper Adam Gilchrist ignoring the slaps on the back of his colleagues after taking a brilliant diving catch to pull out a dummy or whatever. After scoring a try, rugby union players hug, shake hands and show their joy in a more traditional team-orientated, dance-free dummy-less way. Christ (whoops) I'm beginning to sound like Kaka.

Thankfully everything went well upon landing in Milan and I jumped (well, stepped) on the train into the city centre. A taxi to the hotel ... checked-in painlessly ... and a taxi to Milan's training ground to meet the current best player in the universe. It's all going far too well.

In fact, it gets better. Kaka arrives bang on time with a translator, who by a highly acceptable coincidence happens to be stunning. I hoped that her considerable talents did not extend to mind reading.

The rumours were correct. Kaka is an incredibly nice, polite guy and was even happy to talk about being a virgin when he was married. I can say with confidence that this is the first and last time that this line of questioning will feature in any interview I do: footballer virgin grooms. It is difficult to imagine a scenario such as: "So tell me Wayne, were you..."

Back to the hotel by about six o'clock. Turned on the TV and the girl reading the news looked like she had just stepped off the catwalk. They don't do ugly in Italy.

TUESDAY JANUARY 22
Dinner was splendid. Even the waiter looked like Brad Pitt. Incidentally, maybe it is my sense of humour, but did you see the name of Angelina Jolie and Brad Pitt's new baby daughter who was born earlier in the year? Shiloh. That is what she is called. By itself it's a lovely name, but maybe not so lovely when your dad's surname is Pitt. They obviously didn't have spooner-isms in mind when they called the baby Shiloh Pitt.

Back to the hotel by about 10.30 and watched *Die Hard 4* where Bruce Willis at one point went a whole two minutes without hitting or shooting some baddie. Then to the airport still worried that nothing had gone wrong. Even the long term car park coach turned up as I arrived at the bus stop. Kaka obviously has influence upstairs.

THE LAST WORD

My earliest memory of work is receiving my first ever wage packet – about six pounds – and deciding to blow some of it on buying a present for the baby of a pregnant reporter called Doreen.

Aware that it was perceived as unlucky to buy anything for an unborn baby, flushed with money I disregarded tradition. "I just wanted to give you a little something for your baby," I said, handing over a fluffy toy.

"I'm not pregnant…"

I had, in effect, called her a fat bastard. Things got better though as my career developed.

It was great fun. When it wasn't fun, I know now that it was really. Even the bad times were good, though they might not have appeared so when the phone wouldn't work in East Germany and I was on deadline.

Only when we take our foot off the football journalistic pedal and reflect on our careers do we fully realise how lucky and privileged we have been. We all have mates who earn far more than us and while we want their salary, they all want our job.

Football reporters are a privileged bunch, but perhaps we don't appreciate it as we swear at non-functioning pieces of equipment with 800 words to file. Phones that don't work or laptops that cannot get a signal seem the worst things happening to anyone in the world. Nobody is worse off than us when they happen.

However frustrating they are at the time, such inconveniences are mere blips. Being paid to do what most people pay to do – watch football – is brilliant, fabulous, wonderful.

In my next life I want to come back as a football writer again. I hope the Sad Bastard Bar is ready...

Been There Got
The T-Shirt

PLACES

Albania, Algeria, Argentina, Austria, Belgium, Brazil, Bulgaria, Canada, Colombia, Croatia, Cyprus, Czech Republic, Denmark, East Germany, Egypt, El Salvador, Estonia, Finland, France, Georgia, Germany, Greece, Haiti, Honduras, Holland, Hungary, Iceland, Iran, Israel, Italy, Japan, Kosovo, Latvia, Liechtenstein, Lithuania, Luxembourg, Macedonia, Malaysia, Malta, Mexico, Morocco, Nigeria, Northern Ireland, Norway, Poland, Portugal, Republic of Ireland, Romania, Russia, Scotland, Serbia, Singapore, Spain, South Korea, Sweden, Switzerland, Tunisia, Turkey, Ukraine, United Arab Emirates, United States, Wales, West Germany, Yugoslavia.

WORLD CUPS

1966...England

1978...Argentina

1990...Italy

1998...France

2006...Germany

1974...West Germany

1982...Spain

1994...United States

2002...Japan/South Korea

EUROPEAN CHAMPIONSHIPS

1972...Belgium	1980...Italy
1984...France	1988...West Germany
1992...Sweden	1996...England
2000...Holland/Belgium	2004...Portugal

EUROPEAN CLUB COMPETITION FINALS

European Cup/Champions League:
1968 Man Utd 4 Benfica 1
1971 Ajax 2 Panathinaikos 0
1972 Ajax 2 Inter Milan 0
1974 Bayern Munich 4 Atletico Madrid 0
1992 Barcelona 1 Sampdoria 0
1994 AC Milan 4 Barcelona 0

UEFA Cup:
1981 Ipswich 3 AZ 67 Alkmaar 0
1987 Gothenburg 1 Dundee Utd 0
1999 Parma 3 Marseille 0
2000 Galatasaray 0 Arsenal 0 (Galatasaray won 4-1 on pens)
2002 Feyenoord 3 Borussia Dortmund 2
2003 FC Porto 3 Celtic 2
2004 Valencia 2 Marseille 0
2005 CSKA Moscow 3 Sporting Lisbon 1

European Cup-winners' Cup
1971 Chelsea 2 Real Madrid 1
1994 Arsenal 1 Parma 0
1999 Lazio 2 Real Mallorca 1

SUPER BOWLS

XXIII	San Francisco 20 Cincinnati 16 (Miami)
XXIV	San Francisco 55 Denver 10 (New Orleans)
XXV	New York Giants 20 Buffalo 19 (Tampa)
XXVI	Washington 37 Buffalo 24 (Minneapolis)
XXVII	Dallas 52 Buffalo 17 (Pasadena)
XXIX	San Francisco 49 San Diego 26 (Miami)
XXX	Dallas 27 Pittsburgh 17 (Tempe, Arizona)
XXXI	Green Bay 35 New England 21 (New Orleans)
XXXII	Denver 31 Green Bay 24 (San Diego)
XXXIII	Denver 24 Atlanta 19 (Miami)
XXXIV	St Louis 23 Tennessee 16 (Atlanta)
XXXV	Baltimore 34 New York Giants 7 (Tampa)
XXXVI	New England 20 St Louis 17 (New Orleans)
XXXVII	Tampa Bay 48 Oakland 21 (San Diego)
XXXVIII	New England 32 Carolina 29 (Houston)
XXXIX	New England 24 Philadelphia 21 (Jacksonville)
XL	Pittsburgh 21 Seattle 10 (Detroit)
XLI	Indianapolis 29 Chicago 17 (Miami)

ABOUT THE AUTHOR
CHRISTOPHER DAVIES

Christopher Davies has reported on sports events from around the world for over 40 years in a career which has seen him write for *Shoot*, the *Daily Telegraph*, the *Daily Mail*, the *Observer*, the *People*, the *Daily Star*, the *Irish Independent*, *Sports Illustrated* and *Japan Times* amongst many others.

He lives in Bromley, is a member and former chairman of the committee of the Football Writers' Association and loves nothing more than a glass of fine sauvignon blanc with friends.